Invitat... ...ology

General Editor:

Professor Windy Dryden
Goldsmiths College, University of London

Other t...

Invitati...
Vivien I...

Invitation to Person-Centred ...
Tony Merry

Invitation to Rational-Emotive Psychology
Windy Dryden

TO STEPHEN

I had nothing to offer anybody except my own confusion.
Jack Kerouac

Invitation to Psychodynamic Psychology

Alessandra Lemma-Wright

Chartered Clinical Psychologist, Camden & Islington NHS Trust

and

Visiting Lecturer and Reader, Regent's College School of
Psychotherapy and Counselling

W
Whurr Publishers Ltd
London

© 1995 Whurr Publishers Ltd

First published 1995 by
Whurr Publishers Ltd
19b Compton Terrace, London N1 2UN, England

British Library Cataloguing-in-Publication Data
A catalogue record for this book is available from the
British Library.

ISBN 1-897635-62-1

Printed and bound in the UK by Athenaeum Press Ltd,
Gateshead, Tyne & Wear

Contents

Preface

My first encounter with psychodynamic psychology at undergraduate level was something of a non-event but with hindsight and considerably more experience of psychology departments, I am grateful that at least I was then offered an introduction to it, however cursory and bland. Had I been studying elsewhere I might not even have been given a chance to survey this body of theory. This is because psychoanalysis and psychology have had a difficult relationship, as we shall see in the Introduction to this book. Some psychology departments have not considered it as befitting of a scientific discipline such as psychology to be dabbling in something – perceived by them to be – as unrigorous as psychoanalysis. Consequently, psychoanalysis has been a comparatively neglected body of theory within many psychology departments in Britain, although less so in America.

I was, however, fortunate to take part, several years later, in seminars on psychoanalysis led by a tutor whose enthusiasm for, and extensive knowledge of, psychoanalysis made these seminars the most memorable of all. Since then I have myself been an avid reader of the psychoanalytic literature finding in it much that has been of relevance to my work as a clinician as well as to my understanding of myself and my life. My primary aim in this book is to impart to you at least some of the enthusiasm my own tutor originally imparted to me for the field of psychoanalytic enquiry. I hope, however, that you will not accept unquestioningly any of the assumptions underlying this book but merely that you will find enough contained herein to stimulate you to explore further this rich area of psychology.

In trying to give you some idea of what this book aims to achieve as well as what you might expect from it, I find it easier to begin by saying what you should *not* expect. There are many books on psychoanalysis aimed at different levels of readership. This book is not aimed at the seasoned psychoanalytic reader but is written for the newcomer to the field with little or no prior knowledge of psychoanalysis. Although you will find many introductory texts on psychoanalysis, and most are very useful guides, they tend on the whole to be rather theoretically inclined in their rendition of psychoanalytic ideas. Ideas, however, only begin to make sense when we can grasp their scope beyond the circumscribed area of discourse in which they originally evolved. Ideas assume particular meaning and salience for us when we can see them at work as it were; when we can apply them to that which interests or concerns us. Freud was most sensitive to this and although much of his work was concerned with studying abnormal behaviour and at times was heavily theoretical, he also devoted his attention to an understanding of everyday phenomena such as dreams, jokes, slips of the tongue, religion and others. This way, Freud gave us an idea of the scope of psychoanalysis well beyond the analyst's consulting room. In a similar vein the present text invites you to consider the relevance of psychoanalytic ideas to your life, to your understanding of yourself, your relationships and the struggles we all face in coming to terms with the inevitable frustrations of life.

Many of the ideas and concepts presented in this book could be criticised on a number of different grounds and indeed a large body of literature has concerned itself with criticisms of, if not outright onslaughts on, psychoanalysis. Whilst I am myself not uncritical of certain aspects of psychoanalytic theory, as it will become clear to you as you read the book, my primary aim here is not to offer a critique of psychoanalysis. This can be found elsewhere and I can only encourage you to acquaint yourself with the critical literature. Neither am I setting out to defend psychoanalysis although I am clearly partisan to many of the ideas it espouses. I simply hope to give you a point of entry into a psychoanalytic worldview. In doing so it will be clear that I start from the assumption that this particular worldview has something to offer, that it is, in a sense, valuable. I would like to stress, however, that this position in no way implies that I believe psychoanalysis has the final word on human nature – no psychological theory can encapsulate us in such a comprehensive manner even if it might claim that it does so. Indeed, the tone of much psychoanalytic writing can leave one with the distinct impression that analysts believe themselves to be the keepers of the 'truth'. On this matter I can only encourage you to be wary of any form of dogmatism and to not accept more than your own judgement allows.

To speak of the 'value' of psychoanalysis raises, in turn, the thorny question of how one evaluates it. If we are to evaluate it we can approach this task from two sides. On the one hand its evaluation is a personal and individual enterprise with reference to what is meaningful to you and what help psychoanalytic ideas can offer you in trying to understand your emotional life. Indeed, in order to engage with psychoanalysis you *have to* explore its personal resonance. Approaching the subject from a purely intellectual standpoint promises a degree of stimulation but denudes psychoanalysis of its essential radicalism. On the other hand, psychoanalysis may, and some would add *should*, also be evaluated at an empirical level. This is undoubtedly important as some of the claims made by psychoanalysis are far-reaching and have implications at the level of clinical practice with people in emotional distress. As this is not intended to be an academic textbook as such I will not examine in any detail the research studies which have attempted to put some of the ideas to test but where relevant these have been referred to so that you may, if you are so inclined, pursue your own investigations.

A limitation of a book of this nature is that in attempting to convey a very broad overview of the field of enquiry, the subtleties of the ideas presented are at times lost in the process. This is of particular relevance to psychoanalytic theory which presents us with a quite unique combination of respect for the nuances of human behaviour coupled with a tendency towards generalisations and universal claims regarding the validity of its theories. In relaying some of the most important tenets of psychoanalysis this book has emphasised more the latter. I hope, however, that when reading the book you will feel able to maintain a respect for individual complexity.

As an *introductory* text this book cannot hope to be exhaustive in its coverage of psychoanalytic concepts. Neither is it unbiased. On the contrary, the areas covered are highly selective and reflect my own interests and my own personal interpretation of psychoanalysis. I think the latter is true of any book on any subject although it is seldom made explicit. However, my own interpretation of psychoanalysis is born out of an understanding of key psychoanalytic concepts and some of these will be introduced in this book, remaining faithful as far as possible to their original meaning. The aim of Part I will be to give you an account of basic Freudian concepts as they relate to personality development. The other three parts of the book, while introducing psychoanalytic notions, will examine the application of psychoanalytic ideas to everyday concerns and phenomena. Part II will consider unconscious communication between people as well as internally within ourselves, for instance in dreams. Part III will focus on a psychoanalytic perspective on intimate relationships from infancy to adulthood. Finally, Part IV will examine the notions of psychological conflict and change. In keeping with the primary aim of giving a 'flavour' of psychoanalysis this book will, of necessity, leave you with many unanswered questions – and some probably unanswerable – and a degree of confusion which will hopefully spur you on to read more in this area.

Freud, speaking of his models of the mind, wrote: 'the value of a "fiction" of this kind depends on how much one can achieve with its help' (1926: 294). It is in this spirit that this book invites you to consider the relevance of psychoanalytic ideas to your life.

A note on the clinical material used in this book

To illustrate some of the concepts and psychological processes under consideration I have made use of clinical material from my own practice as a clinical psychologist and as a psychotherapist. The people in the anecdotes presented in this book are therefore real but names and other identifying features have been heavily disguised so as to preserve confidentiality. In a few instances, however, composite case studies have been used as it would otherwise have been difficult to preserve the anonymity of the particular individual whose own experiences illustrated well the concepts under consideration.

In the pursuit of clarity the material has also been considerably condensed and only the themes relevant to the concept being illustrated are outlined. Moreover, I have chosen material where the psychoanalytic concepts, in my opinion, seemed to be especially relevant to understanding the individual's predicament. This may give the mistaken impression, however, that the understanding of psychological problems is a straightforward matter, that everything fits, as it were. This could not, however, be further from my own experience of clinical work or from my own personal experience in analysis. Deciphering the multi-layered meanings enveloped in psychological or physical symptoms takes time and courage and can be very painful. The 'reality' of this may sometimes be lost through the process of condensing that which in some instances amounts to several years of personal exploration and struggle by those individuals depicted in the anecdotes. I hope that as you read some of the fragments of their stories you will not lose sight of this.

Throughout the book where the pronoun 'he' is used this refers to 'he' or 'she'.

Every effort has been made to obtain permission to reproduce any copyright material in this book.

Acknowledgements

Writing a book is by no means a solitary enterprise. Many people have made an important contribution in the help and support they have given me. I would like to thank my editor, Windy Dryden, for having 'invited' me to write the book in the first place and for his comments. I am also extremely grateful to Andrea Sabbadini for providing me with a safe space within which to explore psychoanalysis and my personal relationship to it and to David Smith whose excellent seminars on psychoanalysis crystallised my own interest in this area. My thanks also go to my husband Stephen for his unfailing support and for his helpful comments on earlier drafts of this manuscript and to Madelaine Browning, Zack Eleftheriadou, Nina Shepherd and Celia Webster for their understanding, encouragement and support throughout the whole process. Special thanks go to Sandie Meyer, not only for her much treasured friendship, but also for the many lively discussions we have had on psychoanalysis and beyond. Last, but not least, I would like to thank Gill Cruisey for patiently deciphering my handwriting and for her help in typing the manuscript.

Introduction

I do not wish to arouse conviction. I wish to stimulate thought and to upset prejudices.

Freud

Invitation to Psychodynamic Psychology is a very apt title for this book. Not only does it convey its aim, namely to extend an invitation to consider the relevance of psychodynamic ideas to an understanding of ourselves and our interactions with others, but it also touches on another important issue. Psychoanalysis, in both its theoretical and applied form, has for the most part remained the province of a privileged few and it can at times feel as though one does indeed need a formal 'invitation' to this particular ideological club!

Beginnings

Psychoanalysts have long stressed the importance of discovering the historical antecedents in our lives in order to understand our behaviour in the present. In a similar fashion, so as to appreciate some of the contributing factors to the exclusivity of psychoanalysis, let us begin with a historical overview of its development.

Psychoanalysis is a multi-faceted term. It refers to a method for investigating the human 'soul' (Bettelheim, 1984), to the theories arising from such an investigation and to a particular method of psychotherapy, as well as to a theory of civilisation, a profession and an ideological movement. Psychodynamic[1] psychology refers to the branch of psychology which shares the most fundamental psychodynamic assumptions.

Psychoanalysis may be seen as a set of hypotheses about the nature of human beings which itself was the culmination of nineteenth century thought. In the intellectual life of the nineteenth century two basic

---

[1]Psychodynamic and psychoanalytic are terms used interchangeably in this book.

strands of thinking stand out. On the one hand, there was determinism where human behaviour was seen to be externally controlled. On the other hand, there was subjectivism, focusing on our inner life which was considered passionate, irrational and dark. Against this divided intellectual backdrop psychoanalysis was conceived and went on to create an explanatory system – a deterministic system – of our inner, irrational emotional life.

Psychoanalysis was originally developed by Sigmund Freud, a man of great cultivation and scholarship and, importantly, a Jew. Although Freud quickly managed to attract interest in his ideas, psychoanalysis was nonetheless regarded by the world at large as a highly subversive discipline. It undoubtedly posed a serious challenge to the belief in conscious thought as the ultimate datum of human experience by invoking the central idea that there are areas of our experience which are beyond our conscious awareness, but which nonetheless affect our behaviour – from behind the scenes as it were. Also, one of the central themes was sexuality – an emphasis which is likely to have touched a raw nerve in those times. It was Freud's contention that sexuality, along with aggression, both of which he considered to be basic instinctual drives, were central to the development of our personalities. However, psychoanalysis was also thought subversive because it was seen to be a predominantly Jewish movement.

Freud's origins and cultural background are not without significance in understanding the personal, social and political factors motivating and shaping the development of his ideas (Robert, 1977; Roith, 1987). However, Freud himself revealed a significant 'blind spot' in this respect. This otherwise highly perceptive man, who had carried out his own now famous 'self-analysis', failed to make links between his own Jewish roots and his theories. He was nonetheless clear that Judaism was a political impediment to the advancement of psychoanalysis as well as being acutely aware of the impact of his Jewish roots on the acclaim of his ideas. 'Rest assured', he wrote to a colleague, 'that if my name were Oberhuber, in spite of everything, my innovations would have met with far less resistance' (Ostow, 1982). Indeed when his friend and colleague the Swiss psychiatrist Carl Jung – the only non-Jew then affiliated to the psychoanalytic movement – left Freud's following in 1914, Freud was very concerned and convinced that psychoanalysis would now be seen simply as a 'Jewish national affair'.

While it may have been the aim of the earliest psychoanalytic ideology to play down the Jewish connection, the marginalisation experienced by the group cannot be denied. This marginalisation was certainly not just a figment of their imagination. In the 1930s along with the rise of the Nazis, the movement became the victim of real attacks. Freud's writings, together with those of Einstein and H.G. Wells, were burned in public bonfires (Stevens, 1983). Freud himself is said to have remarked: 'What progress we have made. In the Middle Ages they would have burnt me, now they are content with burning my books' (Jones, 1955). However, whilst not literally burnt and effaced into ashes, he was effaced nonetheless by being forced into exile, along with many of his colleagues.

From the beginning Freud saw psychoanalysis as a cause to be defended against attack, and the select analytic institutes which emerged could be seen to be the bastions of his defence (Kirsner, 1990). Freud regarded it as 'very probable' that 'the large scale application of our therapy will compel us to alloy the pure gold of psychoanalysis freely with the copper of direct suggestion' (1919: 167–168). The need to protect the 'gold' of psychoanalysis had the unfortunate effect, however, of also keeping at bay the outside world, fearing its evaluation, criticism and attack, in order to safeguard the orthodoxy.

The very real persecution suffered by the psychoanalytic movement in its infancy left a deep scar and provides some explanation towards what has been described by one author as the movement's 'embattled or siege mentality' (Kirsner, 1990). The movement's paranoia, however, has not just been a feature of its relationship to the outside, non-analytic world. It has also been a striking feature of the quality of the relationships within the psychoanalytic establishment itself, amongst its own rival theoretical offspring. The history of psychoanalysis is one of schisms. Indeed psychoanalysis is an umbrella term covering a number of theoretical schools which, whilst all originating from and honouring some of Freud's original ideas and beliefs, have since evolved very different theories about personality development and the relative importance of particular factors shaping our development.

'Like the metaphysicians of the last century' Smith incisively observes 'analysts have created a proliferation of self-contained "schools" of theory and practice and having abandoned the self-correcting methodology of empirical science, have been unable to rationally decide between rival theories' (1991: 238). Over the years this has become the breeding ground for fanaticism and narrow-mindedness and has lent to psychoanalysis the appearance of a cult or religion (Szasz, 1978). Not surprisingly, the easiest target for criticism has been the behaviour of some analysts who have tended to act more as true believers than as genuine enquirers. In this respect it is of historical interest to note that in 1911 Freud set up 'The Committee' to 'guard the faith' and gave rings to its members – a ritual which concretises the institutional religious flavour of the psychoanalytic movement.

Today the orthodoxy and exclusiveness of the psychoanalytic establishment is safeguarded by making entry into its circles very difficult. In order to train as an analyst or psychoanalytic psychotherapist one has to undergo a lengthy and costly personal analysis. It also helps if one is heterosexual or, at the very least, skilled at concealing one's sexual orientation. Even though no institutions explicitly stipulate a heterosexual

orientation as a prerequisite for acceptance to train, this has long
been an unspoken reality as homosexuality has been viewed by most
psychoanalytic theorists as a form of sexual perversion and therefore
not a desirable quality in those seeking to train as psychotherapists
(Cunningham, 1993; Ellis, 1994).

Psychoanalysis as a form of psychological therapy has also been
restricted to those who can afford the cost. Even though psychoanalytic
treatment is available in the public sector this remains a very scarce
resource and waiting lists for such treatment are long.

The eliteness of the group has been further sustained by the evolution of a very sophisticated and complicated language which at times
obscures the very human processes it is aiming to describe and elucidate, while also alienating those who are not well versed in its language. Many psychoanalytic terms are difficult to comprehend as they
are couched in scientific-sounding terminology, most probably originally chosen by Freud's translators to impress a medical readership
(Hinshelwood, 1994). To complicate matters further the same psychoanalytic terms are used differently across the different schools of
thought. In addition, the original terminology of psychoanalytic writing
has tended to be retained by most psychoanalytic writers long after it
has outlived its usefulness (Smith, 1991). This is but one of many manifestations of the difficulty a significant number of Freud's followers and
successors have experienced in moving on from their ideological
father, elevating Freud to the status of 'corporate superego' (Frosh,
1994). However, the only way we have of keeping the spirit of Freud
alive is to take his observations further, consider certain areas more
deeply and open-mindedly, with the help of the method of enquiry he
bequeathed us.

Psychoanalysis and psychology – an ambivalent relationship

As we have seen so far the psychoanalytic movement was founded on
shaky grounds and this may account, at least in part, for its observed
defensive attitude towards the outside world and the consequent establishment of self-contained schools of thought open only to a privileged
few. The defensive attitude has been a prominent feature of the relationship between psychoanalysis and the rest of psychology – a relationship which can at best be described as highly ambivalent. In order
to appreciate the tenuous position of psychodynamic psychology within the main body of psychological knowledge we need once again to
turn to a historical perspective.

In its theoretical aspects psychoanalysis is no different from other psychological theories. Nonetheless there is a long history of opposition

between psychology, both academic and applied, and psychoanalysis. While some intrepid psychologists might venture as far as to praise Freud for his literary gifts, scepticism if not outright dismissal are the prevailing attitudes held by a significant number of psychologists in relation to Freud and his 'science' of psychoanalysis.

At the same time as psychoanalysis was emerging in the 1880s, psychology was predominantly sensory-physiological in its orientation and was turning to the experimental method as its prime tool for research. The psychologist William Wundt perhaps expressed most comprehensively the scientific forces that were remaking psychology at the time. For him, a genuinely psychological experiment involved an objectively knowable and preferably measurable stimulus applied under stated conditions resulting in a response likewise known and measured. Psychologists were then beginning to adopt a model for their discipline based on the example of the natural sciences. On the face of it psychoanalytic procedure could not be further removed from the idealised view of experimental psychology. Psychoanalysis had its origins in the consulting room, in the evolving dialogue and interactional processes transpiring between the analyst and his patients in the course of analytic treatment. Its data were thus open to the criticism of possible bias in reporting and suggestion on the part of the analyst. Furthermore, the non-observable status of some of its concepts, for instance the notion of an unconscious part of the mind, cast serious doubts on its scientific credentials. Having said this, although an analyst could indeed not experiment in the manner in which, say, the physicist could, the way psychoanalytic theories were derived from observation was nonetheless essentially similar in its underlying logic in both physics and psychoanalysis.

A trend running counter to the prevailing emphasis on experimentation was evident in the writings of William James. His interests were wide ranging and encompassed areas of human experience untapped by experimental psychology, for instance religion and art. Even though he was critical of the notion of the unconscious, like the analysts he was more interested in the problem than the method. However, in spite of William James and those who attempted to extend the scope of psychology to understanding quite fundamental aspects of the human experience, the emphasis on experimentation remained the dominant voice in American and British psychology.

Since the analysts refused to experiment according to the standards set up by the psychologists, they were considered beyond the pale of scientific psychology. Since the psychologists refused to deal with what the analysts considered to be major human concerns, the analysts in turn had little interest in *them*. This marked the beginning of a strained relationship between the two disciplines which has benefited neither.

Freud himself had believed in principle in the scientific method as the only road leading us to a knowledge of reality. His efforts to bring psychoanalysis to scientific status stemmed partly from his original training in neurology and partly from a general overvaluation of the exact sciences which we are only now beginning to redress. And, as some have pointed out, if psychoanalysis had never set itself up to be a science, dispute about its status might not have been so intemperate and the focus of interest might have been better invested in the ideas espoused by psychoanalysis and their relevance to understanding our conflicts and dilemmas. Nonetheless, whilst Freud certainly aspired towards scientific status he was realistic about the limits of his own enterprise. His warning that his observations rather than his theoretical speculations should be most highly valued has unfortunately been largely ignored (Wachtel, 1972).

Many psychologists today feel repelled by the muddle that psychoanalysis has generated around itself and they tend to gravitate towards more rigorous research traditions and programmes. The unerring eye of many critics in spotting absurdities and inconsistencies in psychoanalytic writing and practice has unfortunately not been matched by an equal ability to perceive the valuable contributions that have been made to date and that could be made in the future if the gap between psychoanalysis and psychology could be bridged. To this end the increasing number of university departments offering degrees in psychoanalytic studies is encouraging. Notwithstanding its dubious status within mainstream experimental psychology, psychoanalysis has undoubtedly left its mark. Over the years numerous battles have raged within psychology over some of the most central issues brought to the fore by psychoanalysis.

It has been an unfortunate consequence of the various historical facts reviewed in this introduction that psychoanalytic ideas have either been totally ignored or grossly misunderstood and thereby rejected. This is unfortunate because psychoanalytic ideas can enrich our understanding of ourselves and their repudiation may simply reflect our difficulty in digesting some uncomfortable home truths about human nature which psychoanalysis has starkly highlighted. Whatever its shortcomings as a science this does not imply that psychoanalysis as a body of knowledge should be dismissed as hopelessly subjective. As Farrell (1981) has suggested, it may be that it is the traditional view of science which is too restrictive. Moreover, as Evans has pointed out, 'does something only qualify as truth when it can be validated by the discourse of institutionalised science?' (1995: 13).

There has been some interesting research which has aimed to bring psychoanalytic theories out of the closet into the light of scientific rigour and methodology (see Dixon, 1981; Kline, 1981, 1989; Erderlyi, 1988; Langs, 1993). From within the psychoanalytic field itself there are those who believe that psychoanalysis can contribute to a science of the mind when it becomes in effect no longer the psychoanalysis we know but rather flows into what is presently considered by many to be a more effective science, namely cognitive science. Equally, it is argued, cognitive science, in its present fledgeling condition, will not grow into a science of the mind until it confronts the important questions of real minds such as fantasies and feelings. However, many attempts to test psychoanalytic concepts in the laboratory situation have been severely limited by the overriding weakness and crudeness of some experimental approaches when dealing with truly complex problems. The problem may not necessarily lie with the experimental method per se; rather it may be more a question of how the method is applied by the investigators themselves whereby psychoanalytic ideas are either oversimplified or grossly misunderstood. Attempts to test such ideas highlight the fact that to test a theory may require as much ingenuity as to construct one.

Whatever the ultimate scientific validity of psychoanalytic ideas will prove to be, one of the greatest contributions of psychoanalysis has been to focus squarely on issues relevant to the human experience. In this respect Freud moved where other psychologists feared to tread and in so doing opened up the possibility for us to consider such important areas of our experience as love, sexuality, death, aggression and many more. The commitment of psychoanalysis to understanding the workings of our internal life and its impact on our experiences in the outside world has been unfailing. These were topics that had been largely ignored by psychologists before Freud even though the poets and philosophers had long since begun their musings on such issues. These are the very areas of our experience which are not easily definable, controllable and hence amenable to rigorous testing. However, as Kline so aptly put: 'Models of working memory, computer recognition of origami ducks, prisoners' dilemmas – who in all honesty cares about the findings from such experiments...?' (1988: 142).

Whatever the shortcomings of psychoanalysis in its efforts to become a science, the field taken as a whole has been concerned from the very beginning with the use of that essential of science – scepticism. Freud himself, when writing about dreams, stressed the importance of never trusting that which appears obvious. His caution was not only restricted to working with dreams but reflected a more general attitude towards the material his patients presented him with. It is unfortunate that analysts have not always been sceptical enough in relation to the theories and ideas they have presented, highlighting how even those forewarned have trouble escaping the effects of the self-deluding mechanisms of defence they describe so eloquently.

Beyond Freud

By now you will hopefully have some sense of the place of psychoanalysis within the larger body of psychological knowledge. However, as was previously mentioned, the term psychoanalysis does not refer to a homogeneous school of thought. The current diversity of psychoanalytic schools of thought, you will not be too surprised to hear by now, has a long history. In the 50 years following Freud's first observations and theoretical statements, his ideas triggered divergent movements, each in its own particular direction. In Britain, those who continued to identify themselves as 'Freudian' were by no means a unified group. On the contrary, it included those who remained loyal to Freud, those who became the followers of Melanie Klein – another very important psychoanalytic theorist – those who fell in the middle and who became known as the 'Middle group' and subsequently the 'Independents', as well as those who embraced the approach known as American Ego Psychology.

Today the complexity and heterogeneity of the different psychoanalytic schools of thought can be overwhelming. However, this heterogeneity is deceptive to a degree as on closer examination there is a convergence of basic concerns centring around the importance of our interactions with others from birth onwards and their impact on the development of our personalities. In the context of such theories the human being is seen essentially as a social creature – one whose contacts with reality and particularly with other people are considered to be major determinants of their behaviour. For instance, the quality of a child's interactions with his parent(s) is seen to affect the type of person he will become, the type of choices he will make and, in his own turn, the type of parent he will be. Notwithstanding the similarities there are, however, also important differences amongst the schools centring largely on the origins of psychological problems and, more specifically, on the role played by environmental factors (especially childhood trauma) in their genesis.

It is beyond the scope of this book to review the differences between the various psychoanalytic schools.[2] As all these approaches stem from the original work of Freud it is, however, essential to first understand his basic ideas in order to then appreciate the other psychodynamic theories. This will be the aim of the first part of the book. Nonetheless the ideas of other psychoanalytic theorists will also be presented as they relate to the particular questions which we will explore.

Like any book, this one has its own biases. The ideas which will be presented can best be classified as originating in the 'Independent' school of psychoanalytic thought – a particular school within the British psychoanalytic movement. The 'Independent' position is characterised by a reluctance to be restricted by theoretical constraints. Many of those who ally themselves to this particular group do so largely

[2]Suggestions for further reading on the different schools of psychoanalytic thought can be found at the end of the book.

because they refuse to belong to either of the sectarian groups, namely the Freudians and the Kleinians, which have dominated the psychoanalytic movement in Britain (Rayner, 1991).

Psychoanalysis is a school of thought which can at first be experienced as very confusing and even intimidating. Its key ideas, however, are simple, as I hope this book will show you. A feeling of confusion is nonetheless in keeping with the daunting task we all undertake each day in our lives: to understand ourselves and others with all the confusing, and also conflicting, emotions, thoughts and fantasies to which we are all prey. Perhaps psychoanalysis can help to ease the confusion by clarifying some of the answers to at least some of our many questions.

Part I: Psychoanalytic Theory of Personality Development

No book on psychodynamic psychology can begin without an introduction to some of the basic psychoanalytic concepts and assumptions about human nature. So many psychoanalytic concepts about personality development and personal relationships have infiltrated into various areas of contemporary life and everyday language – the Freudian slip and the Oedipus complex to name but two – that it becomes difficult to envisage thinking about psychological matters without recourse to psychoanalytic notions of development. In order to appreciate these concepts fully it is essential to consider Freud's work as his ideas, though revised by his followers, still underlie much of the current thinking in psychoanalysis.

Psychoanalysis is a complex theory. It is complex because it is also comprehensive, attempting as it does to give a coherent account of our development from birth onwards. The scope of such a project is daunting. The aim of Part I is therefore to render your first encounter with psychodynamic ideas as smooth as possible by introducing Freudian concepts. It does not, however, aim to present the psychodynamic ideas which have been developed since Freud. Rather, it aims to provide you with a map of the territory we will be exploring in this book.

Chapter 1
Who's in charge?

> I recognise that I am made up of several persons and that the person that at
> the moment has the upper hand will inevitably give place to another. But
> which one is the real one? All of them or none?
>
> W. Somerset Maugham

An experience common to all of us is that of feeling, at least some of
the time, conflict within ourselves or with others in our lives. What we
sometimes want to do may be in conflict with what we feel we should
do. Some of our thoughts and wishes may also reveal aspects of ourselves which are at odds with consciously held ideals and these may
then be denied or disowned so as to reduce our experience of conflict.

The idea of psychological conflict, to which we shall return in more
depth in Part IV, is central to the psychodynamic perspective. The very
expression 'dynamic' was itself borrowed by Freud from nineteenth-
century physics to convey the notion of two opposing forces producing
a resultant third force acting in another direction. It was one of Freud's
great insights that our experiences are dynamic – that is, the outcome
of conflicting forces, ideas and wishes. According to the psychodynamic
point of view, conflict, movement and variation dominate our lives.

In order to make some sense of our experience of conflict we need
a framework within which to organise our experience. Freud put forward a model of the mind which serves this purpose. Whilst he revised
his own theoretical model of the mind several times, fundamental to
his thinking, and to that of other psychodynamic schools, is the idea of
different psychic levels or, if you like, different levels of consciousness.[3]

The topographical model of the mind

The first model to be described by Freud is known as the *topographical model*, which consists of three levels. The first level, *consciousness*,

---

[3]It is important to remember that these models only refer to hypothesised structures and do
not relate to actual areas in our brain.

corresponds to that which we are immediately aware of, whatever we may be concentrating on at any given moment – for instance, reading this book. The experience of reading this book may now be said to be part of your conscious experience. Beneath the conscious level lies the second level, the *pre-conscious*, consisting of whatever we can recall without great difficulty. That is, the pre-conscious acts as a kind of storage bin for all those memories, ideas and sense impressions that are readily available to us, but to which we are simply not attending all the time. For instance, whilst reading this book you are probably not thinking about how to drive your car but if you got up to go and drive your car now you would very quickly recall what you have to do in order to drive. The facts are at your fingertips as it were without needing to be part of your conscious working memory. We therefore seem to have bits of knowledge 'tucked away' in the back of our minds that we are not called upon to use but which are nonetheless available to us.

We all process a lot of information every day. As we talk to people or just walk down the street, we are absorbing many things without always being consciously aware that we have actually registered all the incoming information. Let us take as an example the common situation when you are at a party, talking to a group of friends. You are very involved in the conversation and you are not aware of attending to anything else. Quite near you there are two other friends also engaged in conversation. Suddenly your attention is drawn to their conversation as you hear a friend's name being mentioned. In such a situation you had not been consciously attending to that particular conversation. Yet, on another level you were scanning the conversation as you would not otherwise have registered what they had been talking about. Your attention becomes consciously drawn to it once something of relevance to you is registered. This process has been referred to by psychologists as 'pre-conscious processing' and has been successfully demonstrated by experimental studies concerned with subliminal perception. In such studies, stimuli too weak to reach consciousness have been clearly shown to have an effect on our cognitive processes, our emotional experiences and hence on our behaviour (Dixon, 1981). The elicitation of emotional responses without our subjective awareness of their source and the associated assumption that consciousness is therefore not essential to cognition is, as we shall see, consistent with psychodynamic theory.

Beneath the pre-conscious extends that controversial hypothesised part of our mind which has caused so much dispute amongst psychologists: the *unconscious*. Freud used the term unconscious in three different senses. Firstly, he used it descriptively to denote that which is not in our consciousness at any given moment but is nonetheless available to us. This is roughly equivalent to the pre-conscious level and this is no longer a controversial notion in modern psychology. Secondly, he used it to denote the dynamic unconscious, that is, a constant source of motivation that makes things happen. In this sense what is stored in the unconscious is said not only to be inaccessible but also to have ended up in the unconscious because it was repressed. It is this sense of the unconscious that has been severely criticised from various quarters. Thirdly, he used the term in a systemic sense denoting his later understanding of the unconscious not as a gradation of consciousness but as a hypothetical system or structure of the mind.

The unconscious contains all those memories that are not readily available to consciousness because we have repressed them in order to avoid the pain and conflict they may otherwise evoke. According to Freud the unconscious is fundamentally made up of those wishes which are repressed in the face of the demands of reality, particularly the incestuous wishes of infancy. Repression is a concept central to psychodynamic thinking. Although we will return in Part IV to this concept, it is nonetheless important to note that unlike suppression which involves conscious repudiation of an idea or feeling, repression is by definition unconscious. It exists primarily to safeguard consciousness from conflicts and the experience of anxiety.

If we repress a particular memory, this does not, however, mean that it simply vanishes into thin air. Rather it is stored in the unconscious and can resurface in a variety of different guises such as dreams, slips of the tongue and psychosomatic symptoms, as we shall see in Part II. These can be seen to represent the very particular dialect of the unconscious. Furthermore, what we store away in the unconscious is also said to act as a hidden motivating factor for our conscious behaviour. For example, we may find ourselves engaging in quite repetitive self-destructive patterns of relationships with others and yet not quite know why we keep on making the same mistakes. A psychodynamic perspective would suggest that there are unconscious forces motivating and determining this type of behaviour.

Freud, in his early collaboration with his friend Joseph Breuer, an eminent Viennese physician, treated patients suffering from 'hysteria'. A term derived from the Greek word 'hystera', meaning uterus, hysteria had been regarded since the Greeks as an affliction peculiar to women arising from unsatisfied sexual or maternal cravings. Its manifestations included paralysis and fainting spells neither of which could be accounted for in medical terms. Freud and Breuer's view of hysteria is succinctly expressed in their now famous statement that 'hysterics suffer mainly from reminiscences' (Breuer and Freud, 1895: 7). This statement conveys a very important idea, namely that hysterics were believed to be suffering not from an organic disorder but rather from the psychological consequences of traumatic memories which had been expelled from consciousness in order to escape intolerable psychic pain. These memories were not, however, lost, they were merely

believed to have been driven into the underground cave of the unconscious where they then found new, disguised channels for expression.
In the case of hysteria the chosen channel was the body: the psychological conflict was translated into bodily symptoms.

An important implication of all this is that whilst events in our lives
which cause us pain or conflict, and our emotional responses to these,
may not be remembered or acknowledged consciously, they are
nonetheless remembered and acknowledged unconsciously. This suggests that there may be times when we may be, metaphorically speaking, in two minds about some events in our lives. Let us take an
everyday example such as a friend asking you to pick up a book for
her from the library. This happens to be a friend who is frequently call-
ing upon you for favours and you usually oblige. On this occasion you
also agree to help them out even though you are yourself quite busy
and the request is rather inconvenient – you had not planned to go to
the library today and this will take you out of your way. Later that
evening your friend calls to check if you got the book. You are suddenly taken aback as you realise that you have in fact forgotten to go to
the library. You are very apologetic, this is most unlike you, and
explain your forgetfulness in terms of how busy you have been yourself. This may well be the case. However, there is another way of making sense of this same event. It may also be that whilst consciously you
were happy to help your friend and it was really only mildly inconvenient for you, unconsciously you felt much more resentful towards
her for always imposing on you and not really taking into account that
you are also quite busy. Rather than acknowledging these feelings and
telling your friend, you repressed them. However, as we have seen,
what is repressed may continue to affect our behaviour and in this
instance this could explain why you forgot – you were angry with your
friend and did not *really* want to help her.

It is important to remember that if something is unconscious we
truly do not know anything about it. However, central to the theory of
the unconscious we also find the assumption of a dissociated state
in which we simultaneously both know and do not know why we
are behaving in a certain manner or what we are really feeling. For
example, when someone claims that a slip of the tongue reveals an attitude to someone else that we do not know about – instead of saying:
'I'm really happy to see you again', we say 'I'm really sorry to see you
again' – we will not necessarily realise that those are in fact our real
feelings towards that person. Even if this is pointed out to us we may
go to great lengths to emphasise how much we had enjoyed our previous meeting with that person. However, there may be times when a slip
of the tongue might bring home to us the existence of certain feelings
that we had not previously registered consciously. What is stored in the
unconscious only becomes known to us through the way it influences

our life. In talking about the unconscious we have effectively found a very useful way of describing the behaviours, thoughts and feelings that do not really 'fit' into what we know of ourselves.

The pre-conscious and the conscious systems all obey the usual rules of thinking, namely they are logical, reality tested and linear in time and causality. These rules are typical of what is referred to as *secondary process thinking*. Unlike these, the unconscious system obeys a quite different set of rules typical of *primary process thinking*, which is said to be characteristic of childhood. In this part of our mind the information which is processed is said to be treated without regard for secondary process rules. As a result contradictions abound, information is not subjected to any kind of reality testing and mutually exclusive 'truths' may co-exist. Because of these properties the unconscious mind has been likened in the classical Freudian model to an infantile and primitive part of us. If it were to overwhelm the conscious self our functioning would be impossible. Our experience of anxiety is the warning signal that this might occur and in order to protect consciousness defences are called into place. These protect us from the discomfort of anxiety. We shall return to this in Part IV.

The structural model of the mind

In 1923 Freud revised the topographical model and replaced it with the *structural model*. This new model conceptualised the human psyche as an interaction of three forces: the *id*, *ego* and *superego*. These could be seen to be three different agencies of our personalities each with its own agenda and set of priorities. They were said to have their own separate origins and their own highly specific role in maintaining what might be regarded as 'normal' personality functioning.

According to Freud each one of us is endowed with a specific amount of *psychic energy*. The latter notion was used by Freud to understand the workings of our mental life and was characteristic of his tendency to draw analogies between psychological and physical events. This is particularly evident, for example, when Freud spoke of the amount of psychic energy with which a particular object or person was invested, namely their *cathexis*. Cathexis is a psychological concept and refers to the amount of psychic energy which becomes attached to the mental representative of a person or object, that is, to the memories, thoughts or fantasies about a person. This investment of psychic energy is an indication of the emotional importance of the person or object to the individual in question.

In the newborn infant psychic energy is bound up entirely in the *id* which refers to the mass of biological drives with which we are all born. The energy of the id is divided between two types of instincts. The first type are the *Life instincts* aimed at survival and self-propagation. Into this category fall our needs for food, warmth and, above all, sex. The energy of the Life instinct, the *libido*, was considered by Freud to be the driving force permeating our entire personalities and propelling us through life. In his earliest formulations Freud spoke as though our basic drive was entirely sexual and all other aims and desires arose by some modification of our sexual drive. Among analysts nowadays the term 'libido' has lost a great deal of its original sexual connotations and refers essentially to the idea of drive energy; that is, the energy we may invest in our pursuit of particular interests in some topic, activity or in relationship with others.

In opposition to the Life instinct stands the *Death instinct*. Discussions of the Death instinct, including Freud's, tend to be rather vague. It is clear, however, that Freud saw the human organism as instinctively drawn back to a state in which all tension would be dissipated – in short, the state of death. This instinctive attraction towards death gives rise to self-directed aggressive tendencies. However, since self-destruction is opposed and tempered by the life-preserving energy of the libido, our aggression in most instances is redirected outward against the world motivating us to compete, to conquer and in some cases to kill. The notion of an instinct for death may well seem absurd given that much of the time we seem to be preoccupied with our survival rather than any conscious desire to destroy ourselves. This notion in fact continues to cause debate amongst theorists. However, an evening spent watching the news or reading the newspapers may well bring the seeming absurdity of the notion of a Death instinct into question. The intensity of the destructiveness which appears to be a hallmark of human behaviour could readily be understood as an expression of the Death instinct. On the face of it we do seem to be equipped with a large capacity for destructiveness but the fact of human aggression does not, however, necessarily imply the existence of the Death instinct as Freud understood it.

The instincts of the id are essentially biological. They are not amenable to reason, logic, reality or morality. They are, in a sense, reckless. They are concerned only with one thing: the reduction of whatever tensions our organism may experience. This might be, for instance, anything from hunger to sexual need. In short the id is that part of us that is concerned with self-gratification, and more specifically, immediate gratification no matter what obstacle. Our innate tendency to maximise pleasure and minimise pain was referred to by Freud as the *pleasure principle*.

While the id knows what it wants and needs, it is in some respects 'blind' – blind to what constitutes safe or ethical ways of getting what it needs since it takes no account of reality. To fulfil this function Freud said that the mind developed a new psychic component, the *ego*, which he believed to emerge at about 6 months of age. The central function of the ego is to serve as a mediator between the id and reality. Through secondary process thinking – that is, remembering, reasoning, evaluating – the ego locates in reality the counterpart of the id's desires. It anticipates the consequences of using a particular means of self-gratification and then reaches out for that means. There may be occasions, however, when the ego opts to delay gratification until a safer or more appropriate means can be found.

Let us imagine two young people in the first passionate throes of a relationship. They are at a party where the circumstances present an opportunity to go to bed together. They are both very sexually aroused. Their respective ids, if you like, are on the brink of self-gratification. However, the girl decides to go no further as they do not have a condom with them. She would like to have sex but delays her gratification until she can ensure 'safe-sex'. The part of her that is involved in this decision-making process is her ego. Thus, in contrast to the id's pleasure principle, the ego operates on what is called the *reality principle*, the foundation of which is a concern with safety.

Let us now imagine the same scenario but, this time, at the point at which the couple are on the verge of sexual intercourse the girl stops, not because they do not have a condom, but because she feels it is morally wrong to have sex with someone she has just met. In this instance it is not the girl's ego which is in charge; rather she is responding largely to the demands of her *superego*.

The superego refers to the part of us that represents the moral standards of our society and culture which we have internalised and to some extent also personalised. We all hold dear certain principles which we feel must be respected. There are strong rules that we impose on ourselves and on others even if we do not always manage to live up to the standards we set ourselves. Furthermore, the rules that we live our lives by sometimes appear to be entirely arbitrary. These rules may be moral rules, that is relating to our notions of 'good' and 'evil'. However, there are also conventional or social rules which guide our behaviour. For some of us these may be more important still. They may even constrain certain behaviours in public which in private are given free rein.

John worked for a large company where he held a senior position. He was respected by his colleagues for his commitment to his work which he took very seriously. John held very strong views on a number of moral issues, for instance he argued strongly against abortion. He was also frequently critical of others, such as when someone told a rude joke in front of women, which he considered to be inappropriate behaviour.

John's public persona and the rules he abided by stood in sharp contrast to how he behaved in his personal life. His relationship with his wife Joanna was a very troubled one and he occasionally physically abused her to the point that she had to be taken twice to the hospital casualty department. Such behaviour, however, was fully justified by John who believed that his wife deserved such punishment when she failed to live up to his standards of a 'good' wife. While in public he would never be rude or overtly aggressive to others as he believed this to be unacceptable behaviour, behind closed doors John lived by quite different rules. At the time of John's initial referral for psychological help he could not see that his attitude and behaviour in his public and private life revealed many contradictions and paradoxes, as well as very deep-seated problems in his relationships with women.

In addition to those rules that we impose on ourselves we nearly all have a picture of the kind of person we are and the kind of person we feel we ought to be. We judge our behaviour according to the extent to which our perception of ourselves conforms to our 'ideal self'. The rules, the abstract moral principles and the ideal image of who we ought to be can be thought of as a person inside us who has strong views and is always ready to criticise if our behaviour is not up to standard. This person inside us is equivalent to our superego. While most of us have some awareness of the moral rules and standards which govern our behaviour the superego is only partly conscious, that is, we may for instance experience guilt after behaving in a manner which at a conscious, rational level, we do not consider to be in any way inappropriate or immoral.

So where do all these rules come from? The basic answer put forward by psychoanalytic theory is that as we grow up we take into ourselves ideas and attitudes held by others around us. The agents of society which we, as growing children, are in most contact with are our parents. They are said to play an important role in curbing or inhibiting the id's excesses. As children we internalise our parents' standards and values and these come together to form the superego. This account of the formation of the superego is an instance of what is called *introjection*. The idea here is that we take inside our psyche people and their ideas and attitudes. Those aspects of others which we take in continue to act within us in the same way as they were felt to be acting upon us from the outside. Although the identifications of early childhood were believed by Freud to form the nucleus of the superego and to be the firmest, later identifications in adolescence and adult life were not thought to be inconsequential.

Freud observed that to a large extent the parental images which are introjected by the child are those of the parents' own superegos. This means that in bringing up children parents tend to discipline them in a similar fashion to their own parents' approaches to parenting. According to Freud the transmission across generations of certain values and standards was important socially as it resulted in the perpetuation of the moral code of a society.

The superego shares an important characteristic with the id: its disregard for reality. Instead of considering what is realistic or possible it tends to embrace an abstract moral ideal which does not take kindly to 'ifs and buts'. It may, for example, be your ideal always to finish what you have started no matter what you have to endure. You have embarked on a course of study which is very demanding and in the middle of it you have a life crisis. Everyone around can see that what you need is to take a break and be kind to yourself. However, your superego dictates that, crisis or no crisis, you must persevere – not to would be an indication of weakness.

We all vary in the extent to which we prohibit ourselves certain things, in how we conduct our lives and how we judge our own behaviour and that of others. Such variation can be accounted for in terms of the differences between our superegos. If our superego is predominantly friendly and helpful – that is, it functions as a kindly priest giving us some moral guidance but letting us off for our smaller sins – we can tolerate our limitations and those of others without undue distress. However, if our superego is severe – if it functions more as an overzealous fundamentalist priest – we may become overly preoccupied with, and burdened by, a pervasive sense of failure and may adopt a very punishing attitude towards ourselves and all our failings, however trivial. The severity of our superego cannot, however, be explained solely by reference to the severity of our upbringing and the moral codes we introjected. There are enough instances where there is not a clear correspondence between the severity with which the parents opposed the child's instinctual impulses and the individual's superego. Quite lenient parenting may nonetheless produce a child with a very strict superego. Freud's explanation for this was that the intensity of the superego was determined in large part by the child's own hostile impulses towards the parents in the Oedipal phase, which we shall explore in the next chapter, which are subsequently directed against the self in the form of harsh prohibitions.

A conflictual existence

As we have seen, the id, ego and superego have their own exclusive interests and priorities. Hence, these forces are constantly in conflict with one another, the id forever insisting on gratification, while the pragmatic ego, the idealistic superego and the demands of reality all conspire against the id's hedonistic demands. It is up to the ego to satisfy the id without upsetting the superego. The ego's other main function is therefore to mediate between the two warring factions within ourselves. In this respect it has a role akin to that of a statesperson who has to negotiate between two nations in conflict, each with very different demands and where compromise can be a difficult business.

Freud's models of the mind are of course open to criticism and have indeed been heavily criticised if not rejected outright. However, they do provide us with a useful framework which speaks to the common experience of feeling divided or in two minds about certain decisions we need to make or situations and events in our lives. Equally, they can help us to understand those things we say or do which feel at odds with how we would say we are consciously feeling at any given moment. Most importantly, Freud's models of the mind reveal that at the heart of psychodynamic thinking is the notion that to be human is to be divided, in perpetual conflict amongst opposing forces each struggling to be in charge. This conflict is nowhere more evident than in the area of our sexuality and we shall examine Freud's views on sexuality in the next chapter.

Chapter 2
Is it all down to sex?

... in modern civilised life sex enters probably even more into consciousness than hunger.

Edward Carpenter

The central place of sex in our lives is difficult to deny even though, for some of us, it may be equally difficult to acknowledge. Our upbringing, education, cultural background and religious beliefs, as well as the sexual experiences we have or have not had, all contribute to our attitudes towards sex. Whatever our attitudes may be, it would nonetheless be fair to suggest that we all spend some time thinking about sex, fantasising about it, arguing about it, agonising over it and, one hopes, also enjoying it. Sex is the subject of many forms of art as well as of humour. It is also used as a commodity, for instance to manipulate us into buying a particular make of car, seducing us into the illusion that if we buy a bigger and better car we will become as if by magic more sexually attractive and potent. Sex thus preoccupies our imagination, our thoughts and our dreams and is an integral fibre in the fabric of our society.

Sexuality today is a contested zone in the sense that it has become a moral and political battlefield. Perhaps even more importantly sex has become, as Michel Foucault (1981) famously polemicised, 'the truth of our being', thereby suggesting that our identity, our sense of who we are, is intimately bound up with our sexuality – sexuality in this sense is a psychological entity. Sex and sexuality can thus be said to permeate our lives, both social and personal. But would we be justified in reducing all our conflicts and preoccupations to having a sexual origin?

On one level sexual activity is seen by most of us as natural, innate and instinctual. This is of course true – we are constructed on a bedrock of natural impulses – but an overemphasis on the physiological basis of our sexuality detracts attention from the fact that our sexuality also has a history. Indeed, history clearly shows that there have been considerable shifts over time in sexual behaviour and the meanings we attach to it. However, physiology or cultural and social values alone cannot account for our passion, for that which we find attractive, nor for the content of our most intimate sexual fantasies. The social history of sexuality interacts with our own personal sexual history. If we are then interested in understanding the multi-faceted nature of our sexuality we need a framework that not only takes into account physiology and social factors but also gives due emphasis to psychological factors.

The place of sex in Freud's theories

To many people Freud and psychoanalysis are synonymous with sex. Such an association is not entirely mistaken as Freud certainly attributed to dreams, humour and neurotic symptoms a significance that went beyond anything that ordinary common sense might credit them with. In the majority of cases the significance accorded to such phenomena by Freud was sexual in nature. Freud certainly believed that sexuality played a central role in producing conflict and, in particular, in the aetiology of neurotic conditions. He understood neurotic symptoms as substitutes for sexual satisfaction, that is, he believed that sexual frustration played a part in the causation of neurosis. For instance, Freud understood anorexia nervosa as a neurotic behaviour that expressed undeveloped or repressed sexuality. Underlying this understanding was his belief that all appetites were expressions of the sexual drive. Thus, Freud suggested that eating or not eating indicated the presence or absence of basic sexual drives. He believed that the anorectic did not eat because, as a result of a prior association, food had assumed a symbolic, frequently sexual, significance which in turn made it repugnant.

Freud thus stressed the central importance of sex in our lives, but even in this respect, he was more of a follower rather than an originator as the idea that sex was important to us had already been stressed by the pioneers of 'sexology'. Notwithstanding the central place accorded to sex in his theories and those of his followers, Freud emphasised that he was not a 'pansexualist' – that he did not view sex as the sole shaping force of human destiny. On numerous occasions he in fact forcefully denied the equation of all instinctual life with sexuality.

Freud viewed sexuality as being as much a product of nature as of personal history, suggesting that it is in the context of our own individual psychological make-up, of our developmental histories that the biological possibilities of our bodies acquire personal meaning. Psychodynamic thinking thus allows us to understand our sexuality as more than a mass of irrepressible instincts seeking gratification.

Freud's contribution to our understanding of the vicissitudes of our sexual thoughts, feelings and behaviour cannot be underestimated. His challenge, as Wollheim (1991) suggests, was twofold. Firstly, he high-lighted the narrowness of the then conventional definitions of sexuality and secondly he showed sexuality to have a highly complex and lengthy history. Let us now look at these challenges in more detail.

The construction of sexuality

The claim of psychoanalysis that sexuality is central to our mental life can only be grasped if we understand what Freud meant by sexuality. One of his most important contributions in this field was to state clearly that sexuality and reproduction are not necessarily synonymous. This was a first step towards broadening the parameters of what we now refer to as sexual as it implied that what is sexual is not exclusively in the service of reproduction, nor driven solely by the need to fulfil its evolutionary function. Rather, Freud suggested that our sexual life includes the function of obtaining pleasure from various parts of our bodies and not just from our genitals – a function which may then be brought into the service of reproduction but need not necessarily be. This enabled Freud to make a further controversial statement, namely that our sexual instinct and how we satisfy it is not a foregone conclusion. More specifically, what was challenging was that Freud severed the connection conventionally made between sexuality and heterosexuality by suggesting that there is really no predetermined way in which our sexual urges should be satisfied. An important implication of this is that even though our biological sex is a given, our sexuality in its broader sense never is but is, on the contrary, constructed. Familial and socio-cultural factors interact and determine the sexual messages that children absorb as they grow up and which ultimately shape their own gender identity and the expression of their sexuality.

A central tenet of psychoanalytic theory is the notion of universal *bisexuality* which flows quite naturally from the previous views. Freud believed that we are all endowed constitutionally with both masculine and feminine sexual dispositions. Essentially, the notion implies that our sexuality is partly constructed through the repression of its oppo-site – heterosexuality includes homosexuality and vice versa. Seen in this light heterosexuality is therefore no more or less of a compromise formation, it has been argued, than is homosexuality, which we shall explore in more detail in Chapter 14. In any individual one sexual dis-position will prevail but it never enjoys complete monopoly. Indeed, in a letter to his friend and colleague Wilhem Fliess, Freud wrote that he was beginning to understand every sexual act as a process in which four people were involved!

The notion that our sexuality is constructed may be unpalatable. Many people find comfort in the belief that who and what they are are givens. The possibility of choice can lead to inner conflict. That sexual orientation is not innate may then be difficult to accept. Yet psychoanalytic clinical practice with people who are not necessarily suffering from serious psychological difficulties repeatedly highlights what appears to be a rather universal experience, namely that our sense of sexual identity is generally troublesome and confused irrespective of how certain and fixed it may feel to us at a conscious level. Our sexual feelings are charged, conflictual and subjectively meaningful, not just instincts seeking discharge.

Although heterosexuality is the 'natural' order of things in so far as we need a man and a woman to reproduce the species, this line of thinking confuses anatomy with psychology. Freud's radicalism lay precisely in his ability to distinguish between the two as he pointed out that what we desire is what we actually *learn* to desire and that this needs to be considered independently of the biological requirements for the reproduction of the species. That children assume the gender identity and role consistent with the sex of rearing has been repeatedly demonstrated by researchers, for instance, those who have studied the development of children born with both male and female sexual characteristics.

The unresolved elements in all of us when it comes to the experience of our sexuality and our sexual identity undermine the certainty which many theories other than psychoanalysis are inclined to ascribe to our perception of ourselves. Many people struggle with their sexuality. Some may wonder if they are homosexual or not while others may simply explore in their fantasies what it might be like to have sex with someone of the same sex. Such uncertainties and fantasies represent an ever-present potential in all of us.

Freud's notion of a universal bisexuality needs to be considered alongside his views on perversions. According to Freud the abandonment of the reproductive aim is the common feature of perversions. He introduced a useful distinction between the sexual *object* and the sexual *aim*. The former refers to the person towards whom we are attracted while the latter refers to the actual act towards which our sexual urges tend. He showed that there are many forms of sexual behaviour which deviate from the norm in object, in aim or in both and yet which are still sexual in nature. As an example of a deviation in object, Freud cited homosexuality or attraction to children. As deviations in aim he cited sexual practices involving interest in other parts of the body besides the genitals, or the exchange of pain as in sado-masochistic sexual practices.

Rather than placing a firm boundary between such perverse acts and the kind of sexual behaviour which we might regard as falling within the norm, Freud argued that perverse traits are seldom absent from the sexual life of normal people, thereby narrowing the gulf between so-called normal and perverse sexuality. Undeterred by the prevailing views of his society Freud held that adults had within them all the pre-dispositions and experiences that are required to create a perversion. By extending his use of the term sexuality to include all those behaviours which are not in the service of reproduction, Freud enlarged the scope of his enquiry and opened up for us the possibility of thinking about our sexuality in a much broader sense, including perhaps what may feel to some of us to be its 'darker' side.

The roots of sexuality in infancy

Freud's second challenge, and fundamental to his theory of sexuality is the very influential, and perhaps the most controversial, of his ideas, namely that our sexual life does not begin at puberty but starts soon after birth. Of all of Freud's ideas this was the one which was most profoundly shocking and repulsive to the society in which he lived. Even today many people still find the idea that children are sexual beings difficult to accept – even though some adults may abuse the fact of children's sexuality to justify their own sexualised behaviour towards them, as the many instances of child sexual abuse and the explanations given by the perpetrators for their behaviour attest. Some parents do find their young children's manifestations of sexual behaviour difficult to manage and may strictly prohibit them, for instance not allowing masturbation. Such parents may inspire a sense of fear and guilt when the child has sexual experiences that are actually natural and normal for the child. In such cases the child may in turn grow up with difficulties around his sexuality associating it with what is 'bad' and 'dirty' and therefore experiencing it as something which cannot be enjoyed and must be kept secret and hidden away.

The experience of our sexuality is closely connected with the experience of our bodies. Long before any conscious thoughts of sex cross our minds, we all have a sense of our physical bodily identity. This identity is shaped by our early interactions with our carers and the way they handled and made us feel about our bodies – bodies to be cherished and enjoyed or to be ashamed of. The baby's earliest experiences are primarily those of sensation. In the first few months of a baby's life the physical exchanges that occur between mother[4] and baby dominate the relationship – the baby is caressed, fed, changed, bathed and so on. Physical relating is then a primary mode of contact and infancy is characterised by sensual exchanges of this kind between babies and their carers. Indeed Person (1980) has argued for the critical importance of early tactile experience in mediating the relationship between the baby

"'Mother' is not used exclusively in this book to refer to the biological mother but also refers to the role as performed by any other primary caregiver of either sex in ensuring the health and well-being of the baby and in providing the psychological and physical care to ensure survival and growth.

and their carer and assumes that later sexuality develops out of this
early sensuality.

Freud's belief that our sexual life begins at birth led him to describe
what are referred to as the *stages of psychosexual development*. He
argued that we all progress through a series of stages, in each of which
our psyche directs its sexual energy towards a different *erotogenic*
zone, that is, a part of our body which is a source of pleasure. Any such
zone is in the first instance connected with a vital bodily function, for
example the mouth is associated with feeding. The pleasurable sensation
which is experienced around the mouth when feeding is then repeated
but this time independently of the bodily function which first introduced
it, in this instance hunger. Certainly, if you observe babies breast-feeding
you will soon notice that there are times when they are not sucking to get
nourishment but simply because the sensation is pleasurable and for
many babies this is also experienced as very soothing.

Freud first proposed the *oral* stage (0–1 years) where satisfaction is
predominantly derived by the infant via the mouth, for example from
sucking the nipple or the thumb. Second, is the *anal* stage (1–3 years),
where gratification is derived from gaining control over withholding or
eliminating faeces. Again, everyday observations of toddlers highlight
how, as they negotiate their increasing separateness from their parents,
they come to view their faeces as their own possessions which they
want to give up or hold on to. The potential for battles and conflict
between parent and child, for instance over toilet training, during this
period is great. It is at this stage that defecation is said to symbolise giving and withholding. Metaphorically speaking, conflicts at the anal
stage are seen to pose a major dilemma for all children with regard to
the need to adapt to, or to resist, parental control.

During the third stage (3–5 years), the *phallic* stage, children begin
to be more aware of their genitals with consequent curiosity and anxiety about sexual differences and the questions that many parents can
find so difficult to answer! The phallic stage is thought to be particularly important to our psychological development because it is this
stage that provides the backdrop to the Oedipal drama. In Greek
mythology, Oedipus unknowingly kills his father and marries his
mother. Likewise, according to Freud, all children during the phallic
stage long to do away with the parent of the same sex and take sexual
possession of the parent of the opposite sex. Indeed the notion
implicit in the Oedipal phase is that at the core of our psychology lies
desire.

The resolution of the *Oedipus complex* is believed to be especially
crucial to our development. However, if children of both sexes harbour
incestuous wishes towards the opposite-sex parent, then how do they
get beyond this stage? Freud hypothesised that at the same time as the
little boy harbours his incestuous desires towards his mother he also

experiences *castration anxiety* – the child's fear that his father will punish him for his forbidden wishes by cutting off the guilty organ, his penis. Lacking penises girls appear castrated to him and the little boy fears a similar fate. Girls, on the other hand, realising that they have been born unequipped with penises experience the female counterpart to castration anxiety, namely *penis envy*. They are said to harbour angry feelings towards the mother for having created them without a penis. While the boy's castration anxiety is what causes him to repress his longing for his mother, the girl's penis envy is what impels her towards her father, desiring a child by the father – the desire for a child being merely a substitute for her former desire for a penis.

With time both the boy's and the girl's Oedipal desires recede and rather than remaining at war with the same-sex parent who is experienced as a rival, both settle for identification with the same-sex parent, incorporating their values, standards and sexual orientation. As we saw in the last chapter, it is through the incorporation of the parents' moral values in the process of identification that the child develops his or her superego. The resolution of the Oedipus complex was therefore linked by Freud to the development of the superego.

The Oedipus complex has entered the realm of everyday language and is sometimes treated as a psychoanalytic cliché not worthy of further consideration. It has also been criticised by anthropologists who say that Freud was wrong to claim that the complex is universal and we shall return to this notion in Part III. It would of course be ridiculous to suggest that children wish in fact to kill the same-sex parent and have intercourse with the opposite-sex parent. However, observations of young children, and recollections of our own childhood experiences, can help us to appreciate that the timing of the Oedipus complex does coincide with a time in our lives when we may well have wished our rivals out of the way – be they parents or siblings – so as to enjoy greater intimacy with father or mother. Little boys and little girls often express the wish to marry the parent of the opposite sex. This is often a time of passionate love and hate, of jealousy and competitiveness, the outcome of which, psychoanalytic theory would suggest, can have a decisive effect on our personalities.

Between the ages of 6 and 11 years the child goes through the *latency* period during which sexual impulses remain latent and the child's attention is redirected towards mastery of developmental skills. Puberty reawakens the hibernating sexual impulses and the young person begins to rechannel some of his sexual energy towards others.

The shaping of the personality

Central to the psychoanalytic perspective on sex is the notion that the way in which we express and experience our sexuality is the result of our very individual negotiations through the different developmental stages outlined above and this in turn accounts for the wide variations in the manifestation of sexual behaviour. Freud suggested that the way in which our early sexual impulses are satisfied at the different stages of development also shapes the development of our personality. The ease or difficulty encountered by children as they work their way through the oral and anal stages is said to have an impact on all later adult behaviour relating to exchange, control, loving, hating and to such traits as stinginess, generosity and obsessiveness, to name but a few.

At each stage the child has to deal with the conflict between the demands of the id and the amount of gratification which is possible given the demands of reality. Both under-gratification and over-gratification can lead to later conflict. This conflict may then lead to *fixation*. This refers to a situation where our personality can be said to be almost frozen at the stage of development where conflict was experienced. This has led to the attribution of particular personality types to the manner in which the different developmental stages are negotiated. Although the idea is that we all progress through the various stages it is clear that the concept of fixation reflects the acknowledgement that some people may get 'stuck' at some point or other in their development. Thus, for example, clinicians at times refer to people as being 'orally fixated' to describe those who tend to relate to the world in terms of being nurtured. This is not to suggest that such individuals, like the child at the oral stage, want to be literally fed, but it is meant to indicate that the individual wants to be nurtured and soothed in a psychological sense. In addition to the possibility of fixation Freud also believed that *regression* may occur, that is, a return to an earlier mode of gratification. For instance, children who find their privileged position in the family usurped by the arrival of a new sibling may regress to sucking their thumb for comfort even though they had graduated from this particular mode of oral gratification a while earlier.

But how might our experiences during the stages of psychosexual development have an impact on later personality functioning? As an example let us look at what could conceivably happen to a child during the anal stage. Let us imagine a child whose pleasure in playing with his faeces is severely constrained by his parents – that is, the child's natural curiosity about the products of his body is curtailed. In this child's family toilet training is a 'no-nonsense' time and the parents are strict. Bowel control is achieved speedily, if a bit too early, and seemingly without the quite normal 'hiccups'. This scenario, while quite possibly very appealing to those who are parents and still contending with nappies, may, however, have undesirable consequences for the child. They may, for example, develop defences against the forbidden pleasures of playing with their faeces and this may later manifest itself in such symptoms as obsessive orderliness and cleanliness – personality traits commonly associated with an 'anal character'.

Such explanations of the peculiarities of our character are very seductive. They give the impression of clear causal links between events in our life. However, it is seldom so simple and who we become is often *overdetermined*, that is, the end result of the interaction of many factors. In addition, Freud's developmental theory is retrospective as it arose out of his clinical work with adults and not through the observation of children – it singled out adult conflicts as overall definers of what he then considered to be normative stages of development with universal applicability. This manner of constructing theories is clearly problematic. This fact, however, should not be taken as sufficient to dismiss the potentially formative effects of such early experiences and the meaning they hold for us but merely encourages a degree of caution in how we apply such ideas.

The significance of sex: from infancy to adult sexuality

It will be clear by now that even though Freud may have been wrongly accused of reducing all our conflicts down to sex, he nonetheless attached great significance to sex emphasising its pervasiveness in our lives. Several factors contributed to Freud's conclusions, not least the roots of our sexuality in infancy. Given that our sexual life begins so early the likelihood that it will have a powerful influence on us seems a not unreasonable assumption to make. The idea that adult sexuality can stir up infantile feelings is basic to any psychoanalytic approach and points to some not uncommon predicaments in sexual relationships. The emphasis in this approach is very much on the early mother – infant relationship as the starting point of our sexual life.

A common conception arising out of child development studies is that infants at first experience themselves as merged with their mothers and then gradually differentiate separating boundaries between themselves and their mothers. The earliest relationship is thus understood to be in the very first few months a symbiotic one. For the infant this is a reflection of his limited consciousness and total dependence without regard for the mother as a separate person with her own interests. Mothers often feel that they exist only to feed, to soothe and to change nappies! As babies get older they gradually appreciate that their mother is not an extension of themselves nor totally merged with them and therefore not always there to meet their demands. Although the babies, as with older children (and even some adults), may continue for some time to expect this, the experience of frustration and of disillusionment, albeit difficult to accept, is an important one for their development as long as they are not confronted with it too soon.

Psychoanalytic thinking suggests that it is precisely the feelings of omnipotence, comfort and 'oneness' enjoyed in our early merged relationship with our mothers which we continually seek to re-experience in our adult sexual relationships. The experience of merging with another through sexual intercourse is also described in non-psychoanalytic literature though there it is conceived usually in terms of a peak sexual experience than as a common occurrence or, more importantly, as is suggested here, as a revival of an emotionally charged infantile state. However, that which is stirred up so powerfully in us is not so much the early state of merger itself, but the emotions associated with this infantile state (Ryan, 1983). The other person may be felt to be very powerful while the self is experienced as needy, dependent and vulnerable or vice versa. The state of merger may be either longed for or feared depending on the quality of our earliest interactions with those who cared for us. As we will see in the following example the nature of our early relationships with our mothers and fathers may influence our subsequent intimate and sexual relationships.

Mark is 29. He is a successful businessman and is popular with his friends. He is the only child of a comparatively young mother and a somewhat older father. The father, also a very successful businessman, was seldom around throughout Mark's childhood. Even when he was not on a business trip he did not spend much time with Mark and displayed no physical affection towards him. Mark's mother on the other hand doted on her son.

Up until adolescence Mark remembered enjoying his relationship with his mother. She took an active interest in his life and had always been there for him. He recalled frequently being with his mother and sharing many intimacies with her – a feature of their relationship that his friends at the time said they could not share with their mothers. However, their relationship became difficult around the time Mark turned fifteen. It was then that he met his first girlfriend and started to go out more with other friends. Although his schoolwork was fine his mother began to put pressure on Mark to study harder and she clearly indicated to him her disapproval of his social life. Mark remembered feeling very guilty and his mother, according to him, became very depressed around this time. Mark did his best to please his mother and on several occasions he turned down invitations to go away for the weekend with friends so as to not leave his mother alone.

When Mark left home to go to University he felt his mother was heartbroken. Although this did not stop him from going he always felt the need to telephone her at least every other day, send her flowers and spend much of his holidays with her. On one level he resented this but he also felt very indebted to her as she had been such a support to him when he was younger.

As an adult Mark maintained a close relationship with his mother and particularly after his father's death he felt duty-bound to visit her regularly and frequently. Although Mark had various relationships with women throughout this time he found it very difficult to sustain them for long and experienced particular difficulty in his sexual relationships which manifested itself in recurring impotence. It was only after one woman, towards whom he had developed an especially strong attachment, left him that Mark decided he needed to take a look at his life and started therapy.

In therapy Mark's very strong, yet highly ambivalent, attachment to his mother became the focus of the exploration. Mark's difficulty in settling down with another woman, and his recurring problem with impotence, were understood as being in some way connected to his very close relationship with his mother and the rivalry she felt towards any woman Mark introduced her to. In order to appease his mother Mark reached the only compromise which he felt was open to him: he would see other women but he was frequently unable to fully consummate the relationship sexually and would soon disengage himself from any liaison, thereby never establishing any relationship that would seriously threaten his mother. In many respects he had remained his mother's 'little boy'. However, Mark's difficulty in making a long-term commitment to another woman also stemmed from his fear of getting close to women as he anticipated an equally engulfing relationship with them as the one which he experienced with his mother. Women were frightening figures for Mark. Prior to therapy he found various rationalisations to explain to himself why a relationship had not worked out, for instance 'she was just not my type', rather than addressing the nature of his relationship with his mother which lay at the root of his difficulties.

The pervasiveness of sex: sublimation

In addition to his emphasis on the antiquity of our sexuality, Freud also stressed its plasticity and viewed this quality as very significant (Wollheim, 1991). By plasticity Freud meant that several areas and activities in our life can become sexualised even though, on the surface, they may not strike us as having any obvious sexual connections. To account for this state of affairs Freud coined the term *sublimation*. The sexual instinct is said to be sublimated in so far as it is directed towards a non-sexual aim and in so far as its objects are socially valued ones. The main types of activity described by Freud as the result of sublimation are artistic creation and intellectual inquiry.

What can we make of the notion of sublimation? To begin with it should be remembered that Freud believed sublimation to be essential to civilisation as it leads us to invest our energy in activities which are usually socially valued ones besides the pursuit of our personal pleasure. Modelling or sculpting, for instance, may be said to be sublimations of the wish to play with faeces. The sublimated activities are best understood as attempts to harmonise the demands of the id and of our social environment so as to keep both parties satisfied. In this sense sublimation is a defensive measure which is nonetheless adaptive. However, it would certainly be a quite different matter if sublimation was used in the service of a complete denial of sexual feelings or thoughts that would otherwise give rise to emotional conflict. For instance, it is certainly not uncommon to observe people who invest a tremendous amount of energy in their work or hobbies but who may lead quite impoverished sexual lives. In such instances we might speculate that these individuals have sublimated their sexual needs and invested their other activities with the energy which has been diverted away from their sexual lives.

> Michael was devoted to his work for a large charity. He considered his work to be very important and meaningful and he clearly derived much satisfaction from his professional activities. He recognised himself that he felt passionately about the work of the charity and would at times judge harshly colleagues whom he perceived as not working as hard as him.
>
> Michael had friends and he retained close contact with his family. He had, however, reached the age of 30 without having established any intimate relationships. In his early twenties he had a number of fleeting relationships but since he started work for the charity he had felt he had no time for a relationship and that his work was far more important.
>
> He started therapy somewhat reluctantly following the advice of his doctor who suspected that his persistent somatic complaints over the past few years might have a psychological origin. In therapy, Michael was very resistant to exploring his feelings and filled his sessions talking about his work and the various physical ailments which affected him. I drew attention to the fact that work seemed to be the only safe subject we could explore together. It took several months before Michael could begin to talk about how lonely he felt and yet how frightened he was of having an intimate sexual relationship with a woman. His previous sexual experiences had been, according to him, 'disastrous' – he had failed to achieve orgasm and had felt very humiliated. In his work at least he could feel powerful as he knew what he was doing and he was successful. His colleagues respected him whereas he had felt that women would not respect him as he was a failure sexually. Such was the strength of Michael's feelings of failure and powerlessness that he had diverted his interest away from sexual relationships and invested all his energy and passion into his work which provided him with a safe, albeit lonely, haven.

Freud's ideas on sublimation led him to draw particular attention to the link between thinking and sexuality. He believed that curiosity is first aroused in the process of answering the two main questions with which all children struggle, namely how are babies born and what differentiates the sexes. These are familiar enough questions which many of us will recall as having preyed on our minds as well as having been the subject of many playground conversations where some pretended to know what they were still struggling to comprehend. Work with children with learning difficulties which are not organic in origin sometimes reveals their inhibitions in learning as being in part related to their concerns regarding sexual matters, as in the following example.

> Claire is 10 years old. She had been adopted at a very young age and had been told by her adoptive parents that this was the case. They remarked that she had seemed unperturbed by this disclosure and had continued to show a very close attachment to them. However, her teachers at school had

noticed that Claire was underachieving. She was described as being inhibited, showing little curiosity or interest in her surroundings and the experiences she was exposed to at school. Because of this Claire was referred to
me and I assessed her learning difficulties as being emotional in origin and
therefore I offered her psychotherapy. In the course of this work it became
apparent to me that Claire appeared to lack interest and curiosity about
both her past and her present life. It was not so much that Claire was
depressed, although at times she felt very sad, but it was more a sense that
Claire simply did not want to know much about anything as though she
actually feared knowledge and what that might then expose her to.

As her therapy progressed Claire displayed a rather consistent interest in
games involving adult and baby dolls which she would arrange in a variety
of configurations. On one such occasion Claire paired up all the babies,
except one, with their parents. When asked what had happened to the baby
doll which had been left out Claire replied that she did not look like any of
the adult dolls and that this was why she had been left behind. This reflected Claire's experience of having been rejected by her natural parents and
left with a painful sense of difference – like the baby doll Claire also did not
share her adoptive parents' physical appearance.

I encouraged Claire to tell me more about the baby doll that had been
left behind and through this doll Claire was able to express many of her
own feelings and many of the questions she had about her own roots. This
included questions about how she had come to be. As she gave expression
to her curiosity with regard to her own history and more general curiosity
about sexual matters, Claire began to take a more active interest in her surroundings and her schoolwork improved. Claire's difficulties cannot be
explained simply with reference to sexual conflicts as she had clearly also
been affected by the early traumatic separation from her natural parents.
However, her difficulties in exploring this traumatic past led to a shut-down
of her curiosity, in particular about how she had been 'made' and hence
about sexual matters. This then restricted the scope of that which could be
safely explored and questioned and learning of any kind had to be curtailed
as a consequence.

The contemporary relevance of Freud's views on sex

As with many of Freud's ideas it is important not to lose sight of the
cultural and historical milieu in which his ideas evolved and the impact
of these socio-cultural forces on what he chose to stress in his theories.
This caution applies nowhere more so than in his discussions about the
relative importance of sex. Nowadays the polarities of right and wrong,
of proper or improper behaviour in sexual matters, are not as rigidly
fixed as they once were. Repression in sexual matters may therefore
not occur as frequently or as intensely as it did in Freud's time. It is,
however, important not to forget that to speak more openly about sex
need not necessarily entail, in practice, greater openness and freedom
in this area of our lives. Even though we may not treat sex as taboo, our

sexual relationships stand out in our lives as areas which are at times experienced as irrational and as the focus of our strongest and most conflicting feelings. Indeed, sex and sexuality are areas with which we probably all struggle at one time or another.

Freud's emphasis on the centrality of sex in our lives can be traced to the present day in psychoanalytic writings, though later psychoanalytic formulations view sexuality as stemming from the whole development of our personality rather than as determining it.[5] Psychoanalysis helps us to appreciate that our sexuality is shaped not only by cultural and social factors but also by our individual experiences, starting at birth. It is a theory which underlines the complexity and contradictions surrounding the question of gender and sexuality. It reminds us that biology and instincts need to be considered alongside such notions as conflict, fantasy, passion and identity. Understanding the developmental history of our sexuality may help us then to clarify not only the nature of some of our sexual anxieties and fantasies but also our sense of self.

---

[5]This is a view espoused by the Object Relations school of thought which subscribes to a more inherently social view of psychological development seeing us as being formed in relation to, and seeking contact with, others from birth.

Chapter 3
Men and women – how different are they?

Freud is the father of psychoanalysis. It has no mother.

Germaine Greer

In the last chapter we examined the place of sex in our lives. This exploration leads us quite naturally to think about sexual difference. Our identity as men and women is gendered, that is, we all see ourselves first and foremost as 'sexed' beings. Our desires, fantasies, hopes and expectations are partially shaped by our sense of gendered self which is a unique fusion of cultural meaning with individual psychobiographical history.

Human physiology makes us confront the fact that, biologically speaking, men and women are different. However, many people have argued that the differences are not just skin-deep – men and women have also been said to differ psychologically. For instance, it has been claimed that there are differences in their motivation to achieve, in their aggressiveness, in their sensitivity to others' feelings, in the way they express their sexuality and engage in relationships with others and in their dependency needs, to name but a few.

The difficulty in being different

Sexual difference has been one of the dominant issues concerning psychoanalytic theorists. Along with most psychological theories, psychoanalysis has tended to universalise, contrasting men with women and implicitly endorsing a single masculinity and femininity which are seemingly believed to be experienced in a uniform manner by all of us alike. This view has added to the confusion and contradictions which surround the question of sexual difference. The latter has, however, been rendered problematic not only as a result of this monolithic tendency amongst theorists but also because questions about sexual difference have been confounded with the question of equality. Whilst men and women may well be different, the observation of difference has been mistakenly used to make evaluative judgements even though to identify two people as different is, in theory, purely descriptive. The said differences have been used throughout history to deny equal rights to women. The discourse on the differences between the sexes has therefore entered the realm of politics and polemic and this has been an important step in improving the quality of life for women. However, the political dimension of the battle of the sexes, so as to redress the balance in favour of women, has tended at times to imply a kind of 'equality-without-difference' which masks what certainly feel at times like quite fundamental differences between the sexes.

We may well speculate as to why the question of difference between the sexes is such a minefield. Acknowledging difference of any kind is difficult. This is often the case because the one who is perceived as different, as 'other' by virtue of a particular characteristic (e.g. gender, race, culture) may confront us with disowned parts of ourselves. There may be aspects of our potential experience and of our being which we would rather ignore. To think about a man if we are a woman and vice versa is to think about what we are not. What the other is or has may be something that we desperately wish not to be. Conversely, the other may possess attributes we desire to have. Acknowledging differences between the sexes may then confront us with that which we do not have but would like to have and hence elicit and expose our envy. Such considerations may render the task of examining differences between men and women even more arduous and challenging.

A male perspective on women

The discourse surrounding the question of sexual difference is an emotive one and stereotypes of the typical man or woman abound and are deeply imprinted within us. Many men as well as women would say quite confidently that men and women differ – perhaps nowhere more so than in their respective ways of being in relationship to each other. Conceptions of how men and women differ represent our attempts to order and make coherent our unfolding experiences and perceptions as we relate with one another. But the nature of such conceptions depends in part on the position of the observer. On the whole when it has come to describing what is 'female' and what is 'male' psychological theorists have fallen into an observational bias. Explicitly adopting male development and male life as a norm, they have tried to fashion woman out of a male cloth.

The tendency of psychological theorists to project a masculine image when formulating a psychology of women can be traced in Freud's writings. As we saw in the last chapter, Freud built his theory of psychosexual development around the experience of the male child who has to separate himself from the mother, renounce his incestuous desires because of the threat of castration, identify with his father and so resolve his Oedipus complex. On the other hand, the crucial moment in the girl's development is her discovery in boys of a sexual organ perceived to be superior to her own. Whereas the boy is at first indifferent to the girl's sexual organ and only becomes worried about it when he has established a link between the threat of castration and the sight of the female genital, Freud said that the little girl sees the penis, knows that she is without it and wants to have it, hence her penis envy and her feelings of inferiority. The girl therefore is said to see herself as 'castrated' and is also perceived by the little boy in this manner. According to Freud this process is at the origin of the girl's castration complex. He argued that the acknowledgement of the difference between the sexes obliges the girl to give up masculinity and turn to femininity. The girl gives up her desire for the penis, replaces it with a desire for a child and *to this end* turns to her father. The mother is set up as a rival and the girl becomes a 'woman'. In Freud's opinion the Oedipus complex for girls is only made possible, and is initiated by, the castration complex whereas for boys the castration complex heralds the resolution of the Oedipus complex. This observation led Freud to state that in the girl the motive for the resolution of the Oedipus complex, that is, the threat of castration, is missing.

Having linked the formation of the superego to castration anxiety (see Chapter 1), Freud considered women to be deprived by nature of the impetus for a clear-cut Oedipal resolution as they were already castrated, as it were. As a result of this women's superego and sense of morality were said to be compromised. This led Freud to conclude that women showed less sense of justice than men and that they were often influenced in their judgement by their feelings. In addition he attributed to penis envy other traits which he believed were commonly found in women, namely shame about the body, jealousy, narcissism and vanity.

Whilst Freud's views on female development have been very influential he was nonetheless honest regarding the limits of his own understanding of female psychology and acknowledged it to be 'fragmentary and incomplete', advising us to turn to the 'poets' to gain a deeper understanding of women's nature. Yet in Freud's own inimitable fashion – a blend of caution and scepticism coupled with great conviction and dogmatism – he referred to the 'fact' of castration in women, sometimes therefore seeming to suggest that it is anatomical lack alone which provides the motive for female development. It is also true that many psychoanalytic discussions about women seem to refer to a single type of woman and of 'femininity' – one which is principally defined negatively by contrast to masculinity.

Freud himself has been accused by some feminist authors of knowingly rationalising and thereby justifying male supremacy and a patriarchal system through his theories of female sexuality (e.g. Ward, 1984). He is, however, by no means the only guilty party in this respect as much of the early psychoanalytic literature on female psychology by both male and female analysts was dominated by the view of the female as a castrated being (Kaplan, 1991). In Freud's defence we can nonetheless note his critique of the socio-cultural and familial constraints on women's sexuality and his insight into the trap that marriage could become for many women which can be found in his writings and case histories.

Women as the castrated other: the notion of penis envy

You would be justified, at this point, in asking yourself whether it is worth persevering with a theory that is in many respects sexist. Indeed, as Freud himself suggested, you may feel too that it would be more instructive to turn to the 'poets'. It is certainly important to consider whether some of the central tenets of psychoanalysis can be applied to an understanding of the nature of women given their roots in masculine development and measurement by masculine standards. But dismissing psychoanalysis as a whole because of this would be a case of 'throwing out the baby with the bathwater'. What is needed here, as elsewhere, is a return to Freud's observations without his theoretical speculations to see what other sense we can make of what he observed – for, if nothing else, he was certainly an extremely good observer of human behaviour. Let us return in this spirit to one of his most controversial notions, that of penis envy. There are, of course, many assumptions regarding women's psychology that we could focus on in this chapter. The notion of penis envy has been selected because it is one that has received a great deal of attention and which arouses very strong feelings in most people.

Along with many feminist critics we can but speculate as to why the male organ should have such a decisive significance. Why should male envy for the breast or the womb not have an equally powerful effect on men's development? Is the penis a naturally superior organ or is it so significant because of its symbolic importance in a male-dominated culture? Unfortunately Freud was rather hesitant in his response to this, finally suggesting that the penis is central because it is the key to the imperative of reproduction which ultimately governs sexuality. This is not, however, a very convincing argument.

Freud's views on penis envy are best examined in the context of what is readily apparent in the behaviour of young children. Everyday observations of children reveal that they are quite definitely preoccupied by their genitals and often ask questions about their parents' genitals. For instance, the little boy may ask his mother if she also has a 'willy'. The little girl may also show curiosity about the absence of a penis and may be aggrieved by this fact. It is also quite understandable that the little boy who catches sight of the little girl's genital area might be somewhat curious, worried or even frightened by the absence of that part of the body which is so important to his own identity. To accept this is of course quite different from suggesting, as has been the case in psychoanalytic theory, that there is something essentially horrifying about the female genitals.

So far, so good, we might say – Freud was not wrong in pointing out that children of both sexes are interested in their own genitals and those of others. So perhaps rather than clinging to a notion that the absence of a penis actually makes women constitutionally inferior, it may be more helpful to think about the sexual fantasies children have about the differences between their anatomies and the meanings that become attached to such differences. These meanings will evolve in the context of a particular family and a particular society and culture and will therefore also reflect their prevailing assumptions and beliefs about sexual differences. The familial, cultural and societal systems in which we live play an important part in giving particular shape and content to individual psychology.

The male counterpart to penis envy

If we accept that girls might well envy the organ they appear to lack, then why shouldn't boys be equally envious of the organs they lack? Even though this may strike you as a logical progression, the notion of breast envy, which could be seen to be the counterpart to penis envy, is conspicuous by its comparative absence from the literature. This bias has been a common criticism of Freud's ideas found in the feminist psychoanalytic literature (Lerner, 1988). Yet, as Olivier (1989) points out, scanning through any magazine, looking at adverts on television or reading the content of poetry we soon become aware of a very general and widespread interest in breasts – they are quite literally everywhere.

The central place of the breast was stressed by Freud himself who believed that it is at our mother's breast that we experience the first stirrings of our sexuality. The loss of the feeding, pleasurable breast is one of the first frustrations and losses of early infancy. Men's undeniable attraction to breasts may be understood then as a consequence of this early loss and the corresponding desire to recapture the blissful state at the mother's breast. This is a loss, however, that, Olivier (1989) has argued, only women can make good as they have breasts of their own. So perhaps we, both men and women, envy what the other is perceived to have and we have not. The envy then may be common to both sexes. This is evident, as Olivier points out, in children's play where each child is curious about what the other one has and it looks as though they are both respectively aggrieved at discovering that they are missing something. This is a loss that they both explore in pretend games where the placing of the cushion to simulate pregnancy or the ball to simulate a penis or breasts varies with the sex of the child.

Equally surprising is the neglect of the possibility of men's envy of the womb. Men, Kraemer (1994) has argued, are 'peripheral to the business of making babies' – their biological task is over long before the arrival of the baby, rendering fathers redundant within seconds. Here surely lie the conditions for jealous rivalry and envy. Again, everyday observations of fathers reveal that men cope with this envy in different ways and this is likely to be a complex matter. In some traditional societies men whose partners have just had a baby go through a prolonged ritual called a 'couvade', the common features of which are abstinence from male activities like handling weapons, and being looked after by women. The ritual emphasises qualities in the male such as dependency which would otherwise be usually concealed or diminished. Kraemer, who is a male child psychiatrist, has also suggested that the elevation of great stones and the building of pyramids are evidence of men's search for greatness in creativity in their own right, one that, however, depends on the unique resources of the male body, namely its superior strength. Clearly the sense of creative rivalry, stemming from a fundamental difference between the sexes with regard to reproduction, may express itself in a variety of ways besides those mentioned by Kraemer. The activities pursued by men in lieu of actually giving birth provide a very good example of the process of sublimation at work. Some men may initiate new projects at work and become very involved with these while their partners are pregnant or have just given birth. The commitment shown to such activities and the mental space they occupy in men reveal a striking parallel with the mother's own preoccupation with the baby.

The 'dark continent'

In addition to understanding penis envy as the female counterpart to breast or womb envy there may be yet another way of making sense of it. The penis may simply represent for the woman her wish to validate and have permission for female sexual organs. Freud himself referred to the sexual life of women as the 'dark continent for psychology' reflecting his own limited understanding of female psychology. His choice of words is very apt as, certainly with regard to their own sexual organs, many women are themselves kept in the dark, as it were. Indeed, female genitals are not, as a rule, as openly acknowledged or valued as men's. As we grow up we are commonly told that boys have a penis and girls have a vagina. The vagina, unlike the penis, is an internal organ, which is not as readily explorable. But, perhaps more significantly, girls are seldom told that in addition they also have a clitoris. Yet the girl soon discovers her clitoris as the prime source of sexual stimulation and gratification. So the organ which gives her pleasure is not even labelled or validated for her and it remains a forbidden zone. Furthermore, parents will comment more frequently and favourably on the little boy's 'willy' but how often do we hear parents commenting on the little girl's vagina or clitoris. The little boy's genitals are therefore given more prominence and value early on while the little girl is left in comparative darkness about her own genitals. The girl's envy of the penis may thus be understood as arising from the anxiety-provoking nature of her own genitals which she is not encouraged to explore. Having a penis and being a boy may appear a tempting alternative and may reflect her wish to have permission for, and enjoy, female sexual organs (Lerner, 1988). The concept of penis envy may thus not need to be totally disregarded as it may reflect important realities about women's contradictory experiences and feelings about their sexuality dating back to childhood.

Aysha is a young Asian woman who was referred for psychological help for social anxiety. She found it very hard to meet new people, to go out alone and to have intimate relationships with men. Very early on in her therapy she reported a dream in which she was a man, showing off her penis to an audience of people who applauded her. Aysha felt very ashamed of this dream and she sought reassurance from me that she was not 'some kind of pervert'. She also told me that she had had similar dreams in the past.

Aysha came from a very strict Muslim family where she was the youngest of four children. Her mother was experienced by her as a rather benevolent but ultimately powerless figure. She felt she had been a disappointment to her parents who had openly shared their regret that she had not been a boy. She suspected that if they had known that she was a girl that they would have aborted her but the hospital had refused to tell her parents the sex of the foetus.

Aysha presented as very masculine, wearing her hair very short and clothes which would render her body shapeless. Aysha expressed disgust at her own body and the experience of her sexuality was highly conflictual. She could not bear the thought of having a sexual relationship – she was not only afraid of the 'pain' of sexual intercourse but she simply could not imagine any man finding her attractive.

When in the company of women Aysha found that she despised them. She saw them as weak and powerless and could not identify with what she perceived to be feminine values or aspirations. When in the company of men Aysha felt inadequate, never good-enough and eventually realised how much she wished she had been born a boy. To be a man had become equated with being powerful and admired – just as in her dreams the audience applauded her when she revealed her penis.

Aysha's longing for a penis symbolised her longing to be accepted in a family and a community which she felt offered more opportunities and respect to men than to women. As her therapy progressed Aysha explored more openly her sexuality and her disgust for her female genitals. Aysha's knowledge about sexual matters was very limited and she felt she could approach neither her mother or sisters about this. She fantasised that her brother, however, was having a good time with other women and on a very primitive level she felt this was because he had a penis which was worthy of another woman's admiration.

The construction of gender and its roots in infancy

The view of women to emerge in Freud's time, and which is still prevalent today, even if to a lesser extent, was one whereby women were seen to be much closer to nature, irrational beings, ruled by their emotions and, as we have just seen, envying the male penis. Framed in this manner women do not fare well. Indeed, as madness is often seen to signify the breakdown of reason, femininity and madness have frequently been mistakenly aligned. In the West we can trace a clear tendency to overvalue rationality to the detriment of emotionality. This may be understood in itself as a consequence of a masculine identity defined largely in terms of a disembodied and glorified conception of 'reason'. Men have learned to identify with reason but are often deaf to their own emotions, feelings and desires. The expression of their emotions and of their sexuality remains troubling as it demands the very surrender and spontaneity which men have grown up to be suspicious of.

Many men seem to find the experience of intimacy and the acknowledgement and expression of vulnerability more difficult than many women. But why should this be so? Attempts to answer this question from a psychoanalytic perspective have tended to focus on the early formative years and, more specifically, on the relationship which children have with their mothers. It is beyond the scope of this chapter to enter into a detailed discussion of this complex relationship but suffice it to say that, in a general sense, the relationship between mother and child comes to symbolise either nurturance or its rejection, intimacy or its repudiation, bodily pleasure or shame, and guilt at independence or resentment at dependence (Chodorow, 1994). At this point it should also be stressed that focusing on the important role played by mothers in shaping their young children's development is not synonymous with blaming mothers for the consequences of what may later transpire. We have created, for better or for worse, a societal system which hands over to mothers the prime responsibility for raising children even when they do not want it. We do so at our peril and the absent father is as active a participant by his absence as he is in his presence.

Nancy Chodorow, a sociologist and psychoanalytic practitioner, whilst retaining a psychoanalytic perspective in her analysis of the differences between the sexes, has challenged the tacit assumption which renders male identity as the norm. She, along with other authors, attributes differences between the sexes not to anatomy but rather to the fact that women are largely responsible for early child care. This, she argues, gives girls a more continuous experience of relationships since, unlike the boy, they do not have to turn away from their mothers, to dis-identify with them, in order to achieve a sense of sexual identity. Female identity formation takes place in the context of an ongoing relationship since mothers tend to experience their daughters as more like them. Mothers relate to their daughters with a greater sense of symbiosis and identification than they do with their sons. Such an understanding of the differences between the sexes replaces Freud's negative description of female psychology with a more positive one which sees girls, unlike boys, emerging from their early relationships with a stronger basis for experiencing another's needs – a basis for empathy.

The positive reframing of women's psychology whereby women are seen as nurturing types who are sensitive and responsive to the needs of others, presents its own set of problems. The values of care and concern which have been considered to be traditionally 'feminine' are undoubtedly important. Nonetheless, we must not lose sight of the fact that such ways of being revolve around the creation of a personality which, needing to be alert all the time to respond to others, has fewer opportunities to develop and to articulate and so meet its own needs. The stress frequently put on the developing girl on giving and attending to others may thwart her development towards autonomy and differentiation.

The identification that mothers often experience with their daughters is of course also fertile ground for difficult and ambivalent relationships between them as girls may find it difficult to differentiate and separate from their mothers (Eichenbaum and Orbach, 1982). Maternal identification is no guarantee that daughters will feel adequately loved as mothers may more readily perceive, or project into, their daughters all the attributes of themselves which they least like, which can include even their own sense of femaleness.

As we have seen, Freud emphasised the awakening by the mother of the child's sexuality. Following on from Freud's observation some writers have argued that the fact that it is usually the mother who looks after both sons and daughters is all that is required to bring about a fundamental asymmetry between the sexes – the boy has an adequate sexual object from birth in the shape of his mother while the girl is forced to wait until a man appears into her life before she can be desired and find satisfaction. Olivier points out that the little girl may well be experienced by her mother as 'sweet, lovable, graceful and good – anything but sexually alive, tinged with desire' (1989: 44). As fathers are seldom involved in early child care in the same intensive way that mothers tend to be, Olivier argues that the little girl is deprived of the important experience of being desired and female identity is stamped with the desire to meet the man who has been missing from her life for so long.

In Freud's conceptualisation the development of the boy is a more straightforward matter. From the moment of birth he is exposed to, and involved in an intimate way with, someone from the opposite sex, thereby finding himself in the basic Oedipal situation, from the cradle as it were. It is a well-recognised fact in many cultures that sons are highly prized and mothers proudly 'show them off' to relatives and friends in a manner that is less common in the case of daughters. While boys are made to feel special and proud of their sex, girls, on the contrary, introject from very early on a sense that they are somehow inadequate and lacking.

Freud also believed that a mother's relationship with her son was the most 'perfect', least ambivalent and the most fulfilling. Not only is this assumption highly dubious but it is also often the case that the special place held by many sons in their mothers' affections is not without its problems, as it is often accompanied by a corresponding difficulty in mothers in letting go of their 'little boy', allowing him to become a man who can desire women other than his own mother. Perhaps it is in response to this unconscious pressure from mothers to remain young that boys show such a considerable gap in maturity by comparison to girls (Olivier, 1989). If we take this line of argument one step further we may begin to understand some of men's negative attitudes towards women as a consequence of the early mother–son relationship which, whilst gratifying on one level, may have also been experienced as a suffocating trap from which men are forever fleeing. Commitment and intimacy with women in adult life may evoke terrifying fears of female domination as experienced by them as children with their mothers. Mark's story which we looked at in the last chapter illustrates this not untypical male predicament.

Roith (1987) has argued that the woman depicted in Freud's model as the 'castrated other' is the opposite of the mother known to the unconscious where she appears as a powerful figure who is terrifying, seductive and envied. Jukes (1993) has suggested that hatred of women is a deeply repressed aspect of the male character and originates in the early mother–son relationship. Such claims are of course far-reaching and may not resonate with our own conscious experience either as men or as women. However, it does appear to be the case that women are more often the recipients of violence and other types of abuse by men and virtually all over the world women have on the whole been treated as 'second-class' citizens with far fewer opportunities than men. Given this state of affairs there does appear to be something that needs to be explained. While socio-cultural factors undoubtedly play their part in the oppression of women these cannot be considered in isolation from psychological factors. Psychoanalysis can enlighten us on the latter, as we have seen, from its own unique perspective.

Another important implication of the developmental route specific to the boy is that mothers view their sons as opposite, as 'other', and boys, in defining themselves as masculine, need to separate their mothers from themselves and so cut themselves off from the qualities they learn to regard as feminine. Femininity then becomes the receptacle for that which is disowned and feared by men. In this light masculinity reveals its fragile position as it rests on a defensive construction developed over the early years out of a need to emphasise difference and separateness from the mother. This view stands in contrast to Freud's own belief that the development of the little boy was less complicated than the little girl's. However, it is suggested here that Freud's account misses the crucial point that '... masculinity comes to be defined experientially as a movement *away* from ... maternal intimacy and dependence – rather than towards something with a clear and vibrant content of its own' (Frosh, 1994: 112).

The different developmental routes for boys and girls hypothesised by psychoanalysis help to explain why men are so often threatened by intimacy and dependency whilst women appear to be more threatened by separation. Such differences make it harder for men to support others since they so often readily assume that they should pull themselves together without anybody's help. Their sense of reason has a tenuous connection with emotional factors. Men learn to crush their feelings of need, dependency and emotionality to achieve a masculine identity. It is not simply that the feelings are threatening; rather, it is precisely upon the denial of such feelings that the very sense of male identity is built. Masculinity has to be constantly asserted in the denial of femininity or what are perceived to be feminine qualities. Some men find it difficult to be perceived in any way as 'feminine' and may even go to great lengths to avoid anything that could lead them to be seen by others in such a manner. Lacking a model for intimacy men are often left vulnerable to feelings of fear and insecurity, of not knowing physical boundaries either with women or amongst men themselves (Jukes, 1993). Being open about a more feminine side of the self exposes men to the risk of being thought of as homosexual and also to the risk of actually experiencing homosexual feelings. Equally some women find it difficult to integrate the more 'masculine' aspects of their personalities.

The contribution of psychoanalysis to the question of gender

In a world divided along gender lines masculinity and femininity have become central to our concepts of self. Psychoanalysis helps us to understand that the differences we experience as existing between the sexes result, at least in part, from the different developmental tasks facing children of both sexes. For the little boy, the need to renounce his incestuous desires for his mother and to identify himself with his father may have the unfortunate consequence of needing to define himself as opposite to the mother and consequently to women more generally and so deny feminine aspects in himself. For the little girl things might seem easier as the original object of her desires, her mother, is the same person she later identifies with. Her experience of continuity, of sameness, may, as we have seen, pave the way for the basis of empathy. However, there may be a price to pay as she may also learn to deny her own needs or subordinate them to the needs of others. The version that psychoanalysis offers us of 'why' there are differences between the sexes provides a very unique perspective which helps us to appreciate the important role of early experience in shaping our identities as men and women. However, psychoanalysis can only offer us an incomplete picture because much of the early psychoanalytic theorising in this area tells us far more about how men experience women than how women actually are – a tall order for any theory. Freud's original focus on the masculine castration complex, as Chodorow (1994) suggests, betrayed his 'obsession' with the meaning of 'woman' in the male psyche.

The differences which we can observe and with which we struggle in our relationships to each other arise from the interaction between biology and culture which is both a product of, and is mediated by, individual psychology. Even though it was Freud who pointed out our essential bisexuality at birth, it was in fact Jung who saw the acknowledgement and then integration of the feminine and masculine aspects as a most important part of our development. This integration, while desirable, is challenging and seldom achieved. The greatest difficulty we encounter when struggling with sexual difference is that, in theory, masculinity and femininity are constructed categories, positions which are not fixed givens even if in practice we tend to prefer to think of them as immutable aspects of our being. As Frosh so aptly put it: 'though gender distinctions may be constructed and in important senses "arbitrary", they have a hold over us and are difficult, perhaps impossible, to transcend' (1994: 41). The rigid construction of our gendered selves frequently masks deep-rooted fears about the 'other'. It suggests a need to keep at bay anything which could threaten our sense of who we think we are and leads to a denial or repression of aspects of ourselves which could cause conflict.

The problems that men and women frequently encounter in their relationships to each other also raise important questions about the functioning of our society, particularly with regard to the uneven distribution of gender when it comes to child care. Every little girl's and little boy's universe often only stretches as far as their mother and siblings if there are any. Fathers are largely absent from this early theatre. The implications of an almost exclusive female upbringing cannot be ignored. While the media focus their attention on the consequences for children of being brought up in single parent families, the fact that not only do we have absent fathers but also permanently present mothers is frequently glossed over. The Oedipal drama in the 1990s, as Olivier has so vividly depicted, has a dwindling cast, only mother and child. Too much is demanded of mothers who in turn often demand too much of their children, rendering the task of separation and individuation a difficult one. If parenting could be more equally shared children may be helped to integrate the feminine and masculine aspects of their personalities without recourse to defensive structures to deal with the threat posed by the 'other'. Given this state of affairs, many writers have argued that men and women need to work towards role equality within sexual difference so that children may grow to understand that anatomical differences do not entail differences in power and status. This is undoubtedly important but as with any consideration of 'difference' it remains incumbent upon us to also keep in mind the similarities between us, those dilemmas that both men and women share and struggle with.

Chapter 4
Does the past have a hold over me?

Time present and time past
Are both present in time future
And time future contained in time past

T.S. Eliot

The notion, as T.S. Eliot beautifully encapsulated, that time future is contained in time past lies at the core of psychodynamic thinking. A central theme running through the previous chapters has been the importance of our early experiences, from birth onwards, and their impact on the subsequent development of our personalities. What happened to us as children is seen to shape our personalities in a very profound way. As Raphael-Leff so aptly put it: '"Past continuous" is not merely a grammatical term but embodies a psychological truth. The past has a tendency to perpetuate itself' (1991: 211). Indeed all psychoanalytic theories have at their root the belief that the present can be understood in light of the past.

Such a view of human being is a deterministic one which suggests that all events are determined by a sequence of causes and that therefore nothing happens by accident. In the psychological realm this means that we can trace causal links between our behaviour in the here-and-now and our past, early experiences. The belief that it is important to uncover our past is central to all psychodynamic approaches. This goes back to Freud, a committed psycho-archaeologist, who thought that the excavation of the past was essential to an understanding of ourselves. Freud, as we saw in Chapter 1, found meaning in the seemingly irrational symptoms of hysterical patients which had puzzled physicians before him as he understood these as resulting from painful memories which had been repressed into the unconscious and were struggling for expression. In so doing, Freud highlighted the logical continuity in our mental life and unravelled the mystery contained in the neurotic symptoms.

Freud was a determinist, believing that we are 'lived by the unconscious'. He clearly saw us as having limited control over our behaviour

50

in positing the existence of the unconscious which, unbeknownst to us, can profoundly influence our behaviour. Indeed the idea that the past does have a hold over us is an uncomfortable one even though it may go some way towards relieving us of our guilt about past events and actions. If we are able to explain such events in light of particular limitations or specific circumstances beyond our control which led us to behave in a certain manner we can come to feel that it was 'inevitable' that we should have acted in such a manner. For example, parents who frequently hit their children may come to understand this in light of the abuse they themselves suffered at the hands of their parents. This is not to excuse their actions but placing them in the context of a chain of events stemming back to the past may afford some measure of relief through understanding their own developmental history. Acknowledging the impact of the past is therefore not tantamount to denying responsibility for our actions. Even if we suffered a trauma as children this does not absolve us from the responsibility of the harm we might later perpetrate on others, but it helps us to understand why this state of affairs might have arisen. Psychoanalysis thus stresses that our freedom is always hedged by limitations and restrictions, some of which we may overcome.

The hold of the past: an unpalatable truth?

While some people readily embrace the notion that past childhood experiences may exert an effect on adult behaviour, others find the idea less convincing. The notion that the past has a hold over us may be difficult to accept for a number of reasons. Some of us may actually have no conscious memories at all from our childhoods. This fact may itself lead us to conclude that it must therefore have been an uneventful period in our lives. In such circumstances it may be difficult to believe in the significance of something we cannot even consciously recall. Even though many of us have some rather vivid recollections of our early childhoods these are often incomplete and we are at times left with a distinct feeling that we cannot really rely on such memories – could the passing of time not have distorted them after all? Such considerations may then contribute to an underestimation of the potential significance of past events in understanding ourselves in the present.

It is of course true that all memory is to an extent reconstructed, that is, there is not an exact symmetry between our memories and what in fact happened. While we may recall vividly certain events from our past, the vividness of our recall is no guarantee of its precision. Each time we remember something and create a mental image the latter becomes more familiar and this contributes to its subjective authenticity (Rose, 1992; Fonagy, 1994). This does not mean that we are 'liars' or that we purposefully distort the past when we report memories which we feel to be true; rather it is more the case that the recollection of our histories is always a construction about the past from the perspective of the present, reflecting its concerns.

As human beings we continuously interpret and elaborate our memories of our experiences. Gardner (1985) describes an interesting experiment which highlights this tendency. A group of Americans were asked to listen to a story, a Hopi Indian myth, and then to describe its plot. The story might well have seemed incoherent and inconclusive by Western standards yet most of the subjects who remembered the details were able to make sense of it by reworking the details into a logical sequence which was itself coherent by Western standards but which bore little relation to the original story. Their memory of the story thus appeared to be based on an expectation rather than facts. This experiment also highlights the fact that we are semantic beings needing to find explanations for events which are, in turn, constructed by finding a logical sequence that begins in the past, leads into the present and opens out into the future.

It is not only the unreliability of our memories which may understandably make us suspicious of the impact of the past but it also seems to make much more sense to attribute, for example, our feelings of depression or anxiety to an event which took place in the not too distant past rather than explaining such feelings with recourse to something which happened to us as children. Clearly, there will be times when how we feel is related to some very recent event. We may feel anxious because of an exam or a visit to the dentist or we may feel very depressed following a bereavement. Such emotional reactions are in keeping with their triggers and do not warrant a deep search into our past in order for us to make sense of our state of mind. However, the situation would be rather different, for example, if several years following a bereavement we continued to feel very depressed. If we stopped going out, frequently felt tearful, lost interest in the things which used to interest us, this would present a rather different picture. In such a case it may be that the more recent loss triggered earlier unresolved losses from the past which we had no awareness of or had previously dismissed as insignificant.

Finally, the notion that the past does determine our behaviour in the present is one that we do not all readily embrace as it is also threatening to our need to believe in our power of self-determination. The notion of freedom and the responsibility this implies is not one that we necessarily find any easier once we grasp the implications of what it really means to be free. However, on a more mundane level we prefer to believe that we are free in the sense that we can choose our lives, 'make something of ourselves' and that we are in control of our behaviour and thoughts. But if, as psychoanalysis suggests, the past and particularly those experiences we had as children, have such a profound effect on us this casts a shadow on our omnipotent strivings. It serves as a sore reminder that we were once very vulnerable and alerts us to our continued vulnerability and to our limitations as adults – even though we have, of course, considerably more resources as adults to protect ourselves from, and to cope with, adverse or painful experiences.

The re-edition of the past

Even though there are some understandable reasons behind our reluctance to acknowledge the impact of the past we need only take a look at some everyday situations to see the past at work in the present. For instance, the ways in which we respond to particular people in the present may be seen to be under the influence of our experiences in the past. In a general sense we approach new relationships according to patterns from the past, that is, we *transfer* [6] feelings and attitudes from the past which may not be appropriate towards people in the present. More importantly, these represent a repetition, or a displacement, of reactions which originated in regard to significant figures in early childhood. This suggests that we may have developed habitual types of reacting to other people which have become part of our personality, such as a tendency to be afraid of authority so that particular feelings and modes of being may be repeatedly triggered in situations where we are faced with authority figures. It is as if we have a blueprint for particular types of relationships and this influences how we negotiate relationships which we experience as falling within a particular category. In a more general sense Freud's observations on transference crystallised what has now become a widely accepted notion, namely that we bring to each new encounter in our lives our past experience, which conditions us to react in a predetermined manner.

The tendency to transfer on to people feelings and attitudes inappropriate to the present is even more pronounced when there are no cues as to how we should react. In such situations we are more likely to fall back on past experience and anticipate and then behave in the fashion of the old experience even though the present situation may in fact be quite different and warrant a different response. You may for instance find yourself responding inexplicably strongly to a colleague whom you have just met. On reflection it may then become apparent to you that the person reminded you of, and reawakened feelings in you, about some other person from your past. The important point to remember here is that this hypothetical person need not in any obvious way be similar to the person they remind you of but there may well be peculiarities about the person or the circumstances in which you meet

---

[6]The concept of transference is used in a more specific sense in the context of the psychotherapeutic relationship. This will be discussed in more detail in Part IV.

which act as triggers for certain feelings in you.

Let us take as an example:

> Lucy is 30 years old and has worked as a librarian in a university for a few
> years. A senior librarian post is advertised and Lucy applies but is not
> offered the post. The person who is appointed is younger than Lucy. In
> meetings Lucy virtually ignores the new colleague and criticises her to the
> other staff. The new librarian, in her behaviour towards Lucy, is not in any
> way trying to provoke envy or to abuse her senior position. Rather she
> actively tries to enlist Lucy's help with new ideas, hoping to make her feel
> valued. Lucy, however, remains unchanged in her perception of this person.
> A few weeks later another colleague takes Lucy to one side and tells her that
> the other staff have been very critical of the way she has been treating the
> new librarian. Lucy becomes very distressed and begins to talk about a rela-
> tionship much closer to home – the relationship with her younger sister.
> Her sister in fact works in the same university as a lecturer. Lucy recalls her
> father always favouring her younger sister, saying she was the brightest one.
> Lucy admits to feeling very jealous of her and this whole issue is clearly very
> painful to her.

> The knowledge of Lucy's past helps us to understand her present
> predicament and conversely her present difficulties illuminate her past. If
> we apply psychoanalytical ideas we would say that Lucy has transferred on
> to the person of the new librarian feelings which are inappropriate to this
> present relationship and which belong to her ambivalent relationship with
> her sister. Seeing someone younger than herself apparently being more suc-
> cessful than her triggers the unresolved envious feelings towards her
> younger sister whom Lucy perceived to be her father's favourite.

As in Lucy's case the feelings which may be triggered in us by particular situations may be very powerful and it may take a while to disentangle what belongs to the present and what is a residue of the past. If
we are unable to trace the feelings to their original source we may be
in danger of acting on feelings which we do not really understand and
which could have disastrous consequences. For instance, Lucy contem-
plated looking for another job even though there were many advantages in staying where she was. Having established the link between the
present situation and her relationship with her sister, Lucy was then
able to gain a different perspective on the situation and rather than
leaving her job she decided to speak to her sister about her feelings
towards her. Had she not made the link Lucy might have left a job she
actually enjoyed and would have missed an opportunity for resolving
some of her difficulties in her relationship with her sister.

The powerful effect of the past is nowhere more evident than when
we consider the transmission across generations in families of particular patterns of interactions, beliefs and sometimes 'secrets'. Children
who have themselves been abused may in turn as adults abuse their
own children, although this is by no means inevitably the case. It is,
however, frequently true that the ways in which we parent our children

reflect our own experiences of being parented. The ways in which we behave as parents will always carry our individual stamp but on closer inspection we may see how particular beliefs, attitudes and ways of relating with our children have been inherited from our own experiences as children. Our relationship with our mothers and fathers respectively, our subsequent experiences with the Oedipal triangle and our ability to separate from our parents all influence our adjustment to the new role as parents. Selma Fraiberg (1974), an American child psychoanalyst, referred to the 'ghosts in the nursery' when she spoke of those intrusions from the parental past whereby parent and child may find themselves re-enacting a moment or scene from another time with another set of characters, as in the following example.

> Lisa is 25 and the mother of twins, a boy and a girl. Both children suffered quite severe malformations at birth and are now moderately disabled. At the time of their birth Lisa seemed to have coped very well. She nursed her children with great care and was in all ways a devoted mother. Her children made considerable progress, beyond that expected by the doctors. When the children were 3 years old she and her partner separated and Lisa was left with the care of both children. Following their separation, the daughter began to show signs of distress, crying very frequently both night and day. Lisa could not understand what had brought on this change as the separation between the parents had been, according to her, amicable and the children had very regular access to their father.
>
> Lisa became increasingly distressed by her daughter's crying to the point that one day she pushed her away and the daughter fell. Lisa thought she had seriously harmed her daughter but in fact she had only sustained minor bruising. Lisa was nonetheless very taken aback by her actions feeling that when her daughter cried she could almost kill her. Such thoughts elicited great guilt and shame in Lisa.
>
> As Lisa began to reflect on her feelings towards her daughter she remembered that as a child she had been left to cry on her own. Her mother used to tell her that crying was something to be ashamed of and she would therefore never comfort her. Indeed this had made it very difficult for Lisa to share her feelings with her family as she grew up. As an adult, at the time of the twins' birth, Lisa had experienced the same difficulty in talking about her feelings and had felt that she should not show any signs of distress. Although Lisa had coped, she had almost coped 'too well' and it was only as a result of her difficulties with her daughter that her attention was drawn to her own unresolved issues from the past. Her daughter's cries reminded her of her own painful stifled cries fearing her mother's disapproval as well as her more recent grief when faced with her children's disabilities and now the separation from her partner. This had been too close for comfort for Lisa who then had to literally create some distance between herself and her daughter by pushing her away.

Scenarios, such as the one in Lisa's family, are not uncommon in the family 'theatre'. The relationship between child and parent need not be necessarily threatened or deeply affected by these impingements from the past although in some cases the consequences for the functioning of the family may be more serious. Such examples show us the myriad ways in which the past can still be very much alive and active in the present. Indeed when studying the interactions between parents and children, or when thinking about our own experiences in our families of origin, we are repeatedly struck by the importance of adopting what is often referred to as an 'intergenerational' perspective. This stresses the importance of taking into consideration the influences of other generations on the current relationship dynamics in any given family.

As the first child is born into a family, we might imagine that the new parents learn their parenting skills 'on the job'. However, several lines of evidence indicate that the parent–infant relationship is not constructed from scratch from the time of the child's birth, but is determined by aspects of the parents' psychological adaptation prior to parenthood. The relationships children have with their parents may be said to be determined to an extent by the parents' own relationships with their parents and so on. Hence generations hand down to each other beliefs, values and particular interactional dynamics which shape the life of the family and the development of the individuals within it. Intergenerational transmission, then, involves not only organised patterns of behaviour that are brought to the task of parenting, but also organised ways of thinking and feeling in relationships that accompany these interactional patterns.

The complex chain of causation

There has been a significant body of research on 'attachment' which has consistently highlighted the importance of our early relationships with our caregivers to our social, emotional and cognitive functioning. As we shall examine such research in more detail in Chapter 10 we will not detain ourselves on this matter here. Suffice to say for the moment that, on the face of it, such research may be seen to provide compelling evidence to support the psychoanalytic position with regard to the causal influence of the past (Murray-Parkes et al., 1991). However, it is precisely the results which have emerged from such research which, paradoxically, also cast considerable doubt on the tenability of a *strict* deterministic position.

For example, longitudinal studies of children reared in the absence of their biological parents tell us that the outcome for such children is far from gloomy in all cases, suggesting that important relationships later on in life can and do occur and these may successfully influence our subsequent adjustment (Quinton and Rutter, 1985a). Even though we know, from research and everyday clinical practice, that parents with a history of deprivation, neglect and abuse in childhood are more likely than parents with no such history to encounter problems at all stages of family life, such experiences do not always lead to significant psychological problems in adulthood or to a repetition of the abuse they suffered with their own children. Such examples suggest that the way in which the past shapes the present is not consistently predictable. If we described a set of circumstances and events that happened to a hypothetical child we would not necessarily be able to predict what kind of adult they would become even if some of our predictions may nonetheless come close to the 'truth'.

While linear, causal explanations have the appeal of simplicity it is difficult to be very specific about the longer-term consequences of childhood events. This is particularly so since we all vary tremendously and people exposed to the same adverse experiences respond quite differently and show different degrees of resilience in the face of adversity. The social and personal context within which an event occurs may determine its meaning for us and influence its impact. For children, for example, the impact of a traumatic life event is in part mediated by the parent's response. In a time of crisis a supportive and cohesive family environment may help a child to process his experience without adding further undue stress. Moreover, our resilience is not solely the result of positive experiences we may have had which could be seen to act as protective factors in the face of adversity. Not all protection stems from desirable events in our lives – it may well be that for some people the experience of actually overcoming adverse circumstances is used constructively as evidence that they can manage in the face of adversity and therefore lead them to feel stronger within themselves.

Temperament is also likely to play a part. Present evidence suggests for instance that the same stressful life events may result in different effects on children as a consequence of individual differences in temperament (Goodyer, 1990). This, in turn, is likely to contribute to their developing personality as well as to the quality of their interactions with adults and peers. For instance, children with 'adverse' temperamental characteristics such as impulsivity and aggression, have been found to be twice as likely to be the target of parental criticism (Quinton and Rutter, 1985b). Temperament thus appears to exert its main effects through influencing the parent–child interaction, thereby setting up a particular pattern of interaction which may become self-perpetuating.

On the basis of the evidence which we currently have available it would certainly appear that the past does play a part in who we become and how we are able to function in the present, and may influence the choices we make in the present, for instance, our choice of partners, as we will see in Part III. However, its relationship to the present is by no means a simple, linear one. Temperamental dispositions, early experiences, family environment, social and cultural factors all interact. As adults we might find the resilience to manage better the painful consequences of early trauma. We may have formed significant relationships which help us to find the courage to face the past and diminish its hold on the present. Moreover, a strict deterministic position is no longer tenable as modern physics has highlighted the problems with such a position. Events are now no longer regarded as inexorably and absolutely determined but their occurrence is more a matter of high or low probability.

An over-emphasis on the past as a major determining influence denies the inherent complexity of the human condition and the many forces and influences which shape us. However, even if we can no longer say that we are entirely determined by our past we can often trace in our own developmental histories some very interesting and meaningful relationships between the past and the present so that psychological events cannot be considered to just be haphazard. This notion, central to Freud's thinking, is at the core of the principle of *psychic determinism*, that is, that in the mind nothing just happens by chance. Events in our mental life which may at first appear random or unrelated to that which preceded them are only apparently so. The notion of psychic determinism, however, does not imply a simple relationship of cause-and-effect in our mental life. Rather, it is generally recognised that a single event may be overdetermined, the end product of biological, developmental and environmental forces.

To the extent that the past may be said to have a hold over us this is held to be, by analysts, commensurate with the degree to which we remain unaware of its significance. Freud in fact believed that: 'a thing which has not been understood inevitably reappears; like an unlaid ghost, it cannot rest until the mystery has been solved and the spell broken' (1909: 280). If we are able to acknowledge patterns in our lives and trace back their origins we may at least begin to reconstrue that which we cannot alter and achieve a measure of control over our lives. A deterministic position is therefore not necessarily a pessimistic one nor one which denies personal responsibility. It merely points to the limitations and constraints which may be placed on us as a result of early experiences.

Notwithstanding the limitations of a strict deterministic position, psychoanalytic theory remains in some respects a very seductive explanatory system. It can give the impression that links between the past and the present can always be unearthed and that as long as we can unearth the past and recall it we can set ourselves free of the unhelpful patterns of behaviour which constrict or rule our lives. In practice, however, links or patterns between our childhood experiences and our adult lives are not always clear or self-evident. This is because, as was indicated earlier, the pathways from childhood to adulthood are many and varied – taking one route as opposed to another may make all the difference irrespective of the original starting point which may be shared in common with others. It may, however, also be difficult to acknowledge the legacy of the past, not because the links between the past and present are non-existent or unclear, but because to do so would be too painful. When it comes to looking inwards and trying to understand ourselves we do not all follow the same 'emotional maps'; some opt for the less detailed map that only indicates the major routes, others refer to the map that indicates the one-way systems, the dead-ends, the protected areas as well as the major routes which may present fewer obstacles at first glance.

Even when we decide to take a close look at ourselves, when we make a commitment to making as much of what is unconscious conscious, this is seldom sufficient for change to take place. It may be sometimes, but more often personal change requires considerable effort as well as the courage it takes to face the past and those aspects of ourselves which disgust, horrify or sadden us and which appear to be, as if determined to maintain us in situations which cause us undeniable pain.

The search for meaning

So what is the place of psychoanalysis in all this? An important function of psychoanalysis is that it provides a comprehensive account of our development from birth which is also surprisingly coherent given the complexity of its subject matter. Psychoanalytic ideas, however, in explaining the vicissitudes of human behaviour, do justice to our complexity. This 'complex web we weave' can be rendered more comprehensible and more manageable with the assistance of psychoanalytic ideas as they help us to identify links and give meaning to our experiences. We should not underestimate this important function in coping with the chaos which many of us find so difficult to bear, especially if we experience the chaos as arising from within ourselves. We need to construe stories with a beginning and an end so as to order our experience and so disentangle the webs we weave. The ability to create narratives is basic to human existence (Jaynes, 1976). All peoples have had and have their histories. In his novel *1984* George Orwell vividly describes a horrifying world in which historical memory is constantly being re-written to adapt it to the needs of the present rulers with the result that its people lose their identity. The hero of the novel, Winston Smith, sets out on a search for his identity by searching for his own past. His quest poignantly highlights that without such knowledge we are cut off from a vital source of meaning and from the material out of which the self is constructed (Boscolo and Bertrando, 1993).

Psychoanalytic ideas and psychoanalysis in its applied form as a therapeutic intervention offer us a method of semantic interpretation which we can apply to our individual experience and which so often speaks to our experience. But even if they can help us to understand better the adults we become, we should never lose sight of the fact that we are all in a continual process of becoming, in itself a process of coming together of past, present and future with all its limitations and its possibilities.

Part II: The Unconscious

All psychological theories share in common the aim of understanding human being. This aim is a noble one but such is the complexity of human being that it should not surprise us if all the theories leave much that is unexplained or that seems inconsistent and at times perhaps just simply implausible. Over the centuries, we have made great strides in understanding the workings of our bodies and our minds – their resilience as well as their susceptibility to illness and dysfunction – but there is still so much that we do not know.

Of course, the structure and workings of the human mind have not been exclusively the focus of scientific enquiry. The mind has also preoccupied philosophers, writers, poets and artists. Each of these disciplines has contributed its own piece to the jigsaw of the human mind. For its part, psychoanalysis contributed the notion of the unconscious and in a more general sense, alerted us to the mind's more subtle machinations.

Although Freud derived most of his theoretical speculations from his study of people in psychological distress, he also devoted part of his work to studying the functioning of the mind through an examination of such everyday occurrences as slips of the tongue, dreams and jokes, referring to these as examples of the 'psychopathology of everyday life'. He pointed to an underlying connection between such phenomena which one might otherwise consider to be unconnected, and the crucial link was the existence of unconscious processes.

'The division of the psychical into what is conscious and what is unconscious', Freud wrote, 'is the fundamental premise of psychoanalysis' (1923: 13). This statement firmly places the unconscious as the central notion within psychoanalytic theory. Although the unconscious was at the core of Freud's account of the mind, the discovery of the unconscious cannot be claimed by psychoanalysis (Ellenberger, 1970). The question of the unconscious, in one guise or another, was a major preoccupation of nineteenth-century thought in philosophy, literature and psychology. Freud's original contribution in this area was to firmly establish the unconscious as a legitimate field of enquiry in modern scientific psychology which had been up until that point pre-dominantly concerned with the study of consciousness.)

The notion of the unconscious was introduced in Chapter 1, but given its central place within psychoanalytic theory and its particular relevance to understanding our emotional life, it now warrants further consideration. The aim of Part II is therefore to explore in some depth this controversial notion.

Chapter 5
Where did *that* come from?

If there's anything in this book you haven't understood, please regard it as significant.

Arnold Brown

The dynamic unconscious

A common psychoanalytic cliché is that *everything* we do or say or even fail to understand, as the Scottish comedian Arnold Brown suggests in the above quote, is significant, however trivial or inconsequential it may appear to be on the surface. The reason why we may be tempted to not accord any significance to certain events in our lives, or to some of our behaviours, thoughts or feelings, is because to do so may not only be too painful, but also because this requires an acknowledgement that we are not always in control of our actions or feelings. The latter is a notion which few of us readily accept or indeed digest easily even if prepared to entertain the possibility. As it was suggested in the last chapter, we tend to prefer to think of ourselves as the uncontested authors of our lives, in control of our decisions, our behaviour and our emotions. However, the experience of being out of control, of saying or doing things which we had no conscious intention of either saying or doing, is not an uncommon one.

Many of us will have experienced the confusing state of anxiety which seems inexplicable in terms of that which we can pinpoint as a possible cause only for the anxiety to be relieved by the expression of feelings over an incident which we had apparently forgotten.

Alex was the eldest of two sisters. They were both successful in their respective fields. However, Alex had always felt that her sister had been her parents' favourite. She said she was more attractive and entertaining than her and there were many occasions when Alex simply felt overshadowed by her. Yet she loved her sister very much and had always felt obliged to help her out when in need – her sister frequently had financial difficulties and Alex would pay off her debts for instance.

Alex struggled with her ambivalent feelings towards her sister and she would not readily accept my suggestion that she at times felt very envious of her and perhaps even harboured aggressive feelings towards her. Indeed whenever this was even hinted at Alex would accuse me of always seeing the worst in people – after all, Alex would claim, if she hated her sister so much why would she always help her?

Following a therapeutic session which had touched on these themes and during which Alex had become angry with me for attributing to her negative feelings towards her sister, Alex went away on a long boating weekend with her sister and friends. It was her sister's birthday and Alex had put a lot of work into planning the weekend.

When Alex saw me a few days later she reported a heightened state of anxiety. Whilst on the boat with her sister she had a panic attack and she simply could not understand why. She had had a good time on the boat, everything had gone according to plan, so why had she felt so anxious on the boat? The answer to Alex's question only became clearer following a dream she had a few days later which involved Alex in a fight with an old schoolfriend, someone who it transpired in fact reminded her of her sister. Alex recalled feeling very envious at the time of her friend who had 'stolen' her boyfriend from her. Alex remembered having wished her dead at the time as she was so angry with her for this. At this point Alex also remembered a holiday with her family when she was 12 years old and her sister was 4 years old. They had been staying at the seaside with her grandparents whom she felt doted on her sister. One day she had been left temporarily alone on the beach with her sister and had encouraged her to go into the sea with her even though she had been strictly forbidden to do this. She remembered her sister had been very frightened and cried but she had pulled her in nonetheless and had thought at the time that if she let her go she could drown.

As Alex reflected on her associations to her dream she realised that her recent panic attack on the boat at sea with her sister might in some way be related to what had happened on the beach so many years ago. Indeed it seemed plausible to suggest that the recent holiday had reactivated in Alex very powerful feelings of envy and aggression towards her sister, just as she had experienced them at the age of 12 that day on the beach. These feelings were quite overwhelming and elicited great anxiety associated with guilt for harbouring such aggressive wishes towards her sister. However, such feelings were not readily accessible to Alex at a conscious level. Nonetheless, the unconscious associative links between the events on the beach 20 years earlier and her recent experiences on the boat were powerful enough to lead to panic which appeared at first unexplainable with recourse to what was ostensibly happening at the time Alex actually became overwhelmed by anxiety. As Alex uncovered the meaning of her experience her anxiety lessened. She was then able to begin to address consciously the difficult and highly ambivalent relationship with her sister as well as her anger at having been relegated to second place by her family after her sister's birth after several years as an only child.

Not only can our feelings or moods appear mysterious and disturbing when we fail to find a trigger for them but we have also all most probably done something which seemed at odds with our usual behaviour. For instance, we may have forgotten an appointment with a friend even though we might like to think of ourselves as people who are very reliable and never forget appointments, particularly with friends. Or we may have said something which seems out of character, which we feel just slipped out, as if out of nowhere. Such phenomena are 'odd' in the sense that they do not fit in with what we know at any given moment about ourselves.

Most of us have some occasion to say 'I can't think why I did that' or 'I wasn't myself when I said that'. An example of the type of situation that might lead us to say such things is the unexpected argument which may transpire between couples. On such occasions, neither partner intended to quarrel. They got home and had in fact been looking forward to seeing each other. Yet somehow the antagonism builds up and the two people find themselves in the grip of a very powerful argument. The expression 'I don't know what got into me' describes this sort of occasion very accurately. It really does feel as though another person has taken us over and is making us say or do the things that we would not readily own to wanting to say or do. Often we are not even aware that there is something which needs to be communicated. Furthermore, as Balint (1993) has noted, it is not uncommon for one partner not to notice that an emotional message has been conveyed to the other partner and yet unconsciously something has been communicated. For instance, through our gestures or intonations we may convey that we are annoyed about something and yet this 'something' is not made explicit as we may not even be aware that we are at that moment actually annoyed about anything at all. The other partner in the meantime may have registered the message and will respond accordingly. A particular dynamic is then set in motion without either partner having wilfully set out to share their feelings about the particular issue which is at stake.

The situations just described catch us 'unawares' but these are situations that we all come across at some time or another and they do not necessarily impinge in a significant way on our life. Even though we know they take place we cannot always explain why they should and, more often than not, rather than trying to understand why they take place we let them pass. However, if we stop to think about such situations or the 'out of character' behaviours which we cannot readily explain they point to a contradiction. On the one hand, they are ours – that is, it is us for instance who makes the slip of the tongue and not another person. On the other hand, they do not happen as a result of our conscious intentions. Rather they have a quality about them which is accurately expressed in the phrase 'I don't know what possessed me', the idea here being that it feels as if it is not ourselves but some other alien power within us which is responsible for our behaviour. The unexplained moods we may feel locked in or the arguments which seem to spring out of nowhere are things which we never consciously intended, that we never consciously set out to cause to happen, yet the author of such events is undeniably us.

The idea of a dynamic unconscious arises when we carry this line of thinking a stage further and assume that there is something within us that is responsible for what we might otherwise regard as unusual or untypical behaviour on our part and over which we appear to have no direct control. Freud argued that there were mental phenomena that, on the face of it, imply quite inexplicable discontinuities in our mental life – he was referring to the experience of the kinds of phenomena mentioned earlier. The unconscious was the name given by Freud to the container of the things that interfere with our normal conscious intentions. It is said to be dynamic in the sense that it is influential in shaping our behaviour. For example, if we mean to be friendly with someone but in the course of our interactions with them a bitter phrase slips out, we may say that we had an unconscious desire to hurt the other but that this desire had been repressed. The unconscious motives behind some slips may, however, be quite obvious. Likewise, forgetting that we have to do something unpleasant, such as an appointment with the dentist, is readily explainable in terms of the fact that few people have a strong desire to actually go to the dentist! Whatever their underlying meaning, a striking feature of unconscious ideas or feelings is that they strive for expression in consciousness. As Freud himself remarked, 'the repressed will always return'. Our subjective experience of unconscious material becoming or attempting to become conscious is that of anxiety.

Repression

The concept of *repression* is intimately linked to the unconscious as Freud believed that we actually obtained the concept of the unconscious from the theory of repression. There is general agreement across all the psychoanalytic schools of thought that much of the contents of the unconscious have become unconscious as a result of repression. This means that there are some things in the unconscious that, at one time or another, have been conscious and repression is the word used to indicate that this is no longer so. Although repression is very closely connected with forgetting, they are by no means synonymous. The difference between the two is in many respects a matter of the degree of difficulty in bringing something back to consciousness at any given time. Something which has been forgotten can usually be recovered if that would be useful, but a thing that has been repressed can only be recovered back into consciousness after great effort or it may not be possible to recover it at all. Its existence can only be inferred indirectly from an individual's behaviour, fantasies or dreams.

Repression then is a way of ensuring that things are out of sight even though they are obviously not out of mind. This is an important point as it follows that though memories, ideas or feelings may be repressed they nonetheless remain operative within the mind but not within consciousness. In certain circumstances they may reappear into consciousness or make their presence felt in disguised forms – for example, through dreams or the development of symptoms or slips of the tongue. This suggests that although ideas may be unconscious, this does not mean that they are any weaker or have less of an impact. Rather, unconscious feelings and ideas exert powerful influences on our behaviour. Gay's description of the unconscious captures more graphically what has just been described:

> most of the unconscious consists of repressed material ... the unconscious proper resembles a maximum security prison holding antisocial inmates languishing for years or recently arrived inmates harshly treated and heavily guarded, but barely kept under control and forever attempting to escape (1988: 128).

An important question is clearly why should some things be repressed and not others? The answer is generally that an idea has been repressed because it is unthinkable in nature and if allowed into consciousness it would cause conflict and pain. So we may for instance repress a traumatic event in our lives. We also tend to repress those things that challenge our beliefs or fantasies of who we are or would like to be. The things that we repress then tend to be those which would endanger our cherished ideas of ourselves. If remembered, they might prove that we are not the sort of person we would like to think we are.

Repression can be seen in some respects to serve an adaptive function in our psychological development. The things that are repressed are things which pose a threat to our psychological stability. For example, we may repress a painful memory because if we were to remember it we might lose confidence in ourselves and perhaps be unable to cope with our day to day life. Or we may repress the memory of an undesirable action or pattern of behaviour because remembering it would make it difficult for us to develop the better side of our personality. It may be that there are things that would be so difficult for us to face if we did not repress them that it is in some respects easier if they remain repressed. Moreover, there may be feeling or memories which we do at times need to repress in order to give us a chance to rebuild our lives and then face the repressed memories when we are stronger within ourselves. Indeed there are times in our life when it is more salutary to take a closer look at ourselves than at others. For instance, some abused children and adults may need to actually forget that they were abused, erase that memory from their consciousness, in order to build a strong enough sense of self when the traumatic events can be remembered and therefore faced (Alvarez, 1992). Sometimes the repression of such traumatic events, one could say, is essential if we are to grow and develop.

Although, as has been suggested, repression may serve to maintain a degree of stability in our psychological functioning, it has some less desirable consequences because it essentially means that we are disowning some part of ourselves. When we repress something we have thought or done, or something that has happened to us, it is not merely a matter of forgetting that thing, but we are also effectively refusing to see that we are the sort of person capable of behaving in the way that we did. As we have seen, when a memory is repressed it tends to be because that memory is in some way bound up with a tendency within us that we prefer to disown as it may be connected with shameful feelings. From this point of view repression means the loss of an aspect of ourselves and our experience which we would benefit from eventually coming to terms with.

The sense that we 'should' become aware of what we have repressed is the result of the notion, implicit in psychoanalytic thinking, that the development of the whole of our personality is a desirable thing. This means that it is important to acknowledge both the parts of ourselves which we experience as good and desirable as well those that, for reasons of fear, shame or guilt, elicit the need to hide them away, so that both may be hopefully integrated. Repression, while relieving us of a degree of anxiety, may then also preclude us from actually attending to the source of our anxiety, preventing us from resolving the underlying conflict.

Another reason why repression is not altogether desirable is because that which we repress, as we saw earlier, is able to cause all kinds of peculiar distortions in our behaviour precisely because we do not know about it. It is impossible to change aspects of ourselves which we do not consciously own up to. The recovery of what has been repressed can help us to start challenging the peculiarities of our personalities and ways of being which may be difficult for us to face but it also creates an opportunity to come to terms with such parts of ourselves and hopefully to regain a measure of control over our lives.

Projection

Repression we have seen is one way of sidestepping conflicts but there are also other unconscious processes which share this same aim. We shall look more closely at these psychological *defence mechanisms* in Chapter 16 but one additional example deserves some mention at this point and that is *projection*. Projection is another means through which we hide from ourselves the unconscious cause of the phenomena that we have been exploring so far in this chapter. It is a key concept as it describes a psychological process which we commonly use and which helps us to make sense of some of the complex interpersonal dynamics that may evolve between people.

Projection involves attributing motives, feelings and/or thoughts to other people which are really our own. We tend to do this mainly when it comes to thoughts and feelings which cause us some discomfort or dissonance. We may be angry but we say that it is our partner who is angry and therefore fail to acknowledge the sources of our own anger by projecting them into the other person. Or we may be envious of someone else but actually claim that it is the other who is envious of us. Projection is a very convenient means of avoiding such uncomfortable feelings within ourselves. Let us look at an everyday example of projection.

> Mary has been married to Andrew for several years. She is a mild-mannered person who never raises her voice and cannot recall ever really getting angry. Andrew, on the other hand, is a very passionate man who frequently gets angry and is prone to explosive outbursts which Mary finds difficult. She is quite frightened of them even though the physical aggression is never directed towards her. As a child she did, however, witness violence between her parents.
>
> Mary seldom drives her car. When driving Andrew frequently becomes exasperated with other drivers and is verbally abusive towards them. Mary is very critical of Andrew on such occasions and this often turns into an argument between them. On one rare occasion Mary was driving on her own and another car almost ran into her. Not only was Mary shocked by the near-miss, but she was also shocked by her own response to the driver. She found herself quite unexpectedly shouting abuse at the man, using language that she later said she could not even remember having used before. She had also harboured fantasies of getting out of the car and hitting the other driver and subsequently felt very ashamed of such thoughts. Mary was very taken aback by her experience. She found it difficult to come to terms with the part of herself who could harbour fantasies of revenge and who could use foul language. Such an incident was so much at odds with how Mary liked to think of herself.
>
> In this example we would have good reason to speculate that Andrew was the one who usually gave expression to Mary's anger which she safely projected into him so as to distance herself from it. If Andrew had been the driver on that particular day it is likely that he would have got angry and Mary would have not been confronted with those parts of herself she so much needed to disown. Andrew, as the identified carrier for Mary's anger, would, in turn, have been criticised by her in much the same way as she criticised herself following the driving incident.

We do not, however, only project undesirable or uncomfortable feelings or attitudes into others as in Mary's case; we sometimes also project 'good' things – that is, we invest others with positive qualities. This is quite a normal process but it can become problematic if we cannot identify any goodness within ourselves. We may, for instance, always

perceive others in a favourable light, while divesting ourselves of any
positive attributes or qualities. If we have a tendency to always see
others as very good and ourselves as always falling short of some standard, we may in fact begin to wonder whether seeing ourselves as good
actually causes us some conflict and compels us to project into others
all sources of goodness. It is therefore important to remember that we
can project both the good and the bad parts of ourselves. In both these
instances projection is unconscious.

Projection causes us to make wrong judgements about the source of
the uncharacteristic things that we might do or say and also about the
nature and personality of people with whom we relate, but projection
is not merely a matter of what we ascribe to other people. Projection
can also have a very powerful effect upon its recipients as it may arouse
dormant feelings in them. In practice this means that what we might
project may in turn lead the other person to behave in a manner in
keeping with the projected feelings because they may actually identify
with our projection. For example, if we struggle with our aggressive
feelings and therefore project them into a partner, they may then
behave accordingly as our projection touches aggressive aspects of
their own personality. It is as if there is an unconscious match between
the feelings we are seeking to disown and a state of mind that is dormant in the other person but that is awakened by our projection.

These effects of projection are obviously very important when we
consider personal relationships. Many misunderstandings between
people can be avoided if we are aware of our own projections and the
power that projection can have in accentuating in the other person
characteristics that would otherwise play a very minor role if it were
not for projection. Moreover if we use projection excessively we are in
danger of seriously distorting our perception of external reality as we
repeatedly misattribute particular feelings or states of mind to other
people and this, in turn, will affect our interactions with them.

The everyday evidence for the unconscious

One of the greatest difficulties when grappling with such concepts
as repression and projection is that they refer to processes which
are, by definition, unconscious and therefore difficult to prove.
Notwithstanding the numerous methodological difficulties which
plague research in this area, some supporting evidence for the existence
of the unconscious can be found within experimental psychology. Those
interested in studies which have explored the existence of the unconscious and of repression more specifically, are referred to an excellent
book by Matthew Erdelyi (1985).

Empirical evidence is of course important but the most compelling
evidence for the unconscious is really to be found in our everyday

experiences, in interaction with others. When we are with other people and we convey the contents of our thoughts or feelings to them these become a communication. How aware we are of the message we convey in a communication or how receptive we are to the nature of the other person's message will depend on how aware we are of those thoughts, feelings and wishes that underlie the spoken message.

Margaret received a phone call from a friend, Joan, from whom she had not heard for some time. When she picked up the phone and realised who it was she said 'Hello stranger!' and laughed. The friend briefly apologised for not having been in touch and the conversation quickly moved on to other matters. Joan asked Margaret for a lift to a seminar they were both due to attend a few weeks later. Margaret agreed to do this, saying that would be no problem at all. She then told her friend a story about something that had recently happened to another of their friends, Celia. The story went as follows: Celia had just started in her new job and one of her colleagues whom she barely knew had been making unreasonable demands on her. Margaret observed that Celia was just 'too nice' and that she was finding it difficult to set clear boundaries with this colleague. Joan agreed that Celia should be more assertive and that at times she had herself been irritated by Celia's unassuming manner as, after all, Joan said, if people don't say what they really feel how can they expect others to change? The conversation between Margaret and Joan concluded and they finalised arrangements for travelling to the seminar together.

When Margaret and Joan eventually met, Joan said she had felt Margaret had been annoyed with her when they had spoken over the phone. Margaret denied this saying she had probably caught her at a bad time.

Margaret shared the contents of these exchanges with me in one of her therapeutic sessions and at first said she was confused by them and then dismissed the whole thing as insignificant. I pointed out that this exchange appeared meaningful to her otherwise why had she thought of mentioning this to me? Margaret eventually conceded that she had felt quite angry at Joan for not having been in touch and felt 'used' but she simply could not tell whether she was being too demanding of her friends and therefore she was unable to talk openly to Joan about how she had felt for fear that she might come across as unreasonable.

If we look at the content of the exchanges between Margaret and Joan we can see that they contain two levels of communication: a conscious and an unconscious one. At a conscious level this is a normal conversation between two people who know each other, who share friends and interests in common. One person is asking the other for a favour and the other obliges, seemingly quite happily. At an unconscious level the exchange reads quite differently. Margaret, while agreeing to offer Joan a lift and talking with her is actually feeling that she is being taken advantage of, just as Celia feels the colleague is making unreasonable demands on her. Margaret through her story about Celia is conveying to Joan how she *really* feels about not having heard from her for some time and then being asked to help her. She also lets her know just how difficult she finds it to tell people how she really feels just as she tells her Celia has difficulties setting clear boundaries in her relationships. In addition Margaret appears to also be conveying, through her mention of Celia's unreasonable colleague, her own fear that *she* might be unreasonable in her expectations of Joan – a theme which ran through her therapy. Joan for her part unconsciously picked up the communication and though ostensibly talking about Celia, she lets Margaret know that she thinks people should speak their mind and not expect others to divine how they feel.

The exchange between Margaret and Joan is a typical example of how people communicate at different levels of awareness. Margaret could have spoken about many things to Joan. The fact that during that particular conversation she spoke about Celia may be understood in terms of the fact that Celia's story offered a vehicle for expressing what were at the time feelings she was unaware of but which were nonetheless seeking a suitably disguised form of expression.

Words, however, constitute only a small part of our communications with each other as we also communicate by the way we move, by our facial expressions, by our silences and so on. At times such non-verbal communications may be far richer and complex than verbal ones. Furthermore, they may even contradict our verbal communications leaving us exposed as to our true feelings even though we may not even realise that we have revealed ourselves in this manner. Such unconscious communications are by no means uncommon, especially in intimate relationships.

The unconscious, far from being a static subterranean layer is a continuously shifting field. Thoughts, memories, feelings may surface and become conscious, they may surface in a disguised manner, or they remain repressed in the unconscious. In practice this means that communication, including its unconscious aspects, is not as straightforward as we might like to believe. Our intended message to another may in fact conceal another layer of meaning and communication which, if questioned about, we might deny not because we were being untruthful but because we had no conscious knowledge of the unconscious hidden message. In turn, such communications may be perceived subliminally by the other person whose behaviour may be influenced by our message even though it has not been consciously spoken nor processed. The possibility of perceptual information passing directly to our unconscious without having been first registered consciously is supported by studies on subliminal perception (Dixon, 1981).

The unconscious and personal responsibility

The notion of the unconscious is one that has the power to disturb as it challenges us with the possibility of external as well as internal unperceived control. This unease, as Dixon (1981) has suggested, can perhaps be better understood in the context of Western culture which sets the goal of personal freedom above all else.

The notion of the unconscious cannot really be considered in isolation from the question of personal responsibility. All the behaviours that have been described in this chapter are things that happened but not things that we consciously chose to do. We cannot purposely repress a thing because we would have to know about it to do this. If something is repressed we simply do not know about it. When we use projection we also have no idea that we are doing so and tend to think that the other person is the one responsible for all that is going on. This of course raises the problem of who does the repressing or is responsible for the projection and this is an issue which has concerned both psychologists and philosophers.

It is beyond the scope of this book to enter into a discussion about this particular problem but for those who are interested in the philosophical issues this raises, you are referred to Jean Paul Sartre's (1956) discussion of this matter and to Spinelli (1993). Suffice it to say though that even if we are not aware that we are repressing or projecting something, it seems that it must be true that we are in some way responsible for these things. Moreover, it is often the case that those aspects of ourselves which we repress often point to those thoughts, wishes, feelings or actions for which we would rather abdicate our responsibility.

In considering our initial responses to the notion of a dynamic unconscious it is therefore important to remember that to accept its existence does not imply that we are not then responsible for our actions or that we are not free agents. It does, however, mean that such concepts as responsibility and freedom take on a different colouring than within the context of other psychological theories.

The unconscious in perspective

Freud held that a large part of the time our mental functioning proceeds without consciousness. This is a view that stood in sharp contrast to the then prevailing notion that consciousness and mental functioning were in fact synonymous. Since Freud the unconscious has retained its central place in psychoanalytic thinking and is invoked to account for discontinuities in our mental lives. When a thought or feeling appears as if 'out of the blue' it is generally because their causal connection is with some unconscious mental process. Often when we are then able to uncover the unconscious cause we can make sense of what at first seemed odd or unexplainable.

Even though psychoanalytic speculations about the unconscious and how our psyche functions are of great interest and are helpful, we should not forget that we do not really know what the unconscious or our mind is like. Moreover we have no method which allows us to observe unconscious mental processes directly although there are indirect methods which allow us to infer their existence. Given the limits of our knowledge it is fair to conclude that any picture that we make of the psyche is only a convenient way of thinking about it. This means that no picture is the 'right' picture and the picture that has been drawn here is only one of the many ways currently available for thinking about the psyche and how it functions.

Chapter 6
Do my dreams have meaning?

One time ago a crazy dream came to me
I dreamt I was walking in World War III
Went to the doctor the very next day
To see what kind of words he could say
He said it was 'a bad dream,
I wouldn't worry about it none though
Them old dreams are only in your head'

Bob Dylan

Dreams: the 'royal road to the unconscious'

Dreams may well just be in our heads, as the doctor says in Dylan's song, but for anyone who takes them seriously their content and meaning cannot be lightly dismissed. Indeed if Dylan had consulted Freud about his dream he would have been taken a good deal more seriously! This is because Freud appreciated that dreams have the power to disturb us as they invite us to consider concerns, anxieties and wishes which we may not be consciously aware of but which dreams present to us in a sometimes quite surreal, poetic and poignant manner.

In the last chapter we looked at the notion of unconscious processes in a general sense and nowhere is the unconscious more in evidence than when we look at our dreams. Freud recognised that philosophers and scientists were attracted to dreams because they were expressions or manifestations of the unconscious mind. Any activity that refers to a hidden portion of ourselves is appealing and stimulates our curiosity. Today, the fascination with dreams persists. The physiological evidence arising from dream laboratories suggests that we all dream every night, but on the whole we remember very few dreams and even then only parts of them.

From the beginning of his psychoanalytic explorations, dreams held a central position in Freud's work. In 1900 Freud published what he considered to be his most important, and one of his better known

75

works *The Interpretation of Dreams*. Unlike the ancients, Freud did not believe that dreams could predict the future but rather that they contained knowledge of the past. His great interest in dreams was partly founded on what he recognised to be the precious evidence they provided for the deeper workings of the mind, both in normal and abnormal circumstances. The view which Freud expressed in his now famous statement that 'the interpretation of dreams is the royal road to a knowledge of the unconscious activities of the mind' is one from which he never wavered.

Freud's unique achievement was to place dreams into the domain of psychic determinism. In other words, like all other mental activities, he viewed dreams as having both purpose and meaning. His insistence that dreams could be understood in the same way that we make sense of other products of the unconscious helped him both to understand their structure and meaning and advance his treatment techniques by interpreting dreams for therapeutic advantage.

The function of dreams

Very early on Freud asked himself what a dream's purpose is and he concluded that dreams occurred so as to protect sleep – in a sense dreams were viewed as the guardians of sleep. During sleep there are many internal and external stimuli that are sufficiently intense that, if left unchecked, would awaken us. Dreams were seen as a means of somehow incorporating these stimuli into their content so as to protect sleep. For example, a full bladder may lead us to dream that we are urinating and thereby permit us to remain in bed a while longer. Freud referred to his own experience of dreaming of drinking water after having eaten anchovies the same evening and feeling particularly thirsty. Interruption from external stimuli may produce such familiar dream responses as to, say, an alarm clock where the sleeper dreams about getting up, bathing and otherwise preparing for the day. By dreaming about awakening the sleeper can continue sleeping for a while longer.

Once he felt he had established a general purpose for dreams, Freud looked for various motivations that might further elucidate the very intriguing dream process. By analysing his own and his patients' dreams, Freud concluded that all dreams represent wish fulfilments. By this Freud meant that every dream embodies the fulfilment of a wish even if on the surface it does not seem to refer to a fulfilled wish. To illustrate this idea, Freud referred to children's dreams which contain little, if any, disguise and are in essence quite naive in that they reveal their obvious motives. For example, Freud wrote of his daughter Anna who went to bed craving strawberries and that night she dreamt of eating strawberries. The idea of dreams as wish fulfilments is easily illustrated by such fairly simple dreams, especially when they are concerned with somatic needs such as hunger. In these instances we are of course dealing with conscious wishes. The situation is, however, considerably more complex when we deal with unconscious and conflicting wishes. In these circumstances the unconscious wish seeking gratification is far from apparent and the chain of events leading to the construction of the final dream can be highly complex.

Freud's views on dreams generated a lot of interest. Some of his hypotheses have been tested and they have not always received positive results. For example, his hypothesis about dreams as the guardians of sleep is not borne out by modern experimental research which suggests that incorporation of stimuli into dream content does not occur with a degree of consistency which would be expected if Freud's conception of dreams as the guardians of sleep was correct (Erdelyi, 1985). The problem with the wish fulfilment hypothesis is also quite apparent in the case of dreams which have nothing to do with pleasure or which are actually unpleasant. When faced with this challenge Freud did try to defend his thesis of dreams as wish fulfilments but his arguments were not very convincing. He argued that in such dreams their distressing content merely serves the function of disguising something that has been wished for. Along the same lines he understood punishment dreams as gratifying masochistic wishes. He did, however, subsequently revise his ideas and reached something of a compromise whereby he acknowledged that some dreams, even though not technically wish fulfilments, are at least *attempts* at wish fulfilments (Freud, 1932). Within this conceptualisation he understood nightmares or anxiety dreams as representing failures in the attempts to satisfy a wish, more specifically the wish to master in dream fantasy what proved to be overwhelming in reality as, for instance, in the nightmares of people traumatised by war experiences or other disasters. So although some dreams may indeed express our wishes, albeit in disguised form, they are not invariably wish fulfilling.

The wish fulfilment theory is also problematic because by assuming that dreams have an expressive function which releases pent-up energy, it does not allow for the possibility of seeing dreams as attempts at integrating our experience or of actually communicating aspects of our experience both to ourselves and to others with whom we might share the dream. Other theorists have therefore stressed dreaming as a form of communicating with oneself, resembling other waking activities such as talking, consoling or entertaining oneself with one's own imagination. Although many contemporary Freudian thinkers might still subscribe to the view that there is a general tendency in us towards wishful thinking, many do not consider that in order to understand dreams we have to unearth the underlying wish in the dream. Rather dreams are seen to represent the total psychological state of affairs for each one of us at the time that the dream is dreamt. Figures who appear in our dreams are thought to be as likely to symbolise aspects of our own personality as to represent people towards whom we entertain particular repressed wishes (Rycroft, 1979).

There is, however, no general consensus as to the function of dreams and psychoanalytic theorists have variously stressed the dream as a window on to our unconscious conflicts (Brenner, 1969); dreams as attempts at problem solving (French and Fromm, 1964); dreams as an opportunity for integrating recent experiences with the past with a new resolution of conflict (Greenberg and Pearlman, 1975) – to name but a few. While all these conceptualisations of the dream emphasise different functions, they nonetheless all converge on the wider adaptive function of the dream.

The symbolic language of dreams

Both the assumptions that dreams express unconscious wishes or that they represent attempts to communicate with ourselves imply that dreams also have meaning. The question of whether dreams have meaning is a most important one and has attracted a great deal of interest from academics and non-academics alike. Even though it can be inferred from clinical evidence and from the text of some dreams that they have meaning, it is not possible to claim to always be able to discover meaning in every dream.

Theories which subscribe to the view that dreams have meaning and can be interpreted also assert that the imagery in dreams is often symbolic and that individual images occurring in dreams may stand for objects and ideas other than themselves. Freud and many others following him have attempted to take particular symbols or themes that might appear in dreams and to attribute specific meaning to them. Through the analysis of his patients' and his own dreams, Freud found recurring imagery which appeared constant in its meaning and which, he was led to conclude, revealed universal symbols masking universal concerns.

Freud maintained that dreams are sexual, often giving expression to our repressed sexual wishes, and therefore that the images occurring in them are frequently symbols of sexual organs and activities. He proceeded to list numerous symbols for the male and female genitals. Freud claimed that the symbols appearing in dreams were universal, for instance a knife or gun symbolising the penis. Such a claim, as Erdelyi suggests, can be understood to arise from the physical or functional similarity between the symbols and the objects. In 1916 Freud wrote that 'the range of things which are given symbolic representation in dreams is not wide; the human body as a whole, parents, children, brothers and sisters, birth, death, nakedness and something else besides' – the latter referring to the field of sexual life. Although Freud did not view this list as representing a wide range of areas of human experience, Rycroft (1979) has made the very apt point that Freud's list in fact covers a very wide range. Indeed, the range of things symbolised in dreams embraces all aspects of our life cycle, thereby also revealing, according to Rycroft, our deep-seated concerns and anxieties about our biological destiny.

Since dreaming is a private activity, the imagery we use in dreams need only have relevance to us. In dreams we can dispense with language and the lexical and grammatical rules which would usually enable us to communicate with each other despite our differences and our different visions of reality. In other words, we can use in dreams images to refer or allude to ideas, recollections and feelings, without being concerned as to whether the references and allusions would be comprehensible to anyone other than us. The analysis of our own dreams suggests that such references and allusions are not always comprehensible even to us – indeed, many dreams remain a mystery.

The idea that while asleep we send ourselves important messages which we fail to register or to understand may sound, on the face of it, quite absurd. If we are to maintain that dreams have meaning, we then have to explain why it is that we do not usually try to decode their hidden messages, let alone take heed of them. The explanation offered by psychoanalysis is that the meaning conveyed by dreams tends to be of a kind that in our waking state we are more reluctant to understand. This implies that the division of the self into two parts which is characteristic of dreaming tends to be such that the person who constructs the dream possesses insights into themselves which the waking self is reluctant to acquire. This of course suggests that we tend to be to a greater or lesser extent somehow out of touch with our whole selves and that this predisposes us to dismiss as meaningless those nonsense messages which, if we were to grant them some meaning, would compel us to alter and widen our conception of ourselves. The meanings which are conveyed to us by dreams tend to be rejected by the waking self because they arise from a total self which still 'knows' what the habitual waking self has forgotten, disowned or repressed (Rycroft, 1979). This is in keeping with the notion of a dynamic unconscious which was introduced in the last chapter.

Dream interpretation: undoing the dream-work

If dreams are meaningful how do we set about trying to decipher them? While one may disagree with Freud's own conception of why we dream, this should not distract us from the understanding he gives us about their structure and his suggestions for how we might set about the task of interpreting them. According to Freud, all dreams have two components: a *manifest* and a *latent* content. The manifest content refers to the actual remembered dream. This is the story we wake up with and may recount to our friends, partners or even therapists. The latent content refers to the hidden aspects of the dream, those parts that are not within our sphere of conscious awareness or easily brought into it. The latent content contains the meaning of the dream which can be discovered through the process of *free association*.

Free association is a technical Freudian term for elucidating the meaning of an image in a dream by discovering the first idea that occurs to the dreamer when they think of it and then following on from there to wherever the train of thought might lead them. The rationale behind this is the assumption that the free associations to the various details of a dream will converge on to a common theme and that this will help us to discover the thought or wish which actually instigated the dream in the first place. This is an important point as dream interpretation is often imagined to mean that someone else interprets our dream without us having to do any work. On the contrary, dreams are essentially there to be associated to and not to be interpreted by reference to specific symbols assumed to hold a similar meaning for everyone. This is the approach to take if we want to arrive at the very individual meanings that the symbols we use relate to, rather than to just be told that as we dreamt of a knife or a gun, for example, that this stands for the penis. While this may well be the case in some dreams it need not be so in all dreams for everybody! We all develop particular symbols that hold very specific meanings and associations for us.

The *dream-work* is the process by which, according to Freudian theory, the latent content of a dream is translated into its manifest content. In a sense, it is as if we have an internal interpreter which translates our unconscious 'shorthand' into a language that is acceptable to consciousness – acceptable in so far as it does not allow repressed materials free, undisguised, expression which would be experienced as anxiety provoking and threatening to consciousness. If we return to the example of anxiety dreams, Freud took these to be an instance where we could observe a breakdown in the dream-work. In such dreams the latter progressively fails to fulfil its basic function of safeguarding sleep. Disturbing and frightening latent thoughts which the dream would usually attempt to disguise break through the concealment afforded by the dream-work, leading to a very disturbed night's sleep or to waking in a state of anxiety or fright.

It will be clear from what has been said that a greater emphasis is placed on arriving at the latent meaning of the dream, its manifest content merely representing a smoke-screen. Indeed, Freud discouraged analysts from focusing on the manifest content, believing that this tempted the analyst to introduce their own subjective interpretation and to resort to metaphor and allegory while neglecting the dreamer's associations. Freud's caution is important and a warning to anyone undertaking dream interpretation. However, later analysts have shown a renewed interest in the manifest content, suggesting that contained therein we can usually find the expression of conflict (Spanjaard, 1969) and relatively undisguised references to emotionally significant concerns of the dreamer.

The dream-work exploits two main devices to ensure disguise of the latent content of the dream, namely *condensation* and *displacement*. Their purpose is to throw us off our tracks when we try to decipher the meaning of a dream. Condensation and displacement are both primary processes characteristic of unconscious thinking. Condensation is the process by which two or more images are fused to form one image whose meaning is derived from all the images. In dreams condensation of people commonly occurs and involves one figure which represents simultaneously, say, the dreamer's partner and their mother – the reference being in such instances to that which is common in the dreamer's attitude towards both people. Displacement is the term Freud used to describe the process by which the meaning of one thing is transferred on to something else, whereby the latter stands for the former. So a dream which attempts to represent a current conflict in a relationship may manifestly be about an argument at work. Here, the conflict in the person's personal life has been displaced on to the work situation which may feel more manageable and less threatening.

Because of the many distortions to which the dream-work subjects the content of the dream, the end product is frequently puzzling and often 'odd' to say the least. In addition, in the manifest content of the dream, we tend to find that the feelings which triggered the dream and which are typically uncovered later through the undoing of the dream-work, are toned down. Freud quite vividly likened this aspect of the dream-work, that is, the suppression or understatement of affects, to '... the peace that has descended upon a battlefield strewn with corpses; no trace is left of the struggle which raged over it' (1900: 603). Thus when we relate our dreams they may well at first sight appear insignificant or trivial. Yet, through interpretation, we are frequently confronted with passionate feelings and wishes which were struggling for expression.

Dreams may be likened to mystery stories which both reveal and conceal as they unfold. Robert Langs (1988), a most prolific American psychoanalytic theorist, has suggested that we are all really great mystery writers. When we dream, according to Langs, we create our own mystery stories filling them with passion and adventure. We are left puzzled, just like the mystery writer puzzles us with the twists and turns of the story, as we leave behind disturbing clues that intrigue us. We often also throw in a red herring to take us completely off the track.

In this sense, dreams contain clues that need to be deciphered and if we take a look at any of our dreams, some of these clues are very puzzling indeed.

Although we may all be very good mystery writers our detective skills are not, however, always well developed. When it comes to understanding our dreams we may be fooled by the alluring but often deceptive surface of the dream. Langs has suggested several reasons why we are such poor detectives. First of all, Langs points to the nature of the dream itself. He argues that a dream is an expression of our adaptation to emotionally charged situations – that is, it is a means of coping with conflict and achieving a measure of inner and outer peace. If we were able to interpret a dream correctly this would then lead us to face the real causes of our distress so that dream interpretation can actually provoke anxiety as we bring to the surface those things that we have hidden from ourselves. Indeed, even though at times we may set out to remember our dreams, more frequently our fears triumph and our secrets remain hidden away from us as we forget our dreams, ignore them or simply remember just one aspect of them.

Secondly, Langs suggests that part of our difficulty in solving the mysteries contained in our dreams lies in the actual structure of the dream. A dream is, according to Langs, the end of the story. We need to find the origin of our dream in order to begin interpreting it. Dreams do not just suddenly appear out of nowhere. Freud said that dreams were instigated by *day residues*. The day residue is usually an event that occurred on the day of the dream although in some instances it can also relate to the previous day. Freud stressed the often trivial nature of the day residue. Regardless of its exact nature, the day residue has an associative connection to some of the thoughts or feelings which reside in the unconscious. Freud commented that the unconscious feelings or thoughts that are seeking expression through the dream can more easily attach themselves to a trivial or insignificant experience or day residue than to an emotionally meaningful event. The day residue then was seen by Freud as providing the vehicle by which an unconscious wish was expressed and fulfilled in the manifest dream content.

Thirdly, Langs points to the fact that dreams speak to us in an unfamiliar language. They reflect assumptions that are different from our everyday conscious understanding of ourselves and of the world – dreams have their own logic. Because particular objects are used as symbols in the dream to represent other meaningful objects or relationships in our life, the meaning that a particular object holds for us in consciousness may not be the same as the meaning it holds in the unconscious and therefore the place it holds in our dream.

The final reason put forward by Langs for why we fail as dream detectives is the 'red herring factor'. He argues that dreams not only embody clues but they also offer false leads that take us away from their solution. As we are inclined to protect ourselves from the knowledge that is contained in our unconscious, we are easy targets for the deception found in the manifest content of our dreams.

The challenge of dream interpretation

So where do you go from here with your dreams? The first thing to do is to discipline yourself to write them down as soon as you wake up. Postponing this until later may well be too late as you are very likely to forget important elements, if not the whole dream. Once you have recorded it you can set it aside if you do not have time to think about it there and then. Do not worry about remembering your dream exactly – what you remember, even if it is invariably a construction you placed on the dream in the process of recollecting, is still part of the story your unconscious wants you to hear. Find a quiet space where you can begin to associate to elements of the dream – you can start where you like but it often helps if you can identify, through your associations, the trigger for the dream. The rest is in some respects simple: you just continue to freely associate to as many elements to the dream as you like and more often than not a meaningful theme will in time emerge – time and patience are essential. The difficulty, however, lies in allowing yourself the freedom to let your mind wander so that meaningful associations can emerge. Dream interpretation also requires your willingness to hear the message contained in the dream – a message that may be disturbing.

It will be clear by now that undoing the dream-work to arrive at the dream's latent meaning can be very hard work not only because the unconscious is very clever at deceiving us but also because we may actually be reluctant to hear the message contained in our dream. Our own resistance acts as a further hurdle in the process of analysing our dreams. Although lack of awareness comes at a price, it also provides us with a means of self-protection. To this extent dreams are compromises between the needs of consciousness to protect us from the painful consequences of self-awareness and the needs of the unconscious to remind us of that which is being disowned. In this sense, the fundamental mechanisms that we can observe at work in dreams are not specific to them. The laws which govern the translation of the repressed unconscious into its disguised equivalents also apply to the translation of conflicts into psychological or physical symptoms. Both dreams and symptoms represent essentially the same fundamental process: the return of the repressed.

Chapter 7
Fact or fantasy: whose reality is it anyway?

And even the most solid of things and the most real, the best-loved and the well-known, are only hand-shadows on the wall. Empty space and points of light.

Jeanette Winterson

At the crossroads between fact and fantasy

In addressing itself to the most intimate areas of our experience psychoanalysis has shown a particular interest in such subjective phenomena as dreams, as we saw in the last chapter, and also fantasies. All dreams are imaginative in the sense that they consist of images of what is not present conceived as though it were. Fantasies, in turn, share a lot in common with dreams in that they also involve imagination. They are a way of describing the imagery and feelings that are set off by an experience. To talk about fantasies is really to talk about the ideas and feelings with which we invest any new situation. Such fantasies are partly transferred from the past but continue to be modified and developed in the present, in response to the world around us.

In spite of their subjective status such phenomena as dreams and fantasies can feel to us on one level to be very real. The experience of waking up from a dream feeling still totally immersed in it so much so that the mood of the dream may stay with us for hours and impact on our day is not an uncommon one. The contents of our dreams may be recalled so vividly that it feels as if we actually lived through the experience contained within the dream. Equally, fantasies may not only prey on our minds but may also influence our behaviour. It is in this sense that we might say that even though such phenomena are like private snap-shots of how we feel inside, they are nonetheless influential in shaping our behaviour in the external world.

As fantasies are constituted at least partly via language they often have partial resonances with prevailing socio-cultural norms and values which, though individually appropriated, nonetheless exert a degree of influence on their content. This is perhaps most clear when we look at the content of sexual fantasies which are partly shaped through the sexual images and language prevalent in any given culture which lend form and content to our private sexual fantasies.

Most fantasies remain a purely private affair, perhaps only to be shared with those people we feel closest to and trust. The fact that on the whole we recognise their private nature reflects our sense that fantasies are imbued with personal meaning and may therefore reveal a great deal about ourselves as they contain important clues about how we are feeling, what we wish for and what we fear. While we may not actually articulate our fantasies and share them with others, our behaviour may nonetheless betray the fantasies we harbour. There are days when, for example, we feel good, successful and capable of handling anything and we entertain in our minds a correspondingly positive image or fantasy about ourselves. Such fantasies are likely to affect our whole manner and ways of interacting with others. Conversely, if we harboured the fantasy that we are a failure, not worthy of anything, this is also likely to affect our behaviour.

Catherine is a 28-year-old woman who started therapy because she lacked confidence in herself. Although she was an attractive and intelligent woman she harboured a rather different fantasy about herself: she believed herself to be unattractive and not bright. She believed this to be true as she was in fact a rather isolated individual, with few friends and had not managed to sustain intimate relationships with men. While the description of some aspects of her life was indeed accurate, Catherine used this as evidence supporting her fantasy about herself rather than considering the alternative explanation, namely that it was because she harboured the fantasy that she was a rather unattractive and uninteresting woman that she had herself created over the years an environment which confirmed her fantasy. Indeed, because Catherine felt so bad about herself she invariably turned down invitations to go out, she paid little attention to her appearance and tended to apply for low-paid, repetitive jobs, which were well below her actual potential. Catherine's behaviour based on her fantasy expectations had thus influenced those around her who, for instance, eventually stopped inviting her out. In many respects Catherine had shaped her environment in the image of her fantasy.

The converse is also true, however, in that the environment can also spark off corresponding fantasies in us. For instance when parents argue, young children, because they still hold a very egocentric view of the world, may harbour the fantasy that they are somehow the cause of the parents' disagreements, perhaps because of something naughty they did. This was the case for Sammy.

Sammy was a 6-year-old boy who presented with various somatic complaints during a time when his parents' relationship was very strained. Sammy was very preoccupied about his parents and spoke of how frightened he was when they argued. He feared they would separate – he had a friend at school who had no daddy and Sammy said that the other children always picked on him.

When I asked Sammy why he thought his parents argued he replied that it was because he had been sent home from school for throwing some paints on the floor. He had been in trouble before and he had promised his parents he would now be good but he had let them down. Sammy was clearly very distressed about this state of affairs and his fantasised 'badness' was the reason he found for his parents' fighting. He promised me that he would be 'good' believing that this would stop the fighting and it took some time for Sammy to accept that he was in no way to blame for his parents' problems.

Underlying Sammy's fantasy of why his parents argued, we would also say is the accompanying fantasy of omnipotence, that is, Sammy's belief that his actions have the power to cause terrible things to happen, as well as good things. Indeed children in this predicament, such as Sammy, will try to behave well thinking that if they do so they will manage to repair the parental relationship.

If we pause to reflect on our own behaviour we will recognise that we imbue all our interactions with the world, at both intimate and social levels, with our fantasies. This is not to say that we invariably act on them. In most cases, even though we may, for example, harbour the fantasy of being someone other than who we actually are, the fantasy remains just that. However, there may be fantasies which are so powerful that they no longer remain private but cross over into the public domain where we might find ourselves acting on them.

The experience of people in the grips of psychosis provides a very good example of fantasies which become enacted. The psychotic state is characterised by a tenuous relationship with reality and psychotic individuals are often prey to particular delusional beliefs, that is beliefs which have no basis in so-called 'objective' reality. For example, the individual may take themselves to be Jesus Christ and will behave accordingly. In such cases objective reality is totally replaced by fantasy. While such an example may seem extreme, when we look more closely at the function the fantasy serves for the individual, it becomes easier to see the psychotic's fantasies along a continuum with more everyday fantasies. If we are feeling somewhat disenchanted with our lives we may find a measure of relief in our fantasies of how this could be different. We might like to imagine ourselves as living in a different country or holding some powerful position in the world. Freud recognised the human tendency to retreat into a world of fantasy:

> ... in neurosis, too, there is no lack of attempts to replace a disagreeable reality by one which is more in keeping with the subject's wishes. This is made possible by the existence of a world of phantasy, a domain which becomes separated from the real external world at the time of the introduction of the reality principle. This domain has been kept free from the

demands of the exigencies of life, like a kind of 'reservation'. (Freud, 1924: 223–226)

Freud thus suggested that we can all retreat into a kind of psychic reservation, a haven from a reality we may find difficult to bear. The psychotic person who harbours the fantasy that they are Jesus Christ can also be understood as creating this fantasy in the service of psychic survival, to help themselves in their conflict situation. A very interesting study supports this point. The researcher showed that chronically deluded schizophrenic patients scored highly on questionnaires measuring perceived purpose and meaning in life and showed low levels of both depression and suicidal inclination by contrast to a comparable group of schizophrenic patients who were then not deluded. The former group described an alternative perspective on reality which helped them to overcome past hurts and disappointments, finding new fulfilments and satisfactions. One of the patients who actually recovered during the period of the study, having previously possessed an elaborate delusional system centring on his belief that he was the Messiah, explained his experience this way: 'I liked to imagine it [being the Messiah] because I felt so useless without it ... I still feel inadequate now. It's as though I don't know anything. I always felt that everything I said was worthless but as Jesus everything I said was important, it came from God. I just want to hide away now, I don't feel able to cope with people' (Roberts, 1991: 26).

The main difference between the psychotic's fantasies and more everyday fantasies is that the psychotic person actually believes them to be true. They are dominated by their fantasies and in their florid psychotic state usually no evidence to the contrary is likely to make much difference to how they feel. The example of psychosis highlights the difficulties when trying to distinguish fact from fantasy as it confronts us with the question of what we mean by reality. To the participants in the above study their fantasies felt very real to them, so much so that they actually felt happier within themselves than when they were so-called cured. However, in spite of their own claims about how they feel, these individuals would be considered by most professionals to be 'mentally ill' and needing treatment.

Fantasies: a window into our internal world

The relationship between fact and fantasy is a very complex one. Fantasy has two modes: conscious fantasies or daydreams and unconscious fantasies. Psychoanalysis has naturally paid particular attention to the latter. Those theorists from the Kleinian school have argued that unconscious fantasies, conceived of as the representation of instincts, hunger for example, originate for the most part during the first 6 months of life and serve to structure the human mind (Klein, 1930). In the course of her work as a child analyst, Melanie Klein observed that children's play did not correctly mirror the 'real' actions of their family or themselves but rather showed what sense the child made of other people and the world, that is, play reflected a child's 'internal reality'. The child's perceptions of real events were understood to be coloured by their prevailing emotional attitudes and feelings towards others. More specifically, the child's innate aggression hypothesised by Klein was believed to colour the perception of others and the world. This innate aggression was thought to be so overwhelming for the child's comparatively weak ego that in order to manage it the child projected it out into the world which was then, in turn, experienced as a persecutory place.

According to Klein, the contents of unconscious fantasy cover a limited range of themes, namely sexuality, destruction and reparation. The protagonists of such unconscious fantasies are termed *internal objects*. Although the term 'object' conjures up the idea of something inanimate, within psychoanalytic theory internal objects actually refer to mental representations of people or parts of people, the mother's breast for example, which are psychologically significant to our psychic life. They are believed to be housed inside us, populating what has been variously referred to as our *internal world* or our *psychical reality*.

Such ideas, when you encounter them for the first time, may be experienced as quite indigestible, if not unbelievable. This is to be expected since they invite us to consider the existence of a world which is purely subjective and the existence of which can only be inferred. Let us look at an example which might clarify what such theorists propose. Imagine that you are looking at a baby crying and the reason seems likely to be that he is hungry and wants to be fed. Clearly there are physiological correlates to the experience of hunger and we might choose to account for the baby's experience in such terms. However, psychoanalytic theory would propose that such physical experiences are imbued with psychological meaning – indeed Kleinians would argue that biological activity actually comes with pre-formed psychological meaning, that is, that we are all born equipped, as it were, with specific unconscious fantasies arising from our physical and emotional needs. Returning to our hungry baby, the theory would posit that the baby will internally represent the experience of hunger in a very primitive way, as an object located inside their tummy which is malevolently intent on causing painful sensations (Hinshelwood, 1994). While this is what would be termed an unconscious fantasy, the point is that for the baby the experience is nonetheless very real and their distress is also very real to you as observer. What may also be real, however, is that the reason the baby may have to wait is that the mother is either still cooking the meal or the meal is too hot to eat and not because she is wishing to cause pain to her baby. The baby, however, cannot conceptualise his pangs of hunger in this manner and reassure himself that food is on its way. Rather, as we have seen, the baby's reality may be that he is being deprived and this experience is represented in the unconscious fantasy of the 'bad' object inside him which is causing the pain in his tummy.

The latter point conveys the essence of the psychoanalytic perspective on the question of reality, namely the importance accorded within such thinking to our psychical reality and its intimate relationship with external reality. Psychical reality is the world that is real for us but may not be real for anyone else. When Freud (1917a) spoke of psychical reality he was referring to everything in our psyche that takes the force of reality within us. Fantasies may be said then to possess psychical as opposed to 'material' reality but are themselves frequently the result of complex chains of interactions with external reality. It is the unique nature of these interactions which determines how we attribute meaning to our experiences and behave in the external world. To the extent that this is true, while fantasies may at times be based on reality, our interpretation of external reality is coloured by the contents of our internal reality where the former acquires a specific and individual meaning for us.

Fact or fantasy: which one matters most?

The distinction between, and the respective functions accorded to, psychical and material reality are significant in the history of psychoanalysis. It was Freud who stressed the importance of fantasies in the aetiology of neuroses. At first, he believed that hysteria, obsessional neurosis and paranoia were caused by the repressed memories of traumatic childhood sexual experiences. Freud found that his female patients revealed in their analyses much material of an erotic nature. He also found that just about all of them reported not simply erotic feelings and episodes from their current sexual lives but also sexual experiences which appeared to have occurred in their childhoods and which suggested to Freud that they had in fact been sexually abused by adults. This 'discovery' provided Freud with the sexual trauma which his theory required at the time. Because sexual seduction in childhood seemed bound to be traumatic to the child victim and inevitably had to lead to repression because it was such a traumatic experience, it seemed to follow for Freud that such seduction had to be a universal cause of hysteria in later life when the emergence of adult sexuality served to reactivate the earlier trauma. This is what is referred to as Freud's *seduction hypothesis*.

Freud pursued this idea for a few years but gradually became dissatisfied with it and abandoned it in 1897. At this point he concluded that what he had initially taken to be recollections of real traumatic events were, often at least, fantasies founded not on the actual perverse acts of adults, but on his patients' own latent sexual feelings. The recollections were understood to be merely memories of infantile fantasies. This is what is known as the *wish theory*. The wish theory is the cornerstone of one of Freud's most controversial suggestions, namely that children have a very active sexual life. It also led to Freud's ideas on the Oedipus complex.

There has been much speculation as to Freud's underlying motivations for eventually abandoning his seduction theory and he has been severely criticised for this as, it is argued, it reduced to mere fantasy what were in fact the painful consequences of real sexual trauma (Masson, 1984). While such criticisms are often voiced we shall never know what really motivated Freud to change his theory. However, it is clear from his own writings that even after the retraction of his 'seduction hypothesis' he continued to remain aware of the prevalence of sexual abuse and that he was sensitive to the deleterious psychological consequences of such abuse for the victim. We shall not detain ourselves further on this question, important though it is. The relevant point to this discussion is that Freud's replacement of the seduction theory by one in which trauma resulted from an imagined event introduced the notion of unconscious fantasies and highlighted their powerful impact on our psychological functioning.

The either/or nature of the problem, namely real seduction versus fantasy, raised the thorny question of the relative importance of external versus internal reality in the causation of psychological problems. A criticism often levelled at psychoanalysis is that in focusing so much on psychical reality, attention is too often diverted away from the harsh social reality of some people's lives which may be seen to explain some of the psychological problems that they experience. It would certainly be worrying if people's experiences of real trauma were ignored or belittled in favour of a more exclusive emphasis on their fantasies about such experiences. There is now ample research which supports the view that social factors play an important role in the onset of mental health problems. For instance, the now well-known work of Brown and Harris (1978) on depression in women found a greater prevalence of depression among working class than middle class women. This was explained in terms of certain vulnerability factors being more likely among working class women: loss of a mother before age 11, lack of paid employment, three or more children under 14 years living at home and lack of an intimate and confiding relationship. Most of these factors are markers of deficits in social and material resources. A lower social class position is associated with a number of stressful factors which are thought to reduce the individual's resources for coping with everyday stress.

In understanding the development of psychological problems it is therefore important to acknowledge the part played by real social factors. With its emphasis on our internal reality, psychoanalysis may be seen as insensitive to the actual reality of people's lives and therefore as ultimately redundant in helping to bring about much needed change in our society. While such a criticism may be true of certain psychoanalytic theorists who have overemphasised the role of fantasy in the onset and perpetuation of psychological problems, the criticism is more difficult to justify in a general sense. Most analysts readily and sensitively acknowledge the existence of real trauma, injustice and adverse social circumstances and their impact on our psychological well-being. They would, however, also stress the dialectic between fantasy and reality and consider the understanding of this dialectic their province.

What is reality?

In practice the dichotomy between subjective and objective truth or knowing may not be a very useful one. As phenomenologists[7] have long stressed, true reality is both unknown and unknowable (Spinelli, 1989). That which each one of us experiences as real is intimately bound up with our need to construct meaning. Our experience of the world is therefore always the result of an interaction between the raw matter of the world, that is the facts, and our inner reality. The latter can be thought of as a composite of unconscious and conscious perceptions and experiences which acquire meaning over time and, importantly, whose meaning is susceptible to multiple reconstruction over time. If we follow this line of thinking it is then not helpful to speak of a fixed internal reality any more than we can speak of a fixed external reality. Both are shifting fields and as they interact they produce unique realities. If we wish to understand ourselves and the forces which shape us then we need to look inwards as well as outwards. This underscores the dialectical nature of our development from birth onwards, in which our behaviour, which is influenced by our fantasies, changes reality and then, in turn, the changes in reality affect our behaviour.

To highlight the importance of a dialectical perspective on the nature of reality, let us return to the question of memory which we briefly touched on in Chapter 4. An issue of contemporary concern and debate has been the question of 'false memories'. There has been increasing speculation as well as scepticism over the past few years about the veracity of so-called recovered memories of abuse, particularly of abuse involving satanic rituals. The crux of the debate is whether such recovered memories are true or false, that is, whether

---

[7]Phenomenology is a branch of philosophy and psychology which primarily concerns itself with how we arrive at unique interpretations of reality.

they relate to actual experiences of abuse. This is clearly a very thorny area. Many of us find it difficult to believe that some people may be subjected to horrific forms of abuse and it may therefore be more comforting to believe that such abuse does not exist and hence that the recovered memories are false. This may well lead us to ignore the veracity of some accounts but we do know that abuse does occur and occurs with more regularity than we might like to think.

However, we also know from experimental research that in recalling memories we make inferences about what may have happened in order to fill in the gaps and in so doing we frequently confuse the sources and attribute such reasoning to actual memory (Fonagy, 1994). This tendency in fact refers to a common process, identified by Freud in his work on dreams, which he called *secondary revision*. The latter refers to the attempts to normalise the end product of the dream-work so that the gap-filled material is worked over and elaborated into a more coherent whole. Such observations suggest a degree of caution in how we approach memories of any kind if the intended aim is to establish the veracity or otherwise of the recollection. Rose describes well how every time we remember events from the past we recreate memories anew:

> But I have ... in some measure re-invented these memories. Obsessed with the attempt to see how far back in my childhood I can remember I have taken out these internally filed photographs, redeveloped and reprinted them, cropped them a little differently ... enlarged them to fit a new frame (1992: 35).

Research findings in fact support the essentially Freudian notion of the vulnerability of memory to the vicissitudes of desire (Fonagy, 1994). In most instances unless we can make recourse to external corroboration, there is often no way of being able to distinguish accurately between wish fulfilling fantasy and fact. However, this should not be taken to imply either that the traumatic events which we recall are invariably the product of fantasy or that what we recall and believe to have happened is unimportant. Particular recollections may lead us to hold certain beliefs about ourselves and others. Beliefs have consequences of course and it may therefore be important to establish, as far as it is possible, the veracity of our recollections. This would be the case, for instance, if what we believed to have happened to us in the past leads us to take legal action against another person or group of people. However, even in less extreme cases, if we hold certain beliefs about our life and the people in it on the basis of our memories, such beliefs may play a crucial role in shaping our behaviour and attitude towards others. The argument that we cannot really know material reality as such does not mean that we can ignore it – some constructions of the world and our experiences make more sense than others.

The interconnectedness of inner and outer reality

Psychoanalytic thinking has been very influential in encouraging us to take seriously what and how we feel irrespective of the factual status of the events which trigger particular feelings or thoughts in us. Indeed psychoanalytic treatment, following Freud's early formulations, starts on the assumption that neurotic symptoms are grounded *at least* upon psychical reality, on our 'truth', although in some instances there may well be a real trauma which has played its part in the development of psychological problems.

Freud was clear that we should not apply the standards of reality to what is repressed in the unconscious as unconscious processes disregard reality testing and therefore equate reality of thought with external actuality. Given this, fantasies may give rise to symptoms just as readily as any real external trauma. However, while this may be true it is not possible to ascertain whether fact is *more* important than fantasy in our psychological affairs or vice versa. The distinction between the two will be more significant to some people than it will be to others. All that can really be said is that psychoanalytic clinical practice provides numerous examples to suggest that the exploration of our emotional life in light of both inner *and* outer reality is important. Whatever our beliefs are about the world and ourselves we have to become resigned to the fact that it may at times be very difficult, if not impossible, to separate out fact from fantasy, particularly where beliefs are based on past recollections.

Psychoanalysis reveals just how difficult it is to separate inside from outside, reality from fantasy, and invites us to consider the more controversial question of whether it makes a difference at a psychological level if a recollected trauma actually occurred or merely reflects a fantasy. Objective versus subjective truth is too simplistic a dichotomy when it comes to understanding ourselves, given some of the difficulties in establishing what is real which have been examined in this chapter. The difficulties bring sharply into focus the fact that we are all construers of experience and that the meanings we attribute to our experiences are highly personal ones, possibly not shared by anyone else – the unique product of the interaction between our fantasies and wishes, conscious and unconscious, and our raw experiences. Even when our perceptions are accurate, our fantasies may yet enhance, obscure or altogether distort certain aspects of what is actually there.

The fact that our individual realities are so subjective should in no way devalue our experiences nor should we dismiss our fantasies because they are not necessarily based on external reality. There is a tendency, however, to think that the most vital thing is always to check up on whether the facts bear out how we feel. As was mentioned earlier this may be very important for some people, if not essential in

particular instances. But perhaps we are at times eager to stick to consciousness and reality because we associate fantasy with madness.
Fantasies may of course serve a defensive function by offering us an
escape from reality which we may manipulate, in fantasy, to suit our
needs. Also fantasies may be so out of touch with external reality, as in
the case of the psychotic individual, that they may actually interfere
with day to day life.

However, fantasies are not per se something to be avoided, rather
they are a part of our mental life and they add richness and colour to it.
Of course, an important implication of all this, as we shall see in Part
III, is that relationships are never straightforward, as they always
involve the interaction of two quite unique psychical realities with all
their accompanying fantasies. While this may give rise to some complicated scenarios between people, fantasies are ultimately an integral
part of the rich tapestry of life – often painful in its creation but equally
captivating in its intricate design.

Chapter 8
The unconscious – friend or foe?

A full life requires access to the needs and secrets of the unconscious mind, brought into the beacon light of direct awareness where they can be used to influence the course of our lives favourably. Left in the dark, these needs can only cause pain.

Robert Langs

The wisdom of the unconscious

Throughout Part II we have looked at the notion of the unconscious from a number of different perspectives. Its primary role, it has been suggested, is as the keeper of personal truths, wishes and fantasies – not only those aspects of ourselves we wish to keep from others but those we often primarily need to keep from ourselves. However, while the unconscious may serve as a repository for that which we disown, it is not foolproof and memories or fantasies may find their way back into consciousness even if usually in disguised form, such as through dreams or slips of the tongue. At times it may feel as though we are 'tripped up' by the unconscious and we are left exposed. The unconscious then may be experienced as an enemy who is not to be trusted and this leads us to be on guard, just in case.

Most of us would prefer to believe that what we experience and directly perceive accounts for what is most important in life. We might like to dismiss such phenomena as slips of the tongue and forgetting more generally as mere quirks – idiosyncrasies of our being but no more than that. This fact in itself can account for the many criticisms and rebuttals of the notion of an unconscious part of the mind which have marked the history of psychoanalysis. When reading such critiques one is left with the strong impression that there seems to be something quite unpalatable, at an emotional level, about the notion. Yet, even if we may deny the existence of unconscious forces, they make their presence known. The choice we have available to us is then between an insistence that there is no such thing as an unconscious and a commitment to befriending and exploring it. If we opt for the latter we can discover the unconscious as a source of wisdom, capable of helping us in our daily struggles when we are faced with difficult choices or decisions or when we are left with a sense that something is amiss in our lives, the source of which eludes us.

The view of the unconscious as a source of personal wisdom is somewhat at odds with the manner in which the unconscious is conceptualised within classical Freudian theory which has been presented up to this point in this book. Within classical theory, the unconscious part of the mind is said to be ruled by the pleasure principle and hence not capable of making rational decisions – a task relegated to the conscious part of the mind which is governed by the reality principle (see Chapter 1). Before we examine further the alternative perspective of the unconscious proposed here let us take a look at a particular example of a dream, for the unconscious is best grasped when we can see the products of its intricate machinations. The following dream highlights the way in which our unconscious can assist us with some of the difficult dilemmas we are all confronted with at some stage of our lives.

> Carol had been married to John for four years. Their relationship got off to a difficult start as her family disapproved of John. Despite this, Carol and John remained together, struggling with several stressful life events which challenged them over the years. John had been wanting a baby for a few months now but Carol had been more hesitant. She felt that the first few years of their relationship had been intruded upon by her family and that she was still feeling very vulnerable and preferred to postpone a while longer the responsibility of a baby. Furthermore, John had recently been made redundant. However, John's insistence was such that Carol eventually decided to 'give in' as she saw it. After all, she said to herself, everyone has doubts about starting a family and it was probably better to just 'get on with it'. A few days following this decision, Carol had a very vivid dream. She is in a supermarket. She is slowly wandering about, pushing the trolley which feels very heavy. She cannot decide what to buy for dinner. A shop assistant draws her attention to a new product and pushes her to buy this new product – a new ready-made dish – it is quick and he assures her it will please her husband. Carol is unsure about this, however. She recalls having read an article about food preservatives which said they were bad for your health. She then pushes the shop assistant aside, leaving the full trolley and walks out thinking that she will do the shopping another day as she is not in the mood for it.
>
> As we saw in Chapter 6, dreams need to be associated to so as to arrive at their disguised meaning. Carol sets off on this task. She recalls that the shop assistant in the dream wore a shirt very similar to one that John had recently bought. She also recalls that the shop assistant repeatedly said 'come on' as he tried to encourage her to buy the new product. She realises that the expression 'come on' is one that her father-in-law frequently uses. Her in-laws had recently been to visit them and they had asked when they would become grandparents. Carol also associates the full trolley with a

friend of hers whom she feels often buys too much unwholesome food which Carol believes is giving the children bad eating habits. This is a friend that she has known for years and whose only ambition was to have a family. In fact she recently told Carol that she wanted another child. The full trolley is also equated by Carol with the fullness of pregnancy and in the dream she is aware of the heaviness of the trolley and her difficulty in pushing it. This leads Carol to reflect on her ambivalence about the physical aspects of being pregnant.

It is already clear by this stage that Carol's associations to some of the features of her dream point to her current dilemma. The shop assistant's insistence that she buy the new product can be understood as a disguised reference to John's insistence that they should have a baby. If we accept this link then we can see that the dream contains a message to Carol. The ready-made dish which is 'quick' and which the shop assistant, in the dream, assures Carol will please her husband, can be seen as a disguised reference to the hasty decision she rushed into so as to please John. In her dream, Carol is also concerned that the new dish may contain some preservatives which would not be good for her or John. This may be seen to mirror her own conscious anxieties that now is not the right time for John and her to start a family. Finally, in her dream Carol decides she is not in a mood to shop and postpones this till another time, leaving behind the heavy trolley. The dream therefore seems to be suggesting to Carol that she should really trust her instincts and postpone the decision to start a family. After all, as in the dream, this is something she can return to another day. Following this dream Carol spoke with John. Many heated arguments ensued but in the end they both agreed that it might be wiser to wait a while longer and that in fact they both needed some help with their relationship which had become quite strained.

Deploying our unconscious source of wisdom

Langs (1991), the American psychoanalyst whose views on dreams we encountered earlier, has proposed substantial revisions to the classical Freudian model of the mind. He points out that there are two ways in which we can deal with stress in our lives. We can use the 'conscious system method' which involves, for example, confronting issues or examining the advantages and disadvantages of particular decisions. However, the more effective way of handling these issues is, according to Langs, by using the 'unconscious system method'. This is a way of reasoning that involves thinking carried out without awareness and whose solutions or suggestions are conveyed to us in encoded, disguised language. Carol's dream is an example of the latter. While consciously Carol had reached one decision, her unconscious system worked over this decision and came up with an alternative suggestion – one which was more in keeping with Carol's anxieties and with the reality of her situation at the time.

The reason why the conscious system is not ideally suited for reaching decisions is that its capacity for insight is hampered by its use of defences. Carol had in fact been afraid that John would become very depressed if she did not agree to becoming pregnant. She was aware that the loss of his job had affected him a lot and that having a baby was a way of replacing, in a sense, the loss of the job. It also appeared to be a way of avoiding the marital difficulties which later became more apparent. Carol's conscious decision to have a baby was therefore more in keeping with her desire to protect both herself and John from his depression and their marital difficulties – but there was a high price to pay for this. By listening to her unconscious and taking heed of its advice, Carol found the strength to confront the situation with John and possibly avert later difficulties.

Within Langs' conceptualisation the unconscious part of the mind is seen as capable of analysing interactions between people and of making very incisive comments on our own behaviour as well as that of others. This is because, according to Langs, the unconscious has access to perceptual information. This is the critical difference between his model and that espoused within mainstream psychoanalysis. Throughout most of Freud's writing the view that the unconscious part of the mind has no direct access to perceptual information is expressed. However, Smith (1991) has shown that even though Freud did not explicitly refer to unconscious perception, some passages in his writings support a theory of direct unconscious perception even if this theory was never fully developed by Freud. So, for instance, in 1915 Freud wrote 'I have had good reason for asserting that everyone possesses in his own unconscious an instrument with which he can interpret the utterances of the unconscious in other people'. Such a statement supports the view of the unconscious as an 'instrument' or faculty concerned with the interpersonal realm, that is, the perception of emotional reality, which is commonly concealed behind defensive structures.

Like any 'instrument', in order for us to play it and to hear its beautiful, if at times poignant, sound we have to practise playing it and the practice may be painstaking and arduous. No less is required of us if we want to deploy the potential of the unconscious. It is not that the unconscious part of our mind needs to practise its analytical and interpretive skills – the unconscious, as conceived of here, is very adept at analysing incoming information and drawing accurate inferences about our inner life. It is more the case that *we* need to practise and to be committed to giving its views a fair hearing. This is no easy task as we can trace within all of us varying degrees of resistance to any process that may lead to our conscious awareness of those areas of our experience which we would rather ignore. As Langs put it, 'the world of unconscious experience is primitive, horrifying, blunt in its appraisals and raw in its reactions' (1991: 22). In a sense it does not bother with the niceties of the conscious system but 'tells it as it is'.

As we have seen throughout the last few chapters, the unconscious stores a wealth of perceptions, thoughts, memories and feelings. Its contents have been placed there because they would otherwise give rise to discomfort and pain. If we remain unaware of them we reinforce a split within ourselves in that we 'refuse' to face aspects of our being over which we consequently have little control but which nonetheless continue to affect us in subtle, and sometimes not so subtle, ways. It is in such instances that the unconscious may well be experienced by us as an enemy force residing within us, as that which we repress, as Freud himself suggested, invariably comes back to haunt us. But if we can find the personal strength to face our 'ghosts' we then create an opportunity to engage with the repressed aspects of ourselves, to understand them and hopefully to integrate them into the whole of our personality. We also gain access to a rich source of personal wisdom.

This chapter simply cannot do justice to the complexity of the revisions which have been made to Freud's original models of the mind. To go into any more depth on this topic is well beyond the scope of this chapter and this book. However, Langs' views have been introduced as they invite us to rethink the nature of the unconscious often equated with the unruly 'id' seeking gratification. Rather, Langs suggests that the unconscious is in a sense 'intelligent' and can therefore assist us in working through our dilemmas and in picking up important clues in our environment and in our exchanges with others which may simply not register consciously. Such a hypothesis requires testing of course but it does represent an alternative model of the mind which is interesting and controversial to say the least.

We all face dilemmas in our lives and at such critical points we often wish someone else would give us the answer or at least guide us towards the answer. It is at such times that we may even seek professional help in the hope that we will make the right decision. This may of course be helpful, as we shall see in Chapter 18. However, what is being suggested here is that, when looking for such guidance, we need not really search very far. The richest and perhaps wisest source of advice lies within us, waiting to be discovered. We just need to be prepared to hear its message.

Part III: Love and Relationships

One of the areas of human experience where psychoanalytic theories have been most prolific is that of human interaction. Psychoanalysis, with its commitment to studying the development of the individual from birth, and more recently even from our existence as foetuses (Piontelli, 1992), has paid particular attention to the interactions between children and their parents and of adults in relationship to each other. From such observations developmental theories have emerged which have been applied to an understanding of human relationships generally and have also identified the central place of our early relationships in our psychological development. Underpinning a psychoanalytic understanding of all relationships is the central assumption that much of what transpires between us is unconscious. The importance of unconscious communication between human beings can be observed daily in our lives if we take the time to examine our own interactions with those around us.

Part III draws on both Parts I and II and brings them together in applying the notions which they introduced and explored to the intriguing subject of relationships.

Chapter 9
Can I love myself too much?

To love oneself is the beginning of a life long romance.

Oscar Wilde

What is narcissism?

It seems fitting to begin Part III, with its focus on relationships, with a chapter on the relationship we each have with ourselves as this affects how we are then able to relate to others. If we dislike ourselves or feel uncomfortable or dissatisfied with certain aspects of ourselves we may find it difficult to envisage that others will like or love us – how could anyone love us if we believe ourselves to be unworthy of love? On the other hand, we may experience a mixture of feelings; we may be satisfied, for instance, with how we perform at work but less satisfied with how we look or how we behave in certain situations. This may give rise to a degree of conflict and unhappiness and while many of us usually find ways to manage our own lack of perfection, this is not always the case. There are those individuals who experience a greater degree of difficulty in coming to terms with who they feel themselves to be and for whom 'perfection' remains a longed for, but never attainable, ideal. Certain others, however, may behave as though they believe themselves to be perfect and often betray a great, if not exclusive, interest in themselves. They appear to be engaged, as Oscar Wilde put it, in a life long romance where they are both lover and beloved. Such individuals are often referred to as *narcissistic personalities*. Narcissism is now a word we all use and, on the whole, it has come to be used in a pejorative sense to denote self-preoccupation or self-love. To be told that we are narcissistic is unlikely to make us feel good about ourselves.

The term narcissism originates from the Greek myth of Narcissus. Narcissus was the son of the nymph Leiriope who was told by an oracle that her son would live well into old age provided he never knew himself. Narcissus was a beautiful young man who was courted from all sides by both men and women and many were the hearts he had broken. One of his suitors killed himself with a sword sent to him by Narcissus. As the man was dying he called on the Gods to avenge his death. Artemis, one of the Gods, heard his plea and responded to this by ensuring that Narcissus would fall in love while denying him for ever the consummation of his love. One day, so goes the myth, Narcissus was leaning over a pool of water when he caught sight of his own reflection. Its beauty was so great that Narcissus became enamoured with it. Unable to detach himself from this illusory love, tormented by the desire he could never, however, consummate, he plunged a dagger into his breast.

The term 'narcissistic' was first used in the sexology literature in 1898 and it then denoted someone who treated their own body as one would generally treat a sexual object. Freud (1914) at first used the term in a similar fashion to refer to people who find their own bodies entirely self-satisfying. Such an attitude, Freud believed, was frequently seen in male homosexuals who, according to him, took themselves as their own sexual object – that is, they proceeded from a narcissistic basis and looked for a young man who resembled them. Freud, however, went much further than this and elaborated a complex theory of narcissism,[8] arguing that although narcissism in later life could be pathological there exists an early stage of normal narcissism.

Freud described the baby as beginning life in a stage of *autoerotism*. This is the first stage of development where, it was hypothesised, there is no concept of self and other. It is an unintegrated state where the world is not filtered through the concepts of 'you and I'. In this world there are no people, just physical sensations. Eventually, Freud believed, the child develops a self-representation. At first this contains everything good in its experience. Everything that yields pleasure is considered to be 'ME' and everything that is unpleasurable is 'NOT-ME'. The mother's care and concern in response to the baby's needs create the illusion that mother and baby are one. This is the state of narcissism where the baby is in love with himself and thinks he is omnipotent. This blissful state is, however, one from which we need to be gradually disenchanted. As the baby cognitively matures he is forced to realise that there are also 'good' things outside as well as 'bad' things inside. The baby then becomes able to recognise his dependence and so becomes capable of loving another person. This painful transition from omnipotence to a recognition of limitations leads the baby from narcissism to what is termed 'object love' (i.e. love for another person). But what happens to narcissism? Freud believed that we are unable to give up entirely our early gratification so that the belief in our own perfection is transformed into an ideal of at

---

[8]Freud used the term narcissism in a number of different ways which reflected the development of his own ideas in this area (Smith, 1985). The term is used here to refer to illusions of self-sufficiency and this reflects Freud's own theorising on narcissism in the period between 1915 and 1923.

some point achieving perfection, namely the *ego-ideal*. According to Freud we chase our renounced grandiosity throughout life. Indeed, he believed that we never really give anything up but merely exchange one thing for another.

Although Freud made no mention in his earlier writings on the subject of narcissism of its pre-natal origins, he later came to view the foetal state as the origin and model of absolute narcissism (Freud, 1921). During intra-uterine life the illusion of complete self-sufficiency is satisfied – in the uterus the physiological functions and needs of the foetus are automatically fulfilled by the mother's body. If we can speak of a self at this stage we would say that it is omnipotent, 'in a state where time and space do not exist since they result from the gap between the appearance of a need and its satisfaction' (Grunberger, 1991: 219).

Healthy versus pathological narcissism

Freud found evidence of narcissism in children's belief in the magical power of their wishes. Grandiose, omnipotent and magical thoughts and feelings are ubiquitous in the mental life of children. In their games children play out their extraordinary powers, they become the invincible warriors to whose power there is no limit. In play they can make things happen and can exert great control over their make-believe world. All such games reflect the child's fantasies of self-sufficiency which are at the core of narcissism. In the context of play such fantasies are normal and in no way pathological.

Freud hypothesised that narcissism is not just a stage of development but a stable structure within us. He believed that we all remain narcissistic to a degree, even in our relationships with each other. For instance, Freud understood parental love in terms of a revival of the parents' own narcissism. It is certainly the case that parents invest much of themselves and their aspirations in their children. The children's achievements are sometimes experienced as the parents' own achievements, that is, they regard their children as a narcissistic extension of themselves. The parents' narcissistic investment in their children is adaptive. The child is experienced as a part of the parent and this enables them to care for the child, often at the cost of their own gratification (Furman, 1994). It enables them to empathise with and protect the child as a most valuable part of themselves. In order to make such an investment the parents have to have access to a part of the personality which has flexible boundaries with little differentiation between self and others, as in the narcissistic state.

All our relationships contain a narcissistic element – we project on to others many of our aspirations and hope to achieve these through fusion with the other. However, even though we all strive to have relationships which reflect back to us our own importance, value and uniqueness, if we relied exclusively on external feedback for our psychological well-being we would soon run into difficulty. In the course of daily life we all need to invest ourselves with a degree of self-importance and regard while at the same time investing others with similar qualities. If we do not feel ourselves to be at all important, special or worthy in some way we are missing a great spur to our self-growth and the pursuit of our goals. While other people's love and respect for us are a great help, we also need some inner sustenance, that is, a secure belief that we are the kind of person who deserves to be loved, to be successful and so on. In ideal circumstances it is as if we carry an internal picture of ourselves that serves to remind us that we are fundamentally 'OK' as people. If we feel, on the contrary, that we are worthless, it is unlikely that we will feel like investing much energy in the pursuit of relationships or experiences that could make us happy and reflect back a positive image of ourselves. A measure of self-love and selfishness is thus not in itself pathological. We all need this to ensure our psychological survival and growth.

The truly narcissistic personality, however, presents a much different picture. Individuals who are narcissistic in the pathological sense do not, on the whole, elicit sympathy, even if at times they may be very seductive in their manner and temporarily draw us into their world. Their seductiveness often springs from their need for others to bolster their own self-importance. Others are needed and courted only to the extent that they can continually provide 'positive strokes' reinforcing the narcissistic person's feelings of grandiosity – giving them a boost as it were. Because others are needed, they are seduced through what may at first appear to be genuine feelings and concern. However, at a deeper level, and often only from some distance, a certain callousness may be detected; the narcissistic person's niceness and caring is only surface-deep. Their kind, sometimes magnanimous, gestures are only performed so as to ensure a response from the other and if a response is not forthcoming when it is needed then the narcissistic person may reveal another side of themselves – one which may be wounding to the recipient. They may reject the other for what may appear to be trivial reasons which, in the normal course of events, would not warrant such a rejection. The narcissistic person, however, has to expel from their fragile universe anyone who cannot provide them with the constant source of positive reinforcements and assurance that they are important.

Annie, a 27-year-old woman who worked as a freelance writer, was referred for therapy by her doctor because of dermatological problems which he believed to be stress related.

Annie presented as a well-groomed, assertive woman who described her work in glowing terms even though she was at that time without any work.

She felt most authors wrote 'rubbish' and that her own work was of far superior quality. Annie, in fact, begrudged the success of other authors, feeling that her own work was far more deserving of admiration.

She described numerous relationships, especially with women, where she felt the other person envied her and that because of this she now chose her friends carefully. When asked if she had any friends she could trust she replied 'not really' as she felt that people were always resentful of her success.

Annie sought relationships which she felt would in some way advance her own career and she spoke in a very cold and calculated manner about her relationships generally. As she spoke about her friends, relatives and colleagues Annie revealed her difficulty in recognising the desires, feelings and subjective experiences of others.

She related several instances when she felt let down by other people which belied her sense that her needs and priorities were more important and that others should defer to them. Annie expected great dedication from others and was quite intolerant of anyone who seemed to be putting their own needs before hers. She had recently broken off a relationship with a longstanding friend because this friend had pulled out of a commitment at the last minute which had resulted in Annie having to go to a party unaccompanied.

While Annie was in many respects quite a difficult person to warm to she could at times also be very funny, engaging and seductive in her manner. At such times it was possible to see just how she managed to surround herself with people whom she then treated like 'puppets on a string'. When they no longer let her pull the strings she would become very angry, at times even quite sadistic – such was her desperate response to any experience of rejection (real or construed as such) which she simply could not tolerate.

The narcissistic person also finds it difficult to tolerate criticisms as they present a challenge to their frail sense of self. To accept criticisms and to be able to use them constructively we need to feel a certain degree of confidence in ourselves so as to not be totally destroyed by the criticism. At the same time we also need to be able to accept our limitations and to be able to hear what other people have to say as they may know more than us about particular subjects. Acknowledging our limitations forces us to face up to the limits of our self-sufficiency and hence our dependency on others. This, however, is very difficult for the narcissistic person. They usually do not take kindly to being in learning situations where they have to defer to someone else's knowledge or power. As the blows to our narcissism often result from a confrontation with reality, what is often observed in the narcissistic person is a hatred of certain aspects of reality. That which is hated is the evidence that any exposure to real life eventually challenges us all with: evidence of the limits to our omnipotence.

A basic characteristic feature of human beings is that we are relational beings, that is we are always in relation to other people. At the core of narcissism, however, is a hatred of the relational (Symington, 1993). To accept that we are relational beings entails dependency on others.

Dependency makes us vulnerable as we can never have an absolute guarantee that the person we depend on will always be there for us. On the whole, most people manage their dependence on others quite successfully while retaining a sense of themselves and not living in fear of abandonment.

The implications of what it means to be relational beings are not well managed, however, by the narcissistic person. Rather they need to protect themselves from such a reality and they may develop a number of defences to do so. Psychoanalytic writers have focused in depth on the types of defences which can be commonly observed in the narcissistic personality. The first type of defence relies on a denial of separateness. It is a denial that my needs and your needs may not always correspond. The narcissistic personality requires those around them to think and believe the same as them. This affords a much needed control over others and maintains the illusion of omnipotence. If such stringent conditions are not met they are reminded of the separate existence of the 'other' and this raises the possibility of abandonment. The second type of defence involves a denial of connectedness. This creates the illusion that others are not needed. The fantasy that they are entirely self-sufficient serves as a defence against the fear of abandonment. The narcissistic person uses others exclusively for her own ends and here reveals her hidden dependence through a craving for admiration.

The narcissistic wound

It will be clear from these descriptions of the narcissistic personality that what is a basic feature of human being can become a problem that permeates all aspects of an individual's functioning. How does so-called healthy narcissism become pathological? There have been many attempts to answer this question and the psychoanalytic literature is not short of these. Many psychoanalytic theorists argue that pathological narcissism is nearly always the result of a trauma. The trauma need not result necessarily from one specific incident but instead may result from a cumulative process of numerous repeated minor episodes which are experienced as traumatic by a given person (Khan, 1963).

Since the narcissistic image begins to develop from birth onwards, we might well speculate that the traumas in question usually are ones with an early origin. Psychoanalytic explanations of pathological narcissism therefore tend, on the whole, to focus on the nature of the earliest relationships and how these shape the child's emerging sense of self. McDougall (1980) has argued that the narcissistic image of ourselves is essentially an inter-subjective phenomenon, that is, our identity can only come into being through another person. Winnicott, a famous British paediatrician and analyst, stressed that in what he called 'good-enough mothering' the baby sees himself reflected in the mother's expressions. The mother is thought to act as a mirror to the baby. The mother who lovingly looks at her baby and sees a beautiful baby will reflect back to him a positive image. Such repeated experiences will help the baby to take in an image of himself as someone who is lovable and special. The mother's reflection not only gives the baby his mirror image but also a sense of what he represents for the mother. If the mother's attention is diverted away, perhaps because she is too preoccupied with herself, or if she sees in the baby her own reflection, one that she dislikes, she may reflect back to the baby a confused or empty image thereby contaminating him with her own fears and preoccupations. This will, in turn, shape how the baby comes to see himself.

Let us return to Annie who was introduced earlier in this chapter. How can we understand her predicament? Annie came from a middle class background where both parents worked in the media. She was an only child who had been looked after by paid carers as her mother had returned to work within a few months of giving birth. There had been complications at birth which had resulted in her mother having a Caesarean. The mother had been quite ill following the operation and therefore from birth onwards Annie had been cared for by others.

At age 11 Annie was sent to boarding school as her father had been offered an important job abroad and her mother was keen to go with him. During this year Annie began to display behavioural problems at school and she was eventually expelled from the school. Her mother had to return back to England earlier than anticipated and Annie felt that her mother had been very angry with her about this and ignored her even though there were only the two of them at home together.

The relationship with her mother and father seemed to be a very cold and unresponsive one and Annie developed qualitatively similar relationships with others. When her father died when she was 16 years old she did not recall feeling anything about his death except being worried that she would not finish her private education if her mother did not have enough money. Annie's mother remarried within 18 months of her father's death. Annie intensely disliked her new stepfather whom she said had made sexual advances towards her.

At age 18 Annie moved out of the family home reluctantly even though she presented this as being her own decision. The truth was that Annie had felt pushed out by her stepfather and her mother had not tried to persuade her to stay. By this stage in her life, however, Annie had hardened herself emotionally. She was determined she would never be dependent on anyone and superficially at least she gave the impression of being an independent and assertive woman who was very skilled at manipulating others.

Behind the facade, however, was a very frightened and rejected little girl who still yearned for her parents' attention. Her parents appeared, however, to have been so self-absorbed that there had in fact been very little space in their lives for their daughter. Moreover she had actually represented an obstacle to their hedonistic pursuits and although she had never wanted for anything materially, Annie had not really received any emotional care from them. Rather she had been entrusted to various paid carers and institutions throughout her life. Neither parent seemed to have been even remotely 'in love' with their baby girl and one can only imagine what image was reflected back to her by the various carers she was left with.

Annie desperately needed to control others as her experience as a child had been that she had felt repeatedly abandoned not only by her parents but also by the various nannies who had looked after her. It was not possible to know exactly what happened to Annie's mother around the time she gave birth to her but it seemed that for her own reasons her mother had not been available to Annie emotionally. It seems unlikely that Annie could have been filled with a sense that she was special and important to her parents. She also recalled her mother saying to her that she was embarrassed to be seen with Annie as she looked so unattractive.

Over the years Annie developed a 'false self' which was assertive, ambitious, competent and 'full of life' (as she described herself) but which was belied by very low self-esteem, rendering her very vulnerable and sensitive to injury from any criticism or rejection.

Narcissism and self-knowledge

The concept of narcissism is central to understanding many of the difficulties we experience in our relationship to ourselves and hence to others. We all struggle to maintain our narcissistic integrity and feelings of self-esteem which are essential to our psychological well-being. We are all vulnerable, however, to changes in our narcissistic equilibrium as this fluctuates depending on life's challenges. If we fail in some aspect of our life this will reflect back an image of ourselves which may temporarily wound our narcissism. At other times events in our lives remind us of our irrelevance in the wider scheme of things. Such experiences can be more or less successfully integrated when they are set against a degree of self-esteem. Furthermore, life often throws our way a number of opportunities when we can recapture, albeit temporarily, the much longed for state of omnipotence and narcissism when we can feel ourselves to be, once again, the centre of the universe. Falling in love offers such an opportunity as we shall see in Chapter 12.

However, for the narcissistic individual the psychological homeostasis is not so readily restored and maintained and requires the constant upkeep of defences all of which are inimical to genuine relationships with others. People are needed and chosen to reflect the self-image that is so badly missing in the person's internal world. The narcissistic person, while behaving as though he is very important, special and even perfect, feels quite the opposite at a deeper level. At the core of the narcissistic personality we often find a terrible emptiness without any capacity to sustain himself from within.

Even though we may not identify ourselves in the descriptions of the narcissistic personality, it nonetheless remains important to recognise narcissistic elements within ourselves for they can be traced in all of us. This is difficult, however, because, as Symington (1993) suggests, narcissism blinds us to self-knowledge. To know oneself is painful because it entails the recognition of personal limitations, the acceptance that some of our wishes may never come true. Narcissism may blind us to such inner knowledge as it is a blow to one of our most cherished fantasies, namely that we are omnipotent.

This chapter has explored the intimate relationship we each have with ourselves and how it invariably contains a narcissistic element. Although a measure of self-regard and self-sufficiency are essential to our psychological well-being no individual is an island and we shall therefore turn our attention in the next chapter to the importance of relationships with others and, more specifically, the psychological significance of our earliest relationships.

Chapter 10
The first relationship:
most important of all?

We shall not cease from exploration
And the end of all our exploring
Will be to arrive where we started
And know the place for the first time

T.S. Eliot

When we think of our 'first' relationship, many of us probably scan our memories back to our first love which so often becomes securely lodged in our memories. Such 'first' relationships are undoubtedly important and deserve the privileged place we accord them. They mark our initial attempts to separate from our families by establishing bonds with others outside of the family – the kind of bonds which we may have watched our parents enjoying but from which we felt excluded. Indeed Person (1989) points out that the role of the first love in separating the lovers from their families is a theme not only integral to the archetypal 'first love' such as that of Romeo and Juliet, but also finds its way into many popular novels. First love is an important milestone in our development and maturation and often represents one of the most passionate moments in our lives. Our first love is, however, not strictly speaking the 'first'. Rather, psychoanalytic theory would suggest, it is the heir to the first and most crucial relationship we each have with our parents or primary caregivers. These early relationships are understood to be the precursors to, and to some degree, the determinants of, all our later relationships.

Given the structure of our society, the first most intense relationship we have is with our mothers. This is of course not to deny the equally, albeit perhaps differentially, important relationship we have with our fathers. However, as women are still on the whole the primary care-givers, this chapter will focus on the nature and function of the earliest relationship between mother and baby. In what ways can we say that it is important and, in keeping with the theme of Part III, to what extent if any does it influence our ability to establish relationships in general?

The emerging language of love

If we have children of our own or have had the opportunity to observe babies interacting with their mothers, we will recognise the complexity and reciprocity of their relationship. Stern (1977), a psychoanalytic theorist, refers to the interactions that unfold between mothers and babies as a 'dance' which follows its own unique rhythm depending on the respective contributions of each mother and baby. Like any dance, the choreography is all important and some dances are better choreographed than others. Similarly, the 'dances' between mothers and babies show us that there may be occasions when their steps are out of time with each other and this may lead to a breakdown in communication and distress in either or both partners. However, when the dance flows uninterrupted we are privileged to observe a most beautiful and enlivening spectacle.

Observations of mothers and babies have highlighted, amongst many other fascinating findings, the earliest expressions of love. It is certainly not uncommon for mothers to comment that they are in love with their baby and this is frequently evidenced by their behaviour towards them – typically preoccupation with, and idealisation of, their baby. Equally, Stern (1993) argues that babies also fall in love and do so repeatedly but their development increasingly affords them new sets of capacities with which to fall in love, in what he calls a 'deeper' sense.

Stern's observations of many mother–baby couples have led him to conclude that the most basic physical expressions of love, as typically found in adult relationships, are learned by the fourth or fifth month of life. Adult lovers clearly develop highly individualised repertoires of behaviours which act as a boundary to their relationship. However, there are some more global categories of behaviours which are typically observed in adult lovers: couples gaze into each other's eyes without talking, frequently holding their faces only inches away from each other; there is increased physical proximity; vocal patterns alternate and particular gestures such as kissing, caressing and holding the other's face and hands are performed. Very similar repertoires of behaviour are observed between mothers and babies. What is special about such behaviours is that they violate many of the rules that otherwise dominate and structure other relationships in our society. Being locked in silent mutual gaze for prolonged periods is highly uncommon except when we are in love or between a mother and baby. The physical proximity typical of lovers and mothers and babies is much closer than that usually encountered in our society. Finally, speech also has its own peculiar repertoire between lovers and mother–baby couples. Both may use 'baby talk' or may alter the pronunciation of particular words. With the onset of speech, mothers and toddlers also begin to negotiate meanings and do so in highly individualised ways, just as lovers may develop particular code words or jokes which are only meaningful to them.

Also typical of the state of being in love is the exclusive focus on and preoccupation with one person. Similarly, in the first year of life, there is a gradual narrowing of feelings of intimacy and attachment to one particular figure, usually the mother. Babies and lovers likewise show a marked preoccupation with the presence or absence of their attachment figure – a preoccupation that may be either enabling or disabling depending on the perceived stability and security of the relationship. Babies who are securely attached to their mothers tend to be more active explorers of their environment. It is the repeated experience of separation followed by reunion that enables babies, in time, to internalise their mother as a dependable person – one on whose care and concern they can rely. This helps them to feel more confident within themselves and therefore to develop the capacity and desire to explore the world away from the mother, always in the safe knowledge that they can return at any point to their 'secure base' (Bowlby, 1989).

In the early stages of a relationship lovers also display a very similar preoccupation with their partner. The frequent telephone calls, cards or gifts that are exchanged under many different pretexts have in common the aim not only of expressing love but also of reassuring the other of our continuous 'presence' even in our absence. It reflects our continued preoccupation with the loved one. Just as with the baby who feels secure in his relationship with his mother, the lover who does not doubt his partner's love may be filled with energy and encouraged to take on new projects. The lover, however, who lives in the shadow of doubt and uncertainty may find himself temporarily incapacitated, needing constant reassurance of the other's love. So even though being in love is on the whole a life enhancing experience, this may not always be the case.

All the above behaviours serve to delineate the boundaries of the intimate couple and so set it apart from the more mundane relationships we may have with other people in our lives. The similarities in both the behaviour and some of the feelings, between those commonly observed between lovers and mothers and babies, are striking and point to a central hypothesis of psychoanalytic approaches to love, namely that the experience of falling in love and being in love has a very rich developmental history – a point to which we shall return in Chapter 12.

The psychological significance of early relationships

The research which has highlighted the similarities between the behaviour of lovers and that of mothers and babies has emerged from the collaboration of psychoanalytic theorists and developmental psychologists. Such a collaboration has provided important support for the psychoanalytic premise that early relationships are crucial to our psychological development. Even though it is the case that most early analysts viewed babies, exchanges with their mothers as based on oral gratification, for instance the need to be fed, later analysts have stressed babies' pre-adaptedness to play a role in social exchange with their mothers as well as emphasising the importance of mutuality between the baby and mother for subsequent development.

Direct studies of early mother–baby interaction reveal that babies are drawn to engage with other people and to develop particular attachments. Besides the efficacy of the baby's behaviour which solicits protection essential to survival, such as feeding which is solicited by crying, also present at birth are the foundations of a truly inter-subjective communication with the potential for sending out and taking in thoughts and experiences (Trevarthen, 1980). Infants are thus believed to be pre-adapted from birth to interpret affective displays as information regarding subjective state and to be intrinsically motivated to establish affective communication with others. Such behaviours are sensitive to the identity of the habitual caregiver – babies respond discriminatively to their mother's smell, voice, touch and movement. Conversely, babies may withdraw and attempt to defend themselves against abrupt, insensitive handling. In the first few months of life, handling of the baby is the primary mode of communication. In turn, the baby takes in not only the contents of the mother's handling but also the manner of it. The experience of having a nappy changed for instance can be one of intimate exchange and even fun if the mother plays and talks to the baby in the process.

Research suggests that the baby's observed selective responsiveness to people cannot be reduced to a simple attraction for certain salient features like movement or light but rather it very much appears that babies are innately disposed to human qualities as special categories of experience. The fascinating studies in which mothers are asked to simulate a feature of a depressed state, by staring blankly at their babies, poignantly show how babies as young as three months respond by protesting and becoming wary and avoidant (Murray et al., 1989). Such responses have now been consistently demonstrated and suggest that, as psychoanalytic theorists such as Winnicott and Klein believed, babies are able to perceive the form of their parents' expressions in terms of their personal and communicative significance. This means that while babies cannot conceptualise and articulate their experience of relationships as we might do as adults, they nonetheless respond to changes in their parents' moods and adapt accordingly – if repeatedly rejected by their mothers, babies will eventually also begin to avoid them by averting their gaze.

A great deal of research in the field of child development converges on the notion that early relationships are very significant. In addition to the findings mentioned earlier, studies on attachment provide further evidence to support the idea that the quality of the relationships with our parents in the first year of life predicts our later ability to develop and sustain relationships.

Attachment in children has been studied through the application of a simple laboratory technique, the 'Strange Situation', developed by Mary Ainsworth, a psychologist and close colleague of John Bowlby. This technique presents the 12–18-month-old infant with anxiety provoking circumstances. These circumstances include an unfamiliar room, the appearance of a stranger, and two 3-minute separations from the parents. Such circumstances normally give rise to an urgent call by a child for reassurance by the parent. The child's behaviour on the parent's return following the separations provides the most reliable indication of the quality of the parent–infant relationship. Broadly speaking, upon reunion the children react in a number of typical ways: most children, whilst clearly distressed, seek contact with the parent, are satisfactorily comforted and soon resume play. These children are classified as *securely attached*. Other children, those classified as *insecurely attached*, show a number of different patterns. Some are frequently unperturbed by the separation and upon reunion show a mixture of approach towards the parent with clear indications of physical avoidance. This is referred to as an 'avoidant' behavioural organisation which is understood to represent the child's strategy for dealing with the stress of separation rather than indicating an absence of distress per se. Parents of avoidant children are more likely than other parents to minimise the importance of attachment relationships and of experiences of anger and distress in general (Cassidy and Kobak, 1988). Those children referred to as displaying an 'ambivalent' attachment pattern approach the parent in distress, refuse to be comforted but continue to display signs of anger or passivity. The heightened distress and angry behaviour often shown by ambivalent children has been interpreted as a strategy of exaggerating attachment behaviours so as to elicit a response from less responsive parents. When observed at home, mothers of ambivalent infants have been more disengaged and less responsive to infant crying than mothers of secure or avoidant children (Lyons-Ruth et al., 1987). Others still show confusion upon reunion with the parent. This is referred to as 'disorganised/disorientated' attachment behaviour and is believed to have special relevance to family contexts characterised by loss, trauma and parental psychopathology.

Studies which have used this technique have shown that children who were insecurely attached to their mothers at one year of age were in later life significantly more likely to take less positive attitudes into their peer group relationships and displayed more behavioural and social difficulties (Sroufe and Fleeson, 1988). In general, research supports the importance of protective function of parenting and of the quality of parent – child relationships (Egeland et al., 1993). Several studies have replicated such findings and, taken together, these suggest that early, secure attachments may provide a learning experience through which we internalise or represent relationships and may thus exert an influence on our social interactions as adults.

The legacy of early relationships

Our experiences in our earliest relationships may be said to coalesce into what are termed *internal working models of relationships*. This refers essentially to the conceptualisations that children construct, on the basis of their repeated daily experiences with their parents, of the nature and expected behaviour of others. The idea here is that we create mental representations of ourselves and emotionally significant 'others' in affectively organised relationships – representations which may vary across different areas of our experiences or interactions. Based on previous interactions with parents or caregivers, children are assumed to develop particular expectations about relationships, initially with their parents. These expectations may then influence experience in other relationships and, in this sense, all social experiences may be said to involve what analysts have called 'transference' (see Chapter 4). The studies mentioned earlier show us, for example, that securely attached children demonstrate an expectation of an empathic response from the parent whilst insecurely attached, avoidant children appear uninterested in their reunion with the parent, perhaps as a defensive measure to protect themselves from a further painful failure at having their needs heard. Such early relationships then become internalised and give the child some sense of what they may expect in relationships generally.

If we have the opportunity as children to internalise positive working models of relationships – that is, relationships where partners can communicate effectively, can share feelings, where one's needs are met on the whole and where one's individuality is encouraged rather than thwarted – we are more likely as adults to develop qualitatively similar relationships with our partners. This is partly because such early positive experiences influence our self-esteem – they help us to feel that we are people who actually deserve to be loved and respected. Through repeated interactions with a responsive and sensitive parent, children come to view themselves as lovable and worthwhile. To this extent the manner in which our mothers handled our bodies when we were infants and responded to our needs is very important. As was mentioned earlier, in the first few months of life the handling of the baby is the primary mode of communication. The quality of this handling will therefore convey important messages to the baby about the nature of their relationship with their mother. Furthermore, children's perceptions of their behaviour will be co-determined by parental attributions, that is, the meaning parents ascribe to their children's behaviour. Through meaning attributions a whole set of values, reinforcements and prohibitions of emotional colouring contribute to shaping the developing child's experiences and these, through the process of internalisation, may continue to exert their influence over time.

However, not everyone's relationship with their parents is a positive and nurturing one. On the contrary, our early relationships may have been with a parent who was hostile and critical, leaving us with little sense of our own self-worth and with a vulnerability for developing later on in our lives relationships which will bear a striking similarity to our earlier ones, thereby confirming our sense that we are really unworthy of love.

> Sira had grown up in a family where her father physically abused her mother whenever he was drunk. Sira's mother was frequently bruised and had been admitted to hospital several times but she never left her husband. Although Sira's father never hit her he would frequently shout at her, was verbally abusive and could be very critical. Sira's mother also drank and while she never became violent she was often emotionally unavailable to Sira and was not able to protect her from her father.
>
> As an adult, Sira experienced highly ambivalent feelings towards her mother: on the one hand she felt sorry for her and on the other hand she was angry with her because she perceived her to have been very weak. Sira hated her father with whom she had no contact since she left home at the age of 16.
>
> Sira never abused alcohol herself but developed an eating problem with which she battled for several years. She had very low self-esteem and was drawn to relationships with men which simply confirmed what she believed about herself. While the men she lived with were not physically abusive towards her, like her father they were emotionally distant, highly critical of her and her appearance in particular and left her feeling that she could never be good enough. While consciously she claimed she did not want to repeat her mother's mistakes it proved hard for Sira to build a different life for herself as her childhood experiences had left her with a highly distorted perception of herself and her self-worth so that she felt she could not aspire in life to anything better than what she already had.

'History is not destiny'

When we hear about childhood experiences such as those Sira had to contend with we are not surprised to learn that she later experienced considerable psychological problems and was drawn to relationships which simply reinforced her low self-esteem. However, given our present state of knowledge, it is not possible to assert any more than that early experiences, be they desirable or undesirable ones, *predispose* us towards particular types of relationships.

A critical question is how our working models of relationships influence and are influenced by the quality of our current relationships. After all, not all those individuals who experience difficulties in their early relationships will necessarily experience significant problems in their relationships as adults. Moreover, the relationships we establish as adults may provide critically important sources of love, support and encouragement which enable us to overcome past hurts. For instance, amongst the important factors that appear to determine a positive outcome for those parents who suffered deprivation or brutality in childhood, and which positively influences their own parenting capacities, is the presence of a supportive spouse (Fonagy, 1992). We also know that children may be protected from the adverse effects of one relationship by another relationship which is experienced as positive and secure. Main and Weston (1981) observed 60 infants with their mothers and then with their fathers and looked at their patterns of attachment. They found no correlation between the patterns shown with one parent or the other and took this to suggest that the effects of an insecure relationship with one parent can be mitigated by a secure one with the other parent.

Unlike the previous chapters in this book, this chapter has referred more extensively to the findings from experimental research. This is because those psychoanalytic ideas which have received most empirical support are precisely those that have a bearing on the assumed critical importance of early relationships on our development. This is a reassuring finding as the claim that early relationships are formative is one that has important implications and is therefore one that should not be made lightly. However, this is one of the claims that can and should be taken very seriously by all of us even if the variability in the consequences for adult functioning of childhood trauma and deprivation, as we saw in Chapter 4, argues against a strictly deterministic position on this particular issue. In other words, history is quite clearly not destiny (Fonagy, 1992).

Chapter 11
The Oedipus complex –
fact or myth?

The Oedipus Complex, however, is such an important thing that the manner in which one enters and leaves it cannot be without its effects.

Freud

'Two's company, three's a crowd'

In the last chapter the spotlight was on the mother–baby couple and the developmental ramifications of our earliest relationships. Even though the early life of babies may be said to be dominated by their exchanges with their mothers, the world of the infant gradually broadens out. Once the baby emerges from the exclusive intimacy of the mother–baby couple, his attention is drawn to other people in the family and awareness of their relationships with one another comes to the fore. Observing their mother in loving interaction with either father or siblings may arouse intense feelings of rivalry and jealousy in children along with a painful awareness that they no longer control their mother but rather that the mother has a separate existence which takes her away from them even though she is still needed. The common saying 'two's company, three's a crowd' echoes our early ambivalence at having to relinquish sole possession of our mothers and allow third parties into our relationship thereby changing the boundaries of our universe irrevocably.

This later stage of child development is typically associated with the Oedipus complex. Freud coined the term 'Oedipus complex' on the basis of a Greek myth which forms the subject of the play by Sophocles. It begins when an oracle tells Laius, the King of Thebes, that he will die at the hands of his son. So as to prevent this terrible prophecy coming true Laius and his wife Jocasta pierce the feet of their newborn baby and give him to a shepherd to be left to die. The shepherd, however, saves Oedipus who is later adopted by another family. As an adult, Oedipus consults an oracle who warns him that he is fated to kill his father and marry his mother. Through an uncanny twist of fate, this is precisely what Oedipus does, thereby fulfilling the prophecy. The consequences are tragic when he eventually discovers that he is guilty of both murder and incest.

The Oedipus complex essentially refers to the developmental stage when the child is said to wish for an exclusive relationship with the opposite-sex parent, and experiences the same-sex parent as a rival. Such jealous, possessive feelings are also, however, experienced towards the same-sex parent with whom the child also wants an exclusive relationship. Indeed, Freud hypothesised on the basis of his belief in the child's inherent bisexuality that we all experience both a positive and negative Oedipus complex. The former refers to the paradigmatic situation of the Oedipus complex where the focus of the child's desire is the opposite-sex parent, while the latter refers to the homosexual longings directed to the same-sex parent. In both scenarios the child longs for a unique and privileged union with the parent and 'others' are experienced as potential threats to the blissful dyadic unity.

The Oedipus complex: a human universal?

Our ability to navigate our way successfully through the storms of the Oedipal phase is, according to psychoanalytic theory, central to our development and our experiences in later relationships. Such a claim has not received widespread acceptance outside of the psychoanalytic world but has, on the contrary, been heavily criticised or totally dismissed. So let us briefly examine some of the arguments that have been put forward in support of and against the notion of the Oedipus complex. Is it possible to say that there is such a thing as the Oedipus complex and if so what part can it be said to play in our development?

One of Freud's far reaching claims regarding the Oedipus complex was its universality. This was in keeping with his aim to found a science of human being which seemingly cut across individual and cultural differences. It is this claim in particular which has invited criticism and which we shall now focus on. Similarities across cultures, including across psychological phenomena, point to what anthropologists refer to as 'human universals'. Such universals form a heterogeneous set. A great many seem to be inherent in human nature, for example, the existence of universal emotional expressions. Other universals, on the other hand, appear more as cultural conventions that have acquired universal distribution. The Oedipus complex may be seen to fall into the latter category.

Malinowski (1961) is an anthropologist who challenged Freud's claim of the universality of the Oedipus complex. In his criticisms of the complex Malinowski placed great emphasis on the specific family structure which he said underpinned it and which was, according to him, specific to Freud's culture and therefore not generalisable to other cultures. In his study of the Trobriand Islanders, who live on an island off the eastern end of New Guinea, Malinowski claimed that there was no evidence of the Freudian Oedipus complex. Trobrianders have a matrilineal system of kinship and it is the mother's brother who has authority over the children who eventually move in with him at puberty. The husband and father is not even considered to be the procreator of his children as the Trobrianders believe that children enter the mother's womb as spirits. The biological fathers are said to have a good relationship with their sons and they display none of the rivalry which Freud hypothesised between the male child and their father, nor is there any evidence of incestuous wishes towards the mother. Malinowski reported, however, that they have dreams of incestuous relationships with brothers and sisters. According to him then the Trobrianders' matrilineal family system produced a different complex to the one hypothesised by Freud.

In response to such criticisms, analysts (Jones, 1925) and anthropologists (Spiro, 1982; Weiner, 1985) have argued that Malinowski's findings in no way disprove the alleged universality of the Oedipus complex. On the contrary, Spiro argued, for example, that the Trobriand male has a particularly strong Oedipus complex but one that has undergone more stringent repression than in the West. He took the curious absence of the father from the dreams, myths and reproductive beliefs of the Trobrianders as strong evidence of repressed hostility towards the father. Spiro does, however, concede that the Oedipus complex does vary in its outcome and strength. Thus in many New Guinean societies marked by incomplete repression of the Oedipus complex boys are either expelled from their families at puberty or undergo severe puberty rituals that bring them firmly under male control and separate them from their mothers. These rites can be brutal in nature allowing men, Spiro argues, to find an outlet for their own Oedipal hostilities towards their sons.

Unfortunately, the research that has been carried out in this area neither definitively proves nor disproves the theory conclusively and we are none the wiser as to whether the Oedipus complex is a fact of human nature or a myth. It does, however, raise the need to look more carefully at claims of universality as well as at extremist conceptions of cultural relativity (Brown, 1991).

The passion of childhood

Once again we are faced with a theoretical hypothesis for which there is conflicting evidence – a not uncommon predicament in psychoanalytic research. Do we therefore reject the notion of the Oedipus complex outright or do we hold on to it to see if it can help us to make sense of what may be readily observed in relationships between parents and children?

One need not be a committed Freudian to accept as a fact that all little children experience intense emotions towards their parents. These cover a very broad spectrum and certainly include passionate longings for exclusive possession of the parents as well as intense feelings of rivalry with, and envy of, them. Both little boys and girls often reveal through their behaviour their wish to usurp the place of the other parent, and where a parent may in fact be 'absent', the family circumstances may reinforce the child's fantasies. Such feelings are at times expressed very passionately and weave their way into many common childhood games and preoccupations where themes of exclusion and inclusion abound. How these feelings are managed by the child will depend to an extent on the parents' ability to deal with such feelings within themselves and on particular family constellations.

Parents themselves also experience similarly intense feelings towards their children and their task is therefore a challenging one during the years which coincide with the hypothesised Oedipus complex. Parents are required to understand and appreciate their own children's budding sexuality without resorting to either seductive or dismissive responses. The little girl who wants to sit on her father's knee and flirt with him would be upset if her father refused to hold her. It would also, however, be harmful to her psychological development if her father responded to her advances in a sexually explicit manner or in more subtle ways, perhaps fostering the illusion through his attitudes towards her that the little girl can in fact usurp her mother's place.

In families where sexual boundaries are permeable the parents' response to the child's erotised sensuality may be one of overt incestuous assault or erotic contact or may result in more generalised possessiveness, overinvolvement or deep emotional investment in the child. Mark's predicament, introduced in Chapter 3, is an example of a mother–son relationship where the parents' own needs for love and attention were inappropriately realised in their relationship with their children, creating considerable difficulties for them in later life. All such outcomes are undesirable from the point of view of the child's development as they transform fantasies, which in ideal circumstances need to be relinquished, into realities which overwhelm the child's immature ego. The child, rather than becoming reconciled to the futility of the wish to steal one parent from the other, may instead become the parent's surrogate partner, thereby depriving the child of an important developmental experience.

The challenges of the Oedipal phase

The Oedipal phase brings into relief feelings of rivalry and competitiveness and challenges the child with the negotiation of boundaries. Rivalry which is well managed by the parents can lead to constructive preoccupations in the child with fairness and justice (Raphael-Leff, 1991). From a developmental point of view, the child's recognition of his parents as sexual partners encourages an essential relinquishment of the idea of his sole and permanent possession. It involves the recognition of the differences that exist between the relationship parents can enjoy with each other as distinct from that which the child is entitled to enjoy with them. This may give rise to frustration and envy, as the child has to relinquish his sexual claim on the parents and accept the reality of their sexual relationship from which he is excluded. However, such experiences also pave the way for important internalisations which play a part in later relationships. If children are allowed their fantasies and are neither brutally rejected nor invited to enact their incestuous fantasies, they may establish as adults an intimate relationship with a partner who can share sexuality reciprocally and exclusively within the couple, just as they observed their parents doing.

The successful resolution of the Oedipus complex is seen to enable us to internalise a model of exchange that is, on balance, a creative activity. It is further suggested that this appears to be related to the development of thinking and, more specifically, the capacity to allow thoughts and ideas to interact (Feldman, 1989). The Oedipus complex may be then understood to present the child with the experience of the prototype of a relationship of a qualitatively different kind; one in which they are a witness and not a participant. The experience and tolerance of a relationship which excludes the child represents another important developmental milestone, namely the ability to entertain another's point of view whilst retaining our own (Britton, 1989). For if we can be a witness to another relationship we can then also envisage being observed by others. This, in turn, provides us with an opportunity for seeing ourselves in interaction with others as well developing the capacity to acknowledge the reality of other people's experiences and thoughts in our interactions. In a general sense then the Oedipal encounter challenges the child with the toleration of otherness; it confronts them with the experience of conflict so that reality – often a far cry from our regressive wish for perfect harmony in which conflict and difference are denied – can be faced and hopefully worked through (Grunberger, 1991).

Navigating through the Oedipal storm

An example may be helpful at this point to highlight the importance of how families manage the child's Oedipal desires.

Ricky is a 6-year-old boy who enjoyed a close relationship with his mother. He had been a much wanted child conceived after years of infertility treatment and both his parents doted on him. However, Ricky's father held a job which took him away from home a great deal. Indeed until he was 5 years old Ricky spent most of his time with his mother and shared her bed as his father was often away overnight. Ricky established the habit of sleeping with his mother and when his father was at home it became very difficult to get Ricky to sleep on his own. For the sake of peace, the parents said, they often gave in and it was Ricky's father who actually slept in Ricky's room.

A few months before Ricky's sixth birthday his father was offered a new position which would reduce the travelling considerably. Both parents were delighted about this news but Ricky appeared to feel quite differently. It was around this time that he developed a number of psychosomatic symptoms, complaining of stomach pains which made his mother keep him at home during the day. Given that his father was now at home in the evenings it seemed as though Ricky had to find some way of retaining the exclusivity of his relationship with his mother by at least having her all to himself during the day. Whenever the parents announced they would go out in the evening Ricky's symptoms worsened considerably to the extent that the parents felt obliged not to go. This, not surprisingly, created considerable strain in the marital relationship and it was at this point that the parents sought professional help.

From a psychoanalytic standpoint we would hypothesise that the comparative absence of Ricky's father for the first 5 years of his life and the corresponding closeness which evolved between Ricky and his mother rendered the resolution of his Oedipus complex more complicated. The incestuous fantasies which male children are said to harbour in relation to their mothers were to an extent realised for Ricky who had even succeeded in ousting the father from the marital bed. When his father regained a more prominent position in the family home Ricky quite understandably found this very difficult. He felt terribly rejected and was jealous. His symptoms appeared to be his way of expressing his conflicts and of ensuring that his parents did not enjoy themselves to the exclusion of him. Over time the parents were helped to set clearer boundaries and to understand their own reasons for having colluded with the situation which had caused considerable distress to all parties. Ricky himself was also given a space to explore his own feelings.

The above example provides an instance of what can be subsumed under the heading of the Oedipus complex. The resolution of Ricky's Oedipal conflicts had been complicated because of his family's circumstances as well as the parents' own unresolved feelings about their own respective relationships with their parents. But what of more everyday examples you may well ask? Once again, these can be readily found in observations of children with their parents. It is far from uncommon for example for young children to express the wish to marry the opposite-sex parent, or to relish the prospect of being alone with them whilst the other parent is perhaps out of the house. In adulthood also, the early intense emotions first experienced in the triangular relationship with our parents may be revived. The profound pull of the triangle can be seen to exert constant pressure throughout our lives and is most evident when we observe love relationships. Psychoanalytic theory would account for this pull in Oedipal terms.

As our erotic and sexual longings first come together in the Oedipal period, triangular relationships may readily elicit our desire as they prime such early experiences. Person (1989) has argued that it is important to distinguish between two primary kinds of triangles that can be observed in adult love relationships as these encompass qualitatively different psychic realities, namely the rivalrous triangle and the 'split-object' triangle. The former refers to the typical situation where, say, a woman has a relationship with a married man. From her perspective the tension in the triangle revolves around a rivalry and this rivalrous triangle is understood to represent a reincarnation of the Oedipal triangle of early life. From the husband's/man's perspective, however, the triangle is not a duplicate of the Oedipal triangle, rather it is a split-object triangle, the main tension resulting from the division, in emotional life, between two women. Such a triangle may serve the function for the man of avoiding intimacy. This may result from the man's early experiences with his mother where he may have felt suffocated by the intimacy and closeness of that early couple. The appearance of a third person may have been longed for at the time so as to dilute the intensity of the relationship with the mother. The ensuing fear of intimacy may lead such an individual to seek out the insurance of a 'third party' in all their relationships.

Anthony married at the age of 39 after years of 'one-night stands' which he would frequently proudly allude to in his therapeutic sessions. Within a year of being married Anthony became restless – although he said he loved his wife he was aware of desiring other women and was in fact having an affair with a work colleague who was herself married. He described his concentration at work as very poor and he was concerned that his work would suffer.

Anthony was the second of two brothers; his brother was killed in an accident prior to Anthony's birth. Anthony's mother had been very protective of him as she had been anxious that she might also lose her second child. Consequently Anthony had felt very restricted in his activities. Anthony's father left his mother when he was 4 years old. Anthony felt that his parents' relationship had never recovered from the death of his brother – his mother blamed the father for the accident and this had been the source of many arguments between them.

Following his parents' separation, Anthony felt very abandoned by his father. He said he would have preferred to live with him as he experienced his mother as stifling. In addition, he felt that she was unable to acknowledge his achievements as she would frequently refer to how intelligent his brother had been and how well he would have done were he still alive. Anthony had thus felt trapped in a relationship with his mother where he felt relegated to second place and controlled by her. She would insist on knowing his every movement and would accompany him everywhere even when he clearly stated he did not want her to do this. Some nights, Anthony said, she had 'forced' him to sleep in the same bed as her as she was frightened.

Anthony frequently thought that his brother was better off dead as living with his mother had in fact been a fate worse than death. He felt guilty about such thoughts but his resentment towards his mother was very close to the surface. He once remarked that she had really buried both her sons and this reflected Anthony's experience of having been deprived of his independence and autonomy as a child.

On the surface, Anthony's attitudes towards women were positive – he enjoyed their company and he felt for instance that women should be offered the same opportunities as men in the professional world. However, his actual behaviour towards women told a different story. He would relate to women more as objects who could be discarded when he no longer needed them. In the context of the therapeutic relationship this manifested itself in his frequent missed sessions for which there never appeared to be a reason and which he never let me know about in advance. He enjoyed the power he had over me in this way – he would make me wait not knowing whether he would turn up or not. He seemed determined to not be accountable to any woman.

While he enjoyed sexual relationships with women it was difficult for him to be intimate in any other way and he would often describe his partners as 'possessive' or 'suffocating' and would quickly break off the relationship. His wife had been an exception but he was now also beginning to think of her in these terms. His affair followed an argument between them concerning his aloof manner. Anthony felt his wife was being too demanding and his new liaison provided him temporarily at least with a relationship where he could keep his much needed distance.

Anthony feared being overwhelmed by women in the way he had felt with his mother. He found it difficult to allow himself to be dependent on another woman and hence it was hard for him to be intimate except in a sexual sense when he then felt very powerful and in control. Marriage confronted him with a relationship from which he could not flee so easily and his way of diluting the intimacy of his relationship with his wife was by having an affair. As a child his father had seemingly been unable to protect Anthony from his mother and later left him with her. As an adult, Anthony was determined to never again be 'at the mercy of another woman' as he himself put it.

While the above example enlightens us as to some of the possible meanings and motivations – conscious and unconscious – which may lie behind triangular relationships, it would be misleading to suggest that underlying all such relationships are unresolved Oedipal strivings. People find themselves in triangular relationships for many different reasons. For some this will be a transitory or one-off experience reflecting perhaps an unsatisfactory partnership and the genuine desire to find a more rewarding one. For others the pull towards triangular relationships may be traced over a more extended period and suggests the re-enactment of a particular pattern. In the latter case the tendency repeatedly to have affairs may reflect a difficulty in making commitments, a fear of intimacy or a difficulty in sustaining ambivalent relationships so that as soon as the honeymoon period is over the person has to flee, desperate to recreate the blissful moment of early meetings untinged by ambivalence. No love or relationship is totally immune from triadic components but as Person points out 'most often these can be incorporated into the dyadic relationship and need not be corrosive. Particularly where they take form only as fleeting fantasies, such triangles may sometimes be enriching to love' (1989: 237)

The intense emotions associated with the Oedipal phase are not only revived in love relationships but may arise, for instance, at times of pregnancy when the intimacy of the couple is threatened by the arrival of the baby. The baby may subsequently be experienced as a rival, a displacer, and it is certainly not uncommon for fathers in particular to feel left out and jealous of the mother's affection towards the baby. In more complicated cases, to make love with an expectant partner may become unconsciously equated by the man with the enactment of incestuous wishes as the pregnant woman becomes identified with a maternal figure rather than as a sexual partner. Raphael-Leff (1991) has suggested that men finding themselves in such a predicament, perhaps as a result of unresolved Oedipal feelings in their own families of origin, may try to defend themselves from the resurgence of Oedipal feelings and fantasies by becoming helpless or childlike in their relationship or by distancing themselves and seeking out other relationships. The response of both father and mother to the arrival of a baby, especially the first one, will depend in part on their respective experiences, at an unconscious level, in relation to their own parents and siblings.

The Oedipus complex: a useful metaphor

Essentially, the Oedipus complex is about the experience of inclusion and exclusion and the feelings associated with such experiences. It symbolises the widening of the baby's earliest 'universe' – one in which there were only two people closely connected to each other. The loss this involves confronts the growing child with his impotence, all the more accentuated when he has to compete with other adults as well as siblings for the attention and love he so much wants. Although there will be individual differences in how such a phase is negotiated – however we ultimately choose to refer to it – underpinning the experience we often find the recurring feelings of possessiveness, jealousy, rivalry, seduction and the threat or desire to punish the intruder, itself reminiscent of the child's fear of castration.

Throughout life, in triangular relationships, we can observe the reactivation of these feelings. The way in which these feelings are expressed and managed in each family or couple is likely to vary across cultures. Although it remains difficult to state with certainty, as we have seen in this chapter, that the Oedipus complex is a universal fact of life we cannot dismiss it merely as a myth, inconsequential to understanding ourselves. Rather, it serves as a useful metaphor allowing us to consider the passionate feelings of rivalry and envy and our desire for exclusivity to which we are all susceptible. It is nonetheless salutary to remind ourselves here, as elsewhere in our psychoanalytic explorations, that if we believe in the universality of the Oedipus complex we usually have no trouble in finding it reflected back in the myths, rituals and family relations we are observing (Cantlie, 1994).

Chapter 12
What happens when we fall in love?

I hold it true, whate'er befall
I feel it when I sorrow most
'Tis better to have loved and lost
Than never to have loved at all.

Tennyson

The process of falling in love is perhaps one which we are less interested in, or motivated to understand, when we are in love than when we are not. After all, when we are in love we have better things to do. Reflecting on or dissecting the process itself may be more in keeping with the frame of mind of someone who is seeking love or is disappointed by it. Nonetheless, the experience of falling in love is one worthy of exploration as it is an experience we all seek and is one which can be as exhilarating as it can be painful. This chapter will focus on the contributions made by psychoanalysis to our understanding of love. What happens then when we fall in love? What, if anything, distinguishes 'falling in love' from loving someone?

Love as a 'refinding'

There is a general consensus that what is familiarly characteristic of 'falling in love' is the lovers' urgency to be together. The source of such an intense force was illuminated when Freud intuited that love is a refinding. The theme of refinding and its dangers is a powerful one in the myth of Oedipus, as we saw in the last chapter, where he is literally destined to refind his mother Jocasta with tragic consequences.

Freud arrived at his view of love as a refinding through his work as an analyst and his concept of transference. His observations of patients led him to hypothesise that the intense feelings of love and hate which they experienced towards him were in fact 're-editions' of feelings originally experienced towards the parents – the love objects of childhood. These feelings could be re-evoked in the analytic situation with as much intensity and sincerity as when they were originally experienced towards the parental figures. Freud extrapolated from this that romantic love was also a re-edition of the original love objects of childhood. The enormous power the beloved seems to exert over the lover may then be partly explained, in Freudian terms, by the love object having been invested with the mystique of the lost objects from the past. Indeed, Freud maintained that the sexual feelings originally experienced by the child towards the parents are diverted away from them due to the incest barrier which, in theory, precludes such feelings from being acted upon by either parent or child.

The power of love

As we saw in Chapter 10 the physical language of love is already present from birth. One of Freud's greatest insights into love was to highlight the continuity from childhood into adulthood, despite appearances to the contrary, of the lovers' emotional life. All the lovers' unfulfilled yearnings from childhood are transferred to the beloved who is, as a consequence, experienced as a kind of reincarnation of all that is potentially good. They become imbued with a special feeling as they refuel hopes of satisfying yearnings and gratifying wishes from childhood. The loved one becomes invested with the power to transform us and our world. We are invariably energised through love, we feel more confident, able to take on new challenges and we tend to believe that only with the loved one can we really be ourselves. It can feel as if the other person holds some magical power to transform our world and consequently the world can seem like an enchanted place through the eyes of love.

But why should the quest for refinding the lost object take the form of the passionate longing so readily observed in lovers? We can only long for something of which we already have some glimmer of awareness. Reik (1941) gives us an important clue to the motor force in love when he reminds us that longing cannot depend simply upon the memory of love but upon the feelings of loss accruing to that memory; once we felt ourselves to be the objects of unconditional love but no longer so that, according to Reik, 'The need to regain paradise springs from the memory that we once possessed it and lost it' (1941: 111). But what is it really that we are trying to regain?

The experience of being transformed alluded to above, and the function of transforming itself, are equated respectively by Bollas (1987) with the baby's earliest experiences and the maternal function. The baby's experience of his mother's handling of him represents, according to Bollas, the earliest 'human aesthetic'. The latter refers to a very profound experience where the very nature of our self is formed and transformed by the environment. From the baby's perspective, in the early months, the mother actually *is* the environment. If the baby is distressed because he is hungry, his pangs of hunger are transformed by the mother's milk, leaving the baby with a sense of fullness where there was once emptiness. The mother therefore transforms both the baby's internal and external reality, tuning in the external environment to meet the baby's needs. According to Bollas, the mother is a 'transformational object'. The beloved may be seen to perform a similar function to the mother as they literally transform how we feel and how we view the world. Bollas indeed argues that the memory of our early relationship with our mothers manifests itself in adulthood as a search for a person, a place or an event that contains the promise or hope to transform us, changing both our internal and external world. We all invest certain relationships or events in our lives with this hope and falling in love is one such instance.

> Carrie came from a relatively stable family background. Her mother, however, had died from cancer when Carrie was 8 years old. She had subsequently been cared for by her father, to whom she felt very close, and her paternal grandparents who lived nearby.
>
> Carrie was an intelligent woman who was studying for her doctorate when she started therapy. Her presenting problem was that at times she found it hard to motivate herself and she was quite behind with her research. She often found her research meaningless and she was not really sure why she was doing it.
>
> Whilst she was in therapy Carrie met someone with whom she fell deeply in love. From one day to the next Carrie appeared 'transformed'. She started to work very hard, made plans to go away for a long overdue holiday and her general appearance improved. In the therapeutic sessions she was lively and humorous – quite a shift from the early sessions when she was often silent and withdrawn. As we explored together the changes that were taking place in her, Carrie casually observed that this man reminded her of her mother. She told me that when he looked at her she felt so special and important and she then believed that everything would be all right. As a child she felt her mother had performed a similar function.
>
> The loss of her mother had been very traumatic for Carrie. She herself felt that when she started therapy she had been quite depressed, stuck with her work and really wishing that her mother could somehow make it better for her as she used to do when she had been alive. The new man in her life had been invested with this power and this in turn gave Carrie the strength to face some of the difficulties she had been struggling with prior to meeting him. The likeness with the relationship she had enjoyed with her mother and which she was seeking to re-experience was one that Carrie herself had been able to identify. This, of course, also brought to the fore her anxieties about losing this man just as she had lost her mother.

The sense of completeness we experience when we fall in love can be likened to the baby's experience of having all his needs met – having his nappy changed when he is wet, being fed when he is hungry, being kept warm when he is cold or being held when he is distressed.

This may indeed be likened to a kind of 'paradise'. As we watch babies sleep when all these conditions are met we often remark on how blissful they look – just as people in love seem to 'glow' in a very discernible manner. Some psychoanalytic theorists would argue even further that being loved is in fact equivalent to a restoration, inevitably partial, of the first narcissistic state, itself regarded as synonymous with the foetal state (Grunberger, 1991). The refinding which Freud spoke of and which is captured in the transformational power of the beloved helps then to give the love relationship its dimension of pleasure regained, of a kingdom previously glimpsed as babies, then lost and found again when we fall in love.

The relinquishment of omnipotence and the ego-ideal

It has long been postulated within psychoanalysis that the baby's original sense of omnipotence, of being the centre of the universe, is whittled away by the sequential frustrations of childhood such as weaning and toilet training, leading to the child's painful realisation of his helplessness. That which babies experience as the abrupt end of their state of fusion with their mothers when they felt themselves to be omnipotent obliges them to recognise the 'not me' as they see that their mother is a separate person, not at their beck and call. This is seen as the crucial moment when the narcissistic omnipotence that the baby is forced to give up is projected into the parents who become the first *ego-ideal*, that is the inspiring aspects of the parental function. Rather than retaining an increasingly untenable notion of our own perfection, we create an ideal of perfection which is aspired to. The child projects on to his parents his lost omnipotence and for a while sees them as perfect. But, they, too, invariably fail to live up to the child's view of them as omnipotent and perfect. Eventually the child incorporates their image of perfection into his own psyche as a kind of guiding light. The 'lost' ideal parents of childhood are internalised so that they become the basis of the superego and the ego-ideal. The ego-ideal was understood by Freud (1914) to be the heir of the child's early narcissism (see Chapter 9).

Our hope of restoring our lost omnipotence, of regaining the paradise Reik spoke of, rests on our ability to live up to the dictates of the ego-ideal. Alternatively, it rests on the opportunity of uniting with someone else on to whom we have projected that ideal as, for instance, when we fall in love with someone and the feeling is mutual. To the extent that we live up to, or at least come close to, our internalised ego-ideal, all is well. To the extent that we fail to do so, we may feel depressed and our sense of self is diminished. Love may be seen as a roundabout quest for perfection, an opportunity for restoring our narcissism. Through the idealisation of, and our subsequent union with, the loved one we hope to regain our own perfection, as it were. In love then, the lovers hark back to the past and to ongoing, often unconscious, wishes and fantasies seeking to undo many of the inevitable disappointments of early life.

Idealisation and splitting

Psychoanalysis, as we have seen so far, can shed some light on the needs which are being met when we fall in love but can it help us to appreciate what distinguishes falling in love from loving? In addressing the question of love, a common distinction is frequently drawn between romantic love and 'mature' love (for want of a better word), between being-in-love and loving. Romantic love, as Kernberg (1983) suggests, is a normal and indeed essential prelude to a more stable love relationship. In romantic love the normal idealisation of the partner and the experience of transcendence are maximal. Because romantic love is based on idealisation of the beloved, it is believed by love's sceptics that love will eventually fail when confronted by the experiences and frustrations of daily life and the realisation that no one is perfect. Idealisation is a common defence mechanism which involves the persistent overvaluation of the other and the correspondingly persistent refusal to appraise the other realistically. The fate of idealisation is variable, however; it may be preserved, diminished altogether or it may be modulated.

The process of idealisation is central to romantic love and finds its roots in the most archaic and regressive ways of relating – that is, in infancy. To understand the roots of idealisation we turn our attention to the work of Melanie Klein and her followers whose contributions to psychoanalysis have been very influential. Even though in the course of her work Klein did not devote much attention to the love relationship between adults, her work can nonetheless shed some light on the relationship between lover and beloved. More specifically, it allows us to understand the initial stages of the psychic and affective life of the couple. We shall now look at two key Kleinian concepts which are pertinent to this discussion.

Klein believed that a major task facing us is the negotiation of two basic psychic positions in our life, namely the *paranoid-schizoid* and the *depressive* positions. By insisting on the concept of 'position' as opposed to the Freudian notion of 'stages' which we looked at in Chapter 2, Klein highlighted how both these positions are never fully worked through by us. In addition, she showed how the anxieties and defence mechanisms pertaining to them can be re-experienced by us throughout our lives.

According to Klein, from the beginning of existence, the interaction of projective, introjective and splitting defence mechanisms (see Chapter 16) shape the ego of the child. So as to escape from the intense anxiety stirred up by the conflict between the Life and the Death instinct (that is, by the confrontation with destructive feelings) the baby is said to split off such feelings and to project them into the mother. The mother, in turn, becomes identified with the 'badness' and is experienced by the baby as a persecuting figure. At the same time, however, the baby is said to establish a relationship with the 'good' or ideal mother. This is achieved through the projection of the libido, thereby creating a 'good object' which is in tune with the ego's instinctive striving for the preservation of life. The baby therefore is seen to relate to the mother as if she were two different people. The 'bad' mother is the one who frustrates, for instance, when she does not immediately respond to her baby's cries. The 'good' mother is the one who gratifies.

The good and the bad mother are internal representations, that is, they do not necessarily relate to real qualities of the mother. The crucial point to retain is that babies need, for their own psychological survival at this stage, to split the mother in this way so as to preserve their belief that they will be cared for without needing to worry about the destructive feelings which are always in the background and which pose a threat to their survival. The destructive feelings are understood to be part of the baby's innate potential and to be too overwhelming for the baby to tolerate at this stage of development. This is the central dilemma of the paranoid-schizoid position: how to keep 'good' and 'bad' apart, so that the 'good' can be preserved from the fantasised attacks from the 'bad'. This way the baby achieves relative stability by turning an object into an ideal one as protection from the 'bad'. The difficulty experienced by the baby is one with which we all struggle to an extent even as adults – it seems difficult for us to hold emotionally to the idea that someone can be a mixture of bad *and* good qualities.

The process of splitting in the baby enables us to see the benefits that may accrue from the idealisation of the other person. The quest for love mirrors the process of idealisation and splitting in the baby's relationship to the mother. Falling in love calls for the idealisation and splitting process to find a gratifying 'other' – one who does not let us down in any way. That which we often refer to as the honeymoon period in a relationship is precisely the stage when such processes are at their peak. There is a need to avoid all the less than perfect aspects of the beloved and we can go to varying lengths to protect our idealised image of the other.

The analogy drawn here between the lover's experience and that of the baby is not as far-fetched as it might at first appear. When the 'good' mother appears the world feels secure and good to the baby; when she disappears or she frustrates the world becomes frightening and unsafe because in going away she also takes all the goodness with which she has become identified and which the baby has partly projected into her. This last point is equally relevant to the lover's predicament. One of the prices we pay for idealisation of the other person is the loss of self-esteem which follows from the projection into the loved one of all the desirable and good parts of ourselves. This explains in part the experience of depletion and emptiness which we feel if the beloved leaves us, especially if they leave us for good. We are particularly vulnerable to such feelings in the romantic stage of a relationship. Indeed Freud (1914) believed that a common feature of being in love is that lovers have to relinquish a part of their own narcissism with which they invest the beloved. The love of self can only be replenished on the basis of the beloved's return of their love. This led Freud (1914) to state that such dependence means that 'a person in love is humble'. While the idea that falling in love actually involves a depletion of self-esteem may not match our experience of exaltation when we are in love, what Freud is underlining here is that any exalted feeling that accompanies the state of being in love derives from the fact that love is returned. Unrequited love can be a very distressing experience indeed.

Managing ambivalence

In some relationships, if the loved one reveals a shortcoming in the perfection of the image that the lover had formed of them, they may be rejected. It has been suggested that what cannot be called love is when idealisation takes the form of an intolerant demand for perfection (Horney, 1937). Since no one is perfect, at some stage or other both partners will need to face their respective limitations. Given this, we might say that what distinguishes being in love from loving is the ability to establish an ambivalent relationship with the loved one, a relationship in which both their 'good' and 'bad' points can be accepted.

Those individuals who seem unable to achieve such a compromise may be said to be stuck in Klein's 'paranoid-schizoid' position where splitting is the primary mode of defence, and to be unable to move on to the 'depressive position'. The latter is the term used by Klein to refer to the point in the child's development when they can acknowledge that the 'good' and the 'bad' mother are one and the same person, that is, an acceptance that people who love you are not necessarily always good to you but may at times hurt or frustrate you. To achieve this position, the child has to relinquish the idealisation and work through the loss of this fantasised perfect mother and embrace an ambivalent relationship with her. No less is required of the lovers if they are to progress to a more enduring relationship with all its ups and downs. It is important to note, however, that what is lost, as it were, in moving from one position to the next is not necessarily the 'real' attributes of the other but our internal psychic reality and the picture we held of the other person when we needed to idealise them – in short our fantasy of the other person.

The mourning of the loss of the idealised partner seems to be an integral part of mature love. It consists of letting go of the initial splitting and idealisation along with an acceptance of the imperfections in the other person. This implies also the necessity to acknowledge both our hatred and our love and this is no easy task. Some people may in fact need to sustain at all costs the idealisation of the loved one, so frightening is the thought that their hostile feelings might be brought into the relationship if faced with disappointment. In such instances in order to maintain the relationship it may therefore need to be limited to specific aspects. For instance, the loved one may only be met in particular places, times or circumstances as though a change in this routine would introduce the risk of losing the idealised image. Conflict is excluded and avoided at all costs.

> Susan started therapy because she found it difficult to sustain relationships with men. She was nearly 35 years old and she felt she should have settled into a relationship by now. Moreover, she very much wanted a baby and there was a sense that time was running out for her.
>
> Susan described a number of past relationships – they had all been comparatively brief, the longest one lasting 7 months. All her relationships appeared to follow a very similar pattern. She would meet a man and very quickly fall in love with him. Within days of knowing the person she would buy them presents, send them cards telling them how special they were even though she barely knew them. Although she would say how much she missed them and wanted to see them she would not actually see them frequently – there were always excuses followed by reassurances that she did, however, want to see them and that her life was not the same when she was away from them.
>
> On the one hand, Susan idealised her partners – no one could criticise them and she in fact seldom introduced them to friends, fearing their evaluation. On the other hand she needed to keep them at a distance, strictly controlling how often she would see them and where – restrictions which eventually led the partners to end the relationship as they felt she was very withholding.
>
> Susan found conflict very difficult to manage and she therefore could not allow a relationship to develop more fully as this might lead to conflict. She wanted to maintain an idealised relationship which was ultimately a rather empty and shallow one as she could not allow herself to be close to another person. This led Susan to feel very lonely, feeling herself to be a victim in her relationships as the men invariably left her. Yet Susan clearly played an important part in this – a part she struggled to understand in therapy where she behaved in much the same manner as in her relationships with men; that is, she would tell me how 'wonderful' I was and would never disagree openly with me but instead would, for example, miss sessions after I had suggested something she clearly did not want to think

about, so as to avoid a more direct confrontation. Susan's difficulty in managing conflict and her own ambivalence was linked to her fantasy that if she
allowed any negative feelings into a relationship these would destroy the
relationship. This was, in turn, related to Susan's early experiences of relationships which had left her with a sense that relationships were very pre-
carious and could not survive her own aggressive feelings.

Kernberg (1983) suggests that what is most characteristic of many
romantic stories and legends is the ending of the story before the element of time penetrates the love relationship. It is only when a relationship is allowed to develop over time that the hidden presence of
ambivalence and aggression is exposed – feelings that may be experienced as especially threatening. The greater the fear of such feelings,
the more likely it will be that the individual, as with Susan, will frequently change relationships, hoping to keep at bay the inevitable disappointments that are faced by us all if we stay long enough in any
relationship – to keep love free from any blemish is an impossible task.
Others may of course simply avoid relationships altogether as they cannot tolerate the anxiety resulting from any involvement which has the
potential to give rise to such conflicting feelings.

Psychoanalysis reminds us, however, that we are all prey to feelings
of love and hate and that these need to be lived with rather than artifi-
cially kept apart – for even if we are temporarily successful in keeping
them apart they invariably come back to haunt us. Even successful relationships are always delicately balanced and require constant working
at as different strains and conflicts come to the fore over the years.

Love past and present

This chapter has looked at a number of psychoanalytic ideas which
can be usefully applied to understanding the process of falling in love
and what might be considered to be the necessary developments to
establish a more mature love relationship. Falling in love is often felt
to be a novel experience and one which holds the promise of transfor-
mation. However, we cannot really begin to understand that which we
call love and its vagaries until we understand that it is our deepest and
oldest longings which are fulfilled by it. While the experience of falling
in love and loving cannot be explained away by any one theoretical
model, psychoanalysis, once again, reminds us that even in the sphere
of love we can find traces of our earliest relationships and the fantasies and wishes of childhood. Our personal psychodynamics – those
which influence our experience of love and, as we shall see in the next
chapter, our choice of whom to love – are the result of our individual
navigations through the relationships of early life. Love, as Freud
suggested, is in a sense a refinding and is regressive in so far as it
rekindles infantile wishes and feelings. But it is also progressive,

giving us direction and strength and is, in its essence, a 'mutative experience' (Person, 1989).

Chapter 13
Why did I choose *you*?

I think there is a fatality in it – I seldom go to the place I set out for.

Laurence Sterne

The mystery of choice

The question which this chapter will explore is one that we may have all put to ourselves at least once. It is the case that we are attracted to very particular types of people so that, for example, some of us appear to be drawn to partners who are very quiet and distant, others to those who are extroverted and dominant and others still to those who are submissive. Yet our choices, on one level, may feel quite mysterious to us. On closer inspection, however, we can often find a number of factors which have played a part. This suggests that our choices are by no means random or indifferent.

When we enter into a relationship with someone there are many factors that come into play. Our choice of partner is partly determined by considerations of time, place and culture. By the time we settle into our first serious relationship, there are differences between all of us in terms of geography, socio-economic and cultural backgrounds (including the prevailing myths, movies and literature about love pertaining to the culture), our level of education and so on, all of which affect who we are most likely to pair up with. Even though few marriages in the West are now arranged, our choices are still, to an extent, under the influence of such external factors. Indeed, when people are asked why they chose each other they will frequently cite the aforementioned factors with a fatalistic reference to chance also usually thrown in for good measure. While sociological factors play their part in our choices you will not by now be too surprised to learn that psychoanalysis views partnerships as the direct heirs of childhood relationships.

The unconscious pull of the past

We all have an idea of the kind of person we are attracted to and we can, albeit superficially, specify some important physical, social and psychological characteristics of our so-called ideal partner. This picture is partly constructed on conscious wishes and aspirations and on our sense of who would best meet our conscious needs. However, a psychoanalytic perspective would suggest in addition that our choices are also constructed on unconscious priorities regarding those qualities in the other which we intuit would fit with our needs (though we should not forget that the fit need not produce a happy relationship). So, while we can all find conscious, plausible reasons to explain our choices of partner, in addition we can often detect other underlying, *unconscious* reasons which have played an important part in our choice. Moreover, as we saw in Chapter 7, we all live in two worlds – an external and an internal world, the latter populated with significant figures from our childhoods. If there is some unfinished business with such internal figures, the tendency to repeat patterns from the past will be intensified. Indeed, it would sometimes appear that relationships do not take place between two real people but rather between two figures inhabiting their respective fantasy worlds.

If we follow a psychoanalytic lead in attempting to answer the question of why we chose a particular person, we will need to take a close look at ourselves and the unwritten rules that govern our relationships. With this in mind let us turn to some of the pointers that a psychoanalytic perspective affords us.

Often enough, buried in the unconscious, the person we choose evokes the dim memory of our earliest love – the kind of refinding Freud spoke of (see Chapter 12). A partner may be selected, for instance, on the basis that they appear to be very similar to a parent we were very close to but for some the resemblance may be to a parent who was experienced as 'bad'. Where our experiences in our early relationships have been predominantly negative, too laden with anxiety or ridden with conflict, destructive forces may colour present relationships. The man who feels resentful towards a mother he experienced as especially dominant may choose a partner who makes him feel similarly powerless and dependent and which recreates the earlier unhappiness and distress.

Such examples may sound counter-intuitive. After all, would it not make more sense that we should actually want to form a relationship as adults which in no way resembles that which we had with our parents if our experience was a negative one? Consciously this may be of course our stated aim but, as Freud (1920) observed in the course of his work with patients, some people seem to be compelled to repeat past experiences or dynamics, even if the repetition causes undeniable

distress. This tendency is all the more pronounced if we have no awareness or understanding of the dynamics at work. Even though new relationships often represent a conscious wish to start afresh, to not repeat
the same old mistakes again and perhaps even to undo what were
experienced as painful disappointments in our early relationships, the
strong unconscious ties to the first objects of our love often determine
the choice of a partner with whom the earlier unresolved situation can
be re-enacted.

The unwritten rules of relationships

Relationships are governed by rules. Some of these rules are quite
explicit and are negotiated consciously between partners. Other rules,
however, are unconscious, that is they affect the life of the couple but
neither party may be aware that such rules are in fact operating. Such
'unwritten' rules typically lead to unconscious collusions between partners which sometimes serve to maintain troubled relationships which
are resistant to change. Let us look at an example which highlights this.

> Tom and Joy had been married for 20 years and were referred for marital
> counselling following a disclosure by Tom that he had been unfaithful to
> Joy some years previously. Since this disclosure Joy had been feeling very
> depressed and said that she felt her whole life had been a waste. In explor-
> ing their relationship it soon became clear that they also had a very difficult
> sexual relationship, which had been seldom enjoyed by Joy, and they made
> love very infrequently. Joy was convinced that this was the reason behind
> Tom's unfaithfulness. Tom had also been suffering from quite serious bouts
> of depression alternating with manic episodes since just before they married
> and received psychiatric treatment for this. His psychological problems had
> therefore added an extra pressure on their relationship.
>
> The longstanding marital difficulties appeared to have their origins in
> the couple's respective childhood experiences and the sexual messages they
> had received from their parents. Joy strongly identified with her mother, a
> very puritanical woman who had devoted her life to the family and who had
> conveyed her sexual fears to Joy. Joy's relationship with her father had been
> a distant one as he left the family home because of another woman when
> she was very young leaving her mother alone with five children to care for.
> Joy despised her father for this and she generalised such negative feelings
> towards all men even though she consciously denied this.
>
> Modelling herself on her mother, Joy had also devoted her life to the
> family and had accepted Tom's problems as part of her duty as a 'good'
> wife. Her strong affiliation to the Jehovah's Witnesses further reinforced this
> idealised image of the good wife and mother which she strove to live up to.
> This, however, also entailed a repression of her own sexual feelings which
> conflicted with her internalised image of a 'good' woman. Marrying Tom,
> who from the start became highly dependent on her like a child, due to his
> psychiatric problems, conveniently helped Joy to sidestep the difficulties
> associated with her sexuality. She related to him more like a mother than a
> woman.

Tom, on the other hand, came from a family background where the expression of emotions often led to aggressive outbursts and violence. He recalled witnessing, as a young child, his father having violent sex with one of the many women he used to bring home. His own mother had been a devout Catholic – distant but loving in her own way and he felt she had had to put up with an intolerable marital relationship so as to keep the family together. As an adult, Tom found himself repeating some of his own father's behaviour in that he was also unfaithful to Joy. His greatest fear was, however, that, like his own father, he should become out of control of his feelings, particularly his sexual feelings. It transpired that there were in fact some apparent gains in remaining a weak child dependent on Joy. To become a man involved assuming responsibility for his sexual and aggressive feelings. However, Tom feared that, like his father, he would be unable to control these feelings.

Joy reminded Tom of his own mother. One of the advantages of being married to Joy was that her own puritanical upbringing and the rigidity of her religious beliefs served as an insurance against his own sexual desires which he experienced as overwhelming and frightening. Joy, in turn, unconsciously colluded with Tom's need to remain a dependent child as a result of her own fears associated with her sexuality. While both complained of this unsatisfactory relationship, and Tom in particular was unhappy with the lack of a sexual relationship, the status quo had nonetheless been maintained for 20 years.

Tom and Joy's experiences highlight the way in which unconscious residues of earlier conflicts and fantasies which are charged with anxiety or guilt may actually match up so that each partner treats the other in ways which perpetuate rather than resolve the conflicts. Moreover, this actually serves to intensify the fantasies harboured by both parties and prevents them from putting them to the test of reality. Even though we could say that it was precisely such unconscious collusion which seemingly helped both Joy and Tom to deal with their respective anxieties, there is a high price to be paid. Both of them, as with many partners who unconsciously collude with each other, were inhibited in their relationship with each other and had to forsake the joys that come from mutually satisfying partnerships. But while such couples often complain of unhappiness, we can regularly observe them re-enacting some destructive dynamics, blaming each other for the status quo without attempting to resolve their difficulties.

The unconscious needs which keep couples together in spite of evident distress are many and varied. Raphael-Leff (1991) points to a number of typical unconscious collusions which may affect the choice of partner:

1. The partner is chosen because they are most unlike a parental figure we feel ambivalently towards, thereby holding the hope that we can break free from the past.
2. The partner chosen is one who will share with us a similar 'dichotomy',

that is someone who will collude for instance with a mutual idealisation and project on to the world all the 'bad' and denied aspects of both partners.

3. The partner chosen is one who is unconsciously perceived as a symbol of lost, repressed aspects of ourselves and is chosen to enact them.

Such observations converge on the psychoanalytic assumption regarding choice of partner, namely that the personal characteristics of our partners are often selected on the basis that they reinforce, rather than challenge, the defence mechanisms which strive to keep at bay unconscious feelings and fantasies which would otherwise be too threatening to consciousness. This reflects the way in which partners seem to fit into each other's needs in a variety of subtle ways. Not everyone of course experiences the kind of difficulties that Joy and Tom presented but this general rule applies across the continuum without this needing to lead to serious problems in a relationship.

> Jenny began therapy following the death of her mother a few months earlier. She was feeling very low in her mood at times and was concerned that she was withdrawing from her relationship with her husband, Terry.
>
> Jenny was a very quiet, softly-spoken woman who appeared to find the expression of anger very difficult. In therapy she would frequently describe Terry as a very angry person whom she felt 'went over the top'. They often argued about this as Jenny was at times embarrassed by his volatile behaviour and criticised him for not being more in control. Terry and his anger featured a lot in what Jenny brought to therapy so much so that it begged the question of how Jenny managed her own angry feelings. When Jenny was confronted with this she acknowledged that she never got angry and that instead of being angry she became depressed.
>
> Further exploration revealed just how angry Jenny felt towards her mother who had died as a result of an overdose after several previous attempts but these were feelings she found extremely difficult to own up to. She realised that she had needed Terry to give voice to her own disowned anger and that his outbursts were perhaps all the more exaggerated as he was carrying a 'double dose' of anger as it were: his anger as well as hers. Jenny thus used Terry to give expression to her anger and by not challenging her Terry colluded with this. Jenny realised that she had unconsciously chosen Terry at least in part because he could express his anger so openly even if, at a conscious level, she would be very critical of his behaviour.

Pincus (1962), a psychoanalytic practitioner with considerable expertise in marital therapy, has argued that the conflict and confusion that couples sometimes experience may be understood as an attempt to integrate the aspects of themselves which cause conflict. The idea here is that in some way we manage to get them 'married' inside ourselves with the help of our partners into whom we may project disowned aspects of ourselves – aspects which we either projected into our partner in the first place or whom we actually chose because they possessed a particular quality or trait we lacked. In such cases the partner may be seen to act as a kind of container, who holds on to those feelings for us until we are ready to own them. This is an adaptive strategy so long as we are willing at some stage to reclaim what is ours through a recognition and understanding of such disowned feelings. However, if we fail to claim back such disowned aspects of ourselves, not only do we remain cut off from important features of our personalities but we also become prey to such qualities in other people. For example, if we establish a relationship with a person because they are prone to envy so that they can conveniently carry that part of us, we suffer the effects of living with envy all the time.

All relationships involve both positive and negative interactions and mutual projections. Projection is a process common to all relationships and is therefore not exclusively the province of troubled relationships. If we can accept this basic premise then it also follows that any difficulties in a relationship are not due exclusively to one or other partner but are always the result of an interaction underpinned by unconscious agreements between the couple. This should not be taken to mean, however, that individual partners need not assume responsibility for their own actions. Indeed, such an understanding should not be used, as it has been at times, to justify for example violence between couples whereby the woman who is beaten by her partner is often said to be colluding with this. While there may well be aspects of the woman's personality and early experiences which may illuminate why she chose an abusive partner, this in no way justifies the violence of which she is a victim. While there are often unconscious reasons which bring and keep people together in destructive and unhappy relationships it is nonetheless important not to lose sight of the socio-cultural factors which may also make it difficult for partners to separate, such as financial considerations, particularly if children are involved. A psychoanalytic perspective on such matters, while helpful, can only offer an incomplete picture.

Healthy conflict

Although it has been suggested that there is often a bias in the choice of partner in favour of one who can act as a carrier for the undeveloped or rejected parts of ourselves, not everyone chooses someone who complements them in this way. Some people appear to need to engage with someone with whom they can very closely identify so as to strengthen their own self-image. Underlying such relationships is often a denial of difference and hence an attempt to avoid the envy, anxiety and the hostile feelings which might be aroused by its acknowledgement. The need to protect a relationship from the expression of negative feelings and from conflict while not uncommon is ultimately restricting. As we saw in the last chapter, the need to sustain the idealisation of the loved one may lead the lover to restrict the relationship in all manner of ways.

Whilst constant rowing and disagreements may be symptomatic of deep-seated problems in a relationship, longitudinal studies of marital interaction have, however, found that disagreement and angry exchanges amongst couples, which have been usually considered harmful to marriage, may in fact not be harmful in the long term. Even though the experience of conflict correlates with concurrent reports of unhappiness by the couple, they were found in one study to be predictive of improvement in marital interaction over a period of three years (Goffman and Krokoff, 1989). It appears that such couples develop a sense of confidence that they can weather conflict together whereas its avoidance may reinforce pre-existing fantasies that conflict would be disastrous thereby precluding the testing out of such fantasies in reality.

Working at relationships

Psychoanalysis has afforded some important insights into the unwritten alliances and misalliances that can be traced in any relationship. It helps us to appreciate some of the factors that undoubtedly play a role in shaping our choice of partner. It also helps us to understand why we may remain in relationships which, on one level, make us unhappy and feel unrewarding.

Intimate relationships reactivate both the good and the bad experiences from childhood and unresolved conflicts from the past are often stirred up by the intimacy of the couple. This means that relationships are fertile ground for both creative and self-enhancing experiences as well as inhibiting and self-destructive ones. Relationships which are mutually satisfying are those that are built on an undertaking by both partners to translate what was at first a largely unconscious choice into a conscious commitment (Lyons, 1993). This can be a painful process and some may give up along the way opting for a relationship that is transitory or for one which, whilst gratifying defensive needs, thwarts individual development and that of the partnership.

This may sound rather pessimistic but it reflects the reality of many partnerships which are not sustained through love but through motives based on, and revealing of, personal anxieties and conflicts. However, in relationships, as Balint (1993) has pointed out, we seem unconsciously to hope to find a solution to our intimate problems. She argues that we seldom give up trying to put things right for ourselves even when to all intents and purposes we seem to be doing quite the opposite. Sometimes even the most destructive and hostile behaviour can be understood as a desperate attempt to put right what is unsatisfactory, even if from an observer's point of view we may well judge the attempt to be misguided.

Rewarding relationships require constant effort – they do not just happen but many relationships fare well on the whole. What enables such relationships to survive and grow is the commitment by both partners to recognise the reality of their respective needs and to accept the other even if they fall short of what they had originally and, often unconsciously, projected into them.

Chapter 14
I'm homosexual: is there something wrong with me?

Psychoanalytic research ... has found that all human beings are capable of making a homosexual object choice and in fact have made one in their unconscious.

Freud

In the last few chapters we have looked at relationships generally and the love relationship in more detail. All that has been said so far applies equally to both heterosexual and homosexual relationships. However, Part III would be incomplete without a more specific consideration of homosexuality from a psychoanalytic perspective. This is all the more important as any lesbian or gay individual who braves the psychoanalytic literature on the subject of sexuality may well be left wondering if in fact there isn't something 'wrong' with them. Such an impression is reinforced by the majority of psychoanalytic writers who have used the terms 'homosexuality' and 'perversion' interchangeably. To be called a 'pervert' is humiliating and degrading to say the least. Yet in the context of much psychoanalytic writing such is the fate of those individuals who have not followed the path of heterosexuality.

The whole question of homosexuality, as it applies to both gay men and lesbian women, represents one of the most controversial and problematic areas of psychoanalysis. It has consequently been the focus of much psychoanalytic writing to such an extent that Chodorow (1994) has suggested that the question of heterosexuality by comparison has not received as much attention. This, she argues, reveals the prevailing consensus amongst psychoanalytic writers that heterosexuality does not require explanation as it is the 'normal' course of events unlike homosexuality which represents a deviation from 'normal' development. It is well beyond the scope of this chapter to do justice to the complexity of all the issues in question. In view of this, this chapter will be more humble in its aim and will merely sketch the area of controversy and refer to some of the psychoanalytic literature on homosexuality, hoping that if this area is of interest you will find here a guide to your own explorations.

The causes of homosexuality: the limitations of the explanations

The standard psychoanalytic question, as Strubin (1994) suggests, when faced with a homosexual individual has been 'what went wrong?'. From this question two areas opened themselves up for psychoanalytic investigation. Firstly, the search started for those factors in the individual's development which could account for the deviation from the heterosexual norm. Secondly, given that it was assumed that something had gone wrong the next question was 'how can we put it right?' Indeed, some analysts to this day view homosexuality as a problem even if most have given up trying to 'cure' it as clinical experience repeatedly shows that this is a very difficult thing to achieve and ethically highly dubious.

Analysts have tended to locate the causes of homosexuality in difficulties in the developmental period pre-dating the Oedipus complex where both the male and female homosexual are said to remain identified to the mother precluding the later developments and identifications which would ensure a heterosexual orientation (see Chapter 2). The other typical pattern believed to underlie a homosexual orientation can be traced back to difficulties during the Oedipal period itself when, it is suggested, the boy or girl fails to resolve the Oedipus complex. The fear of castration is said to lead to the adoption of the negative Oedipal position, that is, love for the same-sex parent. In this context, men are said to assume the role of the female with their father and so later with other men, and women are said to assume the role of the male to the mother and so later with other women (Socarides, 1979; Rosen, 1979). The problem here, according to psychoanalytic theory, is that both the male and female homosexual identified, as children, with the opposite-sex parent. This was, in brief, the essence of Freud's own understanding of homosexuality.

Psychoanalytic speculations about the causes of homosexuality have been numerous and have highlighted a number of factors assumed to be implicated in its genesis. Limentani, in keeping with most of the more classical psychoanalytic literature on this subject, reveals a rather confusing picture of the possible causes of homosexuality. It is worth quoting his views verbatim as the views he espouses reflect a more general problem with psychoanalytic theorising in this area:

... a parent may or may not be absent. The father may be strong or weak. The mother may be distant or excessively seductive and domineering. The mother may be over-preoccupied with the father or totally indifferent to him. Lack of love is of as much importance as too much. (1977: 210)

In a similar vein it has also been suggested that the absence of a father may encourage homosexuality. While this may be true for some individuals and a strong case could be made for the importance of the presence of both parents to a child's development, such a statement cannot be generalised. The main problem with such causal accounts is that, in covering all possibilities, they actually tell us nothing about why people become homosexual. While some of the factors mentioned by Limentani in the above quote may well apply to particular individuals, they do not actually allow us to predict any particular outcome. What is most worrying about such statements is that they should have any place in an account of human behaviour which claims scientific and rigorous thinking as part of its credentials and psychoanalysis does indeed make such claims.

A further problem with psychoanalytic theorising in this area has been the tendency to extrapolate general theories about homosexuality from clinical psychoanalytic work which, by definition, is with individuals who are experiencing psychological problems that may or may not be related to their sexual orientation. Moreover, to construct general theories on the basis of such clinical experience is laden with methodological problems, not least that the samples studied are too small. These are, of course, criticisms that can justifiably be levelled at psychoanalytic theorising generally but they are all the more noteworthy when it comes to theories about homosexuality where there has been the unfortunate association between the latter and psychological difficulties.

While psychoanalytic theorising on homosexuality is rife with problems this should not be taken to imply, however, that we should dismiss all the observations that have been made by analysts on the subject but merely to encourage a degree of caution in accepting unquestioningly the universal claims regarding the theories. This cautionary note is in keeping with the findings from reviews of studies which have attempted to find common personality characteristics or family backgrounds in male homosexuals and which have not yielded any conclusive results or clear patterns in support of psychoanalytic hypotheses. Rather, such studies suggest that homosexuality can be found in individuals with very different personality structures, with varying degrees of individual psychopathology (that is, both psychological and psychiatric problems) and with different family backgrounds (see Friedman, 1988). Similar findings apply to female homosexuals.

Freud's views on homosexuality

In reviewing the psychoanalytic literature on homosexuality one can only wonder how Freud's own humanism and openness in relation to the question of homosexuality could have led to such an unproductive dead-end on this issue. It is important to note Freud's views on homo-sexuality as they are certainly not representative of the general trend in psychoanalytic thinking which followed his work. Freud's view was that the child's early sexuality was in a state of what he called *polymor-phous perversity* by which he meant that the child's early sexuality is not anchored in its aim to a particular object, that is, either to a female or male person, but is indiscriminate in this respect. One important implication of this, as we have seen in earlier chapters, is that hetero-sexuality is not itself indelibly inscribed in our psyche at this stage as the only natural way in which sexual feelings should be expressed.

Freud was clear that homosexuality existed in many forms and indeed it does make much more sense to speak of 'homosexual*ities*' (Strubin, 1994). While Freud, committed as he was to his scientific aim, inevitably tried to explain homosexuality in terms of his own theories, he was nonetheless clear that homosexuality was not the only type of sexual behaviour which needed to be explained as he indicated in the following passage:

> Psychoanalytic research is most decidedly opposed to any attempt at sepa-rating off homosexuals from the rest of mankind as a group of special char-acter ... all human beings are capable of making a homosexual object choice ... thus from the point of view of psychoanalysis the exclusive interest felt by men for women is also a problem that needs elucidating and is not a self-evident fact based upon an attraction that is ultimately of a chemical nature (1915: 56).

While Freud may not have viewed homosexuality as an illness as such he nevertheless saw it as resulting from a halt in normal sexual development as he makes clear in his response to a letter from the mother of a homosexual man:

> Homoerotism is assuredly no advantage but it is nothing to be ashamed of, no vice, no degradation, it cannot be classified as an illness; we consider it to be a variation of the sexual function produced by a certain arrest of sexual development. (quoted in Jones, 1955: 208)

Challenging the stereotypes

By contrast to many of his contemporaries and his followers, Freud was undoubtedly more open-minded on the question of homosexuality even if he clearly ultimately believed in one particular healthy develop-mental path, that of heterosexuality. However, his point that there is as much to be understood and explained regarding heterosexuality remains very important. This point has been central to the work of Stoller (1975), a psychoanalytic practitioner who has steadfastly held on to the view that heterosexuality is an acquisition and not a natural given, in much the same way as homosexuality is, and that the experience of sexual conflicts is not exclusively the province of those who become homosexual. A person whose sexuality is not normal – in the statistical sense that heterosexuality represents the norm – is not necessarily ill. We will find both psychologically healthy and unhealthy homosexuals as well as heterosexuals.

There are many assumptions regarding the peculiarities of the homosexual person which we all make and which many of us tend to take for granted. A common one regarding male homosexuals in particular is that they have unsteady relationships. Again, this may be true of some but it is also true of some heterosexual men and women and we also know that a large number of homosexual men and women are in stable relationships. As Cunningham (1993) – a lesbian psychoanalytic practitioner – has pointed out, a person's choice of sexual partner need not necessarily carry any information regarding the type of person he or she is. However, a person's choice of sexual partner is all too often seen to colour the whole personality and to affect the functioning of the individual both professionally and personally.

Although psychoanalysis may be justifiably accused of pathologising homosexuality, it is also true that for some people the path of homosexuality may be conflictual and one which deserves to be understood and here a psychoanalytic perspective may be very enlightening. Some homosexual individuals feel ashamed of their own sexual wishes and may conceal their orientation. Homophobia, that is the pathological fear of homosexuals, is not exclusively the province of heterosexuals, as homosexual individuals may also struggle with it when they cannot come to terms with their own sexual orientation and wish to disassociate themselves from it. It is not always easy in such cases, however, to know where the source of the conflict lies: is it the fact of desiring someone from the same sex or is it the result of having such desires in a culture where most people are heterosexual and where homosexuality is certainly not a passport to success? The latter scenario is likely to lead to much confusion and anguish for those who, for whatever reason, deviate from the heterosexual norm. Indeed, as Marmor (1982) suggests, it is unsurprising that in Western culture, where homosexuality is often a derogatory and humiliating label, there should be homosexual people whose self-image and emotional stability are affected.

> Angie is a 35-year-old woman who entered therapy because of confusion she experienced over her sexual identity. Since she was a teenager she had felt drawn to women but she had only had one sexual relationship with a woman. Because of her own upbringing she felt it was wrong to have homosexual relationships. Such was her anxiety about this that she renounced her desire to be in a relationship with a woman and engaged in numerous unsuccessful relationships with men over a period of 10 years. She, however, spoke fondly of her only relationship with a woman, the only time she had

felt loved in her life, and she yearned for this experience again which, she said, had given her confidence in herself.

Angie revealed during the course of her therapy that she had been sexually abused by her uncle over a period of years when she was younger. She said she could not trust men whom she believed were only driven by sex and the need for power. Her own father had been a very distant man whom Angie felt had ruled her mother's life.

Angie had always been much closer to her mother, who had done her best, she felt, to protect her from her uncle. However, she did not think her mother could understand her attraction to women and she therefore found herself unable to turn to her at a time when she very much needed her support.

At 35 Angie felt she needed to 'sort herself out' as she was very unhappy and had thoughts of killing herself. Her homosexual feelings were a source of conflict and distress for her. Although she was quite clearly drawn to women she simply could not allow herself to have another relationship with a woman. She viewed her desire as unnatural and she feared her friends' and parents' rejection if they were to find out. By all accounts the community she frequented held quite homophobic attitudes and her own parents appeared to have instilled in her considerable fear regarding sexual matters.

It is difficult to say with any certainty how much of Angie's distress and confusion with regard to her sexuality would have been alleviated if it were not for the hostile attitudes towards homosexuality that her family and community had conveyed to her. Choosing the homosexual path would most certainly have created quite real problems in her immediate environment. Although these factors were taken into account it remained important to also acknowledge Angie's highly ambivalent relationship with men in light of her early experiences and the impact of this on her sexuality.

For Angie, as with other homosexual individuals, the experience of their sexuality is ridden with conflict. The conflict may well be exacerbated by the negative attitudes towards homosexuality which are prevalent in some communities but this is not always the case. Rather, the person's early experiences in their families of origin may, in some instances, offer a more meaningful account of why the choice of a homosexual partner is a conflictual one and causes distress to the person.

The answer to homosexuality

The question of why some people are homosexual and others are not is an important and interesting one. Over the past decade biological hypotheses have gained in popularity. These have suggested that sexual orientation is inborn, that there is a gene for homosexuality. The latter position has brought relief to some homosexual people as it reflects their own experience that they were 'born this way'. Moreover, it removes the whole discourse from the realm of morality. However, such a position also introduces some problems as it removes the question of sexuality from the area of psychodynamic concern implying that our developmental histories are incidental. It may also serve to deny conflict where it exists for an individual, as well as denying the element of choice which it might be equally important to hold on to (Hurry, 1994). A gene for homosexuality has not so far been found even though there is some evidence that in some individuals there might be biological factors which shape and influence the emergence of homo-sexuality (Friedman and Downey, 1993). While one may disagree with the prevailing view espoused by psychoanalysis on the question of homosexuality, one of its important contributions in this area has been its emphasis on the fact that here there is something that needs to be understood with respect to psychological factors and not simply bio-logical ones.

> Tony was a 30-year-old man who had had a number of homosexual relation-ships since his late teens. He had one relationship with a woman when he was 20 years old but was unable to have sexual intercourse with her. He described himself as 'gay' but experienced considerable anxiety regarding this and harboured very ambivalent feelings towards women generally.
>
> Tony's father died when Tony was 4 years old and his mother never remarried. He was an only child and he recalled a rather lonely childhood even though he felt his mother had provided well for him and had indeed encouraged him with his studies where he had been very successful. However, Tony also experienced his mother as a very strict and prohibiting figure. She had frowned upon his social activities as an adolescent, empha-sising the importance of work. She had never been welcoming of any girl-friends that Tony brought home and he experienced her as very intrusive with regard to sexual matters. She used to look through his drawers to check for any pornographic material and would frequently enter his room in the evenings without respecting Tony's wish that she would knock first. He said that he had felt emasculated by her and his dreams and fantasies revealed a fear of women which accounted at least in part for his choice of men as the object of his sexual desire.
>
> Tony described feeling safer with men even though his relationships with men were punctuated by the anxiety which resulted from his fear that his partners would invariably leave him. This is a fear that he later under-stood as arising from the abandonment he experienced when his father died – a man he remembered otherwise in a very idealised way and whom he believed, in fantasy, had been killed by his suffocating mother.

While the genetic and the psychoanalytic hypotheses respectively will hold particular appeal for different people, the truth of the matter is that there does not appear to be a single cause or specific develop-mental path that determines sexual orientation, be it heterosexual or homosexual. Genetic research raises some interesting issues but is, at present, as ultimately inconclusive as any psychoanalytic speculations.

The threat of the 'other'

A survey of the psychoanalytic literature and the prevailing social atti-tudes towards homosexuality starkly highlight the extent to which many of us fail to achieve psychic bisexuality. As we have seen, Freud believed that both masculine and feminine dispositions exist psychically in all of us but that in the course of development one becomes more prominent than the other even if the other never totally disappears. Evidence of the presence of the other sexual disposition can often be traced in fantasies, dreams and free associations.

> Steve is a 30-year-old man who worked as a teacher. He was happily married with two children. He started therapy because he was unsatisfied in his job but feared leaving it as he had little confidence in his own abilities. One day he arrived at one of his sessions in a rather agitated state reporting an incident involving a male colleague. They had been playing tennis and when they had gone into the showers he had found himself staring at his colleague's naked body. That night he had a dream which involved him having sexual intercourse with this man. He had woken in a state of anxiety. When he explored his dream further his associations led him to recall his fondness for his father, a man he admired greatly but whom he recognised had difficulty in expressing any affection towards his son. Steve now realised how he had yearned for physical closeness with his father when he was a child and also recognised how he had internalised his father's difficulty in being close to men. For Steve such closeness triggered anxiety about his own homosexual longings towards his father.
>
> As we have seen in previous chapters, homosexual longings towards the same-sex parent are part of normal development. However, Steve had never resolved such feelings towards his father largely it seemed as a result of his father's own difficulty in this respect.

Psychic bisexuality entails the ability to identify with both the desire for our own sex and the opposite sex. However, as Cunningham (1993) points out, our hostility towards those individuals who present us with the sexual possibility which we have not pursued (for whatever reason) would not be so great if we did not have such considerable difficulty in integrating both masculine and feminine aspects within ourselves. She suggests that homosexuals are feared because we have projected into them our disowned parts which we experience as too difficult to incorporate into our preferred self-image.

You may be feeling after reading this chapter that psychoanalysis has little to offer those who 'choose' the homosexual path. Although an understandable response given the problematic nature of some psychoanalytic theorising on homosexuality, this would be an unfortunate conclusion to draw. This is because there are some psychoanalytic theorists who do not espouse such views and who are committed to the development of psychoanalysis, in both its theoretical and applied form, paying heed to the complexities and vicissitudes of individuals' lives and relationships (see O'Connor and Ryan, 1993). At its best, psychoanalysis can help us to understand ourselves and find our own truths. There may be much that can be gained from the exploration of our sexuality, not because we should aim to change the object of our desires, but merely because all the choices we make in our lives have something to tell us about what we value and why and ultimately who we are.

Part IV: Psychic Pain and Psychic Change

Although psychoanalytic ideas have been applied extensively outside the clinical realm to an understanding of everyday phenomena, psychoanalysis originated in the consulting room. It was essentially Freud's work with patients who complained at times of quite disabling symptoms that led to the development of psychoanalysis. Indeed, the term psychoanalysis itself is better known for its association with a form of psychological treatment characterised by its intensity (five times weekly sessions over a period of years) and its reliance on the use of the couch from which patients are invited to share all the contents of their thoughts. In view of the longstanding application of psychoanalysis to the understanding and treatment of psychological problems Part IV will devote itself to examining this applied area.

Chapter 15
Are we all neurotic?

A neurosis would seem to be the result of a kind of ignorance – a not knowing about mental events that one ought to know about.

Freud

What is neurosis?

Nowadays we use the term 'neurotic' quite freely without always being
clear of its meaning. We are as likely to call the person who constantly
bites his nails neurotic as we are the person who is readily prone to
anxiety in social situations. Even though the criteria we use to define
someone as neurotic, in the everyday sense of the word, can be highly
idiosyncratic we do tend to use the term to denote, on the whole, a
way of being that is somehow at variance from a particular cultural
norm. One general criterion that we adopt when designating someone
as neurotic is therefore whether their mode of living and behaving
coincides or not with any of the recognised patterns in our culture.
Our conception of psychological normality is to a large extent arrived
at through the approval by the majority of certain standards of behaviour and feeling which are then imposed on the members of a given
group.

Neurosis was originally a medical term first used in 1769 by William
Cullen to describe what were then believed to be organic diseases of
nerve tissue; those suffering from these disorders presented with complaints such as dizziness or poor appetite and these were taken to be
indicators of an underlying physical problem. While they were at first
considered to be suffering from 'weak nerves', the development of psychoanalysis led to a growing awareness that these physical complaints
could have their foundation in psychological as opposed to physical
mechanisms.

The term neurotic became a household word through the exposi-
tion of Freud's views on this matter. Even though clear demarcations

hold a certain appeal, especially when we are dealing with human behaviours which have the potential to threaten our need to believe in a stable and orderly world, Freud challenged such demarcations in the context of mental health as he had also done in relation to sexuality and perversion. Freud quite clearly stated that we are all neurotic. He believed that it was not possible to distinguish clearly so-called 'normal' from neurotic people. Where there was a difference it was held to be one of degree rather than kind.

The constraints of civilisation

Freud's views on neurosis are central as he himself held that the theory of neurosis reflected the whole of psychoanalysis. The previous chapters in this book have already covered some of the main concepts which underpin a psychoanalytic understanding of neurosis, namely the notion of a dynamic unconscious and the theory of psychosexual development.

The dynamic unconscious is relevant to our understanding of neurosis because Freud (1917b) held that neurosis resulted from an *unconscious* conflict between the ego and the id. He argued that neurotic symptoms were born of unconscious conflicts and the blocking or imbalance of energy flow which resulted from them. In addition, Freud thought that his neurotic patients were stuck somewhere in the past. Because of fears and anxiety neurotic individuals held on to their past, precluding development and change. Indeed, psychoanalytic treatment often revealed that neurotic patients were carried back by their symptoms or the consequences to some particular period in their past.

The theory of psychosexual development is also integral to an understanding of neurosis as Freud argued that the conflict underlying neurosis had an essentially sexual basis. As we saw in Chapter 7, Freud first believed that neurosis resulted from the repression of painful memories which, once recalled, frequently revealed traumatic sexual experiences in childhood. Thereafter he came to believe that, in many cases at least, no such traumatic seductions had taken place and he was led to the development of the 'wish theory' stressing the role played by fantasy and desire. In this later theory Freud understood neurosis as resulting from a regression of the libido which had not been granted expression due to social constraints. As a result the libido was said to flow back to an earlier stage at which it had become partially fixated during the course of development. So, for example, the obsessional patient was said to regress to the anal stage. Neurosis was thus seen to result from the conflict between instinctual drives, which seek a form of gratification, and social demands which prevent their gratification. Conflict may also arise between the instincts and the dictates of the individual's superego.

According to Freud civilisation put limits on the free expression and experience of our instincts, especially the sexual and aggressive ones. Although Freud's initial emphasis had been on the sexual roots of neurosis, he later recognised the important role of aggression in neurosis. In exchange for family and societal acceptance the child has to repress sexual and aggressive feelings. Neurosis was thus located by Freud in the battle between emotions and social conformity. Living in any society involves a degree of frustration of our own personal desires and their fulfilment. We cannot all go around doing whatever we feel like doing regardless of other people or the rules of society. If we do, however, then it is likely that we either break a law and our behaviour becomes criminalised or our behaviour is taken as evidence of some mental disturbance and may be labelled as 'mental illness'. Although some people's behaviour may fall into either or both of the latter two categories, most people have to find a way of living with their needs in the face of an often unsatisfying or restricting reality.

The neurotic compromise

In his later work, Freud emphasised more the role of anxiety in neurosis, a point made by Karen Horney (1937), an analyst who stressed the part played by social factors in neurosis. She held that neurosis is brought about only if the conflict between instinctual drives and social demands generates anxiety and if the attempt to allay the anxiety leads to defensive tendencies. When the expression of desires which are conflictual or in some way forbidden is blocked, repressed fears and longings may yet resurface and give rise to neurotic symptoms and inhibitions. These serve to prevent the troubling contents of the unconscious from entering consciousness where they would give rise to considerable anxiety by seeking gratification. Symptoms represent *compromise formations* which express in disguised form unacceptable sexual and aggressive impulses. Thus do they allow us to carry on with our daily lives.

The price to be paid for this 'neurotic compromise', however, is psychic pain. Freud was well aware of this when he remarked that neurosis can take up so much of our psychic energy which could otherwise be put to creative use. Nonetheless neurotic symptoms could perhaps be said to be creative insofar as they represent attempted solutions to conflicts which help us to restore a measure of psychic equilibrium. Indeed throughout our lives much of our psychic energy is used to maintain the solutions we have found to the conflicting claims of instinctual life and reality. Some of these compromises may enable us to enjoy our lives. Others, however, lead to extensive personal restrictions or inhibitions and are maintained at the cost of psychic, as well as sometimes physical, well-being.

Neurotic conflict

Neurosis, as we have seen so far, is believed to be rooted in conflict. What distinguishes neurotic conflict from the conflict that psychoanalysis postulates as common to all human beings is not its content nor that it is believed to be unconscious but the more accentuated nature of the conflict in the neurotic person, which may give rise to considerable suffering. In neurotic conflict the ego strives to keep the dangerous drives, that is the id, from gaining access to consciousness. This places the ego under considerable pressure and impoverishes the ego which may then fail to keep up its defensive efforts, thereby allowing the drives discharge in the disguised form of neurotic symptoms.

> Jane complained of dizziness when she was out alone. Although she had never actually fainted she was so concerned that this could happen that she stopped going out alone. In fact she only felt safe if her husband John went out with her. Medical investigations did not reveal any organic cause for the dizziness and hence Jane was referred for psychological help. Jane was rather puzzled by her dizzy spells and while she said she believed that there was no organic cause to her symptoms she was not all that pleased that she had been referred to a psychologist as she described her life as 'very contented'.
>
> When we started exploring the onset of her symptoms Jane told me that the first time she had felt dizzy was in the local library. When I probed further Jane said that on that particular day she had exchanged a few words with a new male librarian who had helped her to find a novel she had been looking for. She recalled feeling very hot in the library and then feeling very faint. The librarian had offered her a chair but she had instead decided to leave, feeling that she needed some fresh air. She had returned to the library a few weeks later and had a similar experience after another exchange with the same librarian who had in fact remembered her and asked her how she was feeling. Jane had been most surprised that he should have remembered her – she did not think she could make an impression on anyone. It was following this second visit to the library that Jane started to feel dizzy whenever she went out alone.
>
> Although Jane did not readily volunteer information about herself and her private thoughts she had described the male librarian in considerable detail and when I remarked that not only had he remembered her but she also very clearly remembered him, Jane finally acknowledged that he was a handsome man and she blushed. She quickly added that she could not see the point of discussing this when she was there to see me about her dizziness. Despite her obvious difficulty in discussing very personal issues, Jane persevered with her therapy and she gradually spoke of her marriage. It was clear that Jane was far from fulfilled but she was also very reluctant to explore her relationship with John as she had tried to convince herself that she had everything she wanted.
>
> Jane had been married for 8 years. She had married John because, she said, 'it was the thing to do'. He had a good job and prospects and at least superficially, Jane felt they complemented each other well. However, within the first year of marriage Jane and John encountered difficulties in their sex-

ual relationship and Jane found herself withdrawing from him. Despite such difficulties they remained together and Jane tended to deny the extent of their difficulties.

Once Jane was able to say that she had in fact been quite unhappy for some time, the meaning of her symptoms could be explored less defensively. When Jane met the male librarian she had been very attracted towards him. This had made her feel very anxious. Her dizziness and fear of fainting were understood as symbolic representations of losing her self-control. She had after all striven so hard to deny any difficulties in her relationship with John and she had been brought up to be faithful to her husband. Having sexual fantasies about another man thus triggered considerable anxiety. Going out alone became threatening because Jane was faced with the possibility of meeting men she might find attractive and of not being able to restrain herself. Being out with her husband served as an insurance against her sexual fantasies and desires. Her symptoms of dizziness and the subsequent fear of going out alone in case she should faint thus represented a means of keeping at bay the sexual feelings and the associated anxiety and guilt.

Jane's anxiety was so great that in order to keep it at bay she had developed a very rigid and constraining pattern of behaviour which served a purpose but at considerable psychological cost. This is not untypical in people with neurotic problems. Indeed, Horney (1937) pointed out that neurosis was characterised by rigidity in the person's responses. In the course of our lives the demands made on us by society generally and those close to us more specifically require us to remain sufficiently flexible so as to adapt to such demands and to the changes that may need to occur in our lives. However, the neurotic individual may find such adaptation problematic as they lack this kind of flexibility – things may have to be done in a certain manner and any deviation from a pre-established pattern may give rise to anxiety.

Although many people have set routines in their lives, most can adapt if circumstances demand. The neurotic person is the one who, under such circumstances, would experience anxiety if, say, they were unable to adhere to their usual routine. It is not having a routine per se nor the fact that one experiences a degree of inconvenience if it is disrupted which is the hallmark of neurosis, but rather it is the inflexibility in the person's responses. It is as though the mental mechanisms used in the service of defence become in the neurotic person permanent features of the personality.

The costs and benefits of neurosis

Horney pointed out that a discrepancy between potentialities and accomplishments is also characteristic of neurosis. This relates to the 'cost' of a neurosis whereby people who have the potential to do well in their lives prevent themselves from fulfilling this potential. Clearly there may at times be external circumstances beyond one's control which prevent people from achieving this, physical illness for instance, but this is not what Horney had in mind. She was referring to those individuals who somehow manage to 'stand in their own way' because of the neurotic prohibitions they develop, as the following example illustrates.

Sarah is 29. She is an intelligent and articulate young woman who developed obsessive compulsive symptoms whereby she had to repeatedly wash her hands. Although at first the symptoms were not interfering with her day-to-day life, they gradually worsened and she calculated that she was spending several hours each day just washing herself. When asked about what she imagined would happen if she resisted the urge to wash her hands, Sarah replied that she feared that if she did not respond to the voice inside her that told her to wash her hands, her mother would die.

On one level Sarah realised that her belief was irrational – that there was no logical link between washing her hands and her mother's well-being or any reason why her mother might be at a higher than normal risk of dying at present – yet she felt compelled to perform her ritual repeatedly. In all other respects Sarah led a very 'normal' life. She had a good job, several friends and had recently started a relationship. It was, however, when she began to explore her sexual life in more detail that some light was shed on her symptoms.

Sarah had been brought up in a strict Catholic family where sex had been a taboo subject. She had not been allowed out with boys as a teenager and even though she had had a relationship whilst at university this had been more 'platonic than anything else', as she put it. However, a few months preceding the onset of her symptoms, Sarah had met a man she was attracted to. She had got to know him quite well and eventually slept with him even though this went against the family's strong beliefs regarding pre-marital sex. Consciously Sarah had told herself that as she loved this man and she hoped to become engaged, there was nothing wrong in sleeping with him. She had in fact also been quite relieved to discover that she had enjoyed the experience. However, unconsciously this first sexual relationship appeared to have given rise to conflict and anxiety in Sarah. Her symptom of compulsive handwashing encapsulated her conflict and the anxiety triggered by her guilt could only be relieved temporarily once Sarah washed her hands.

Over a period of many months Sarah reflected on her predicament. One day she recalled that when she was 6 years old her mother had found her masturbating. On this occasion she had hit Sarah and shouted at her a great deal, took her to the bathroom and told her to wash her hands as she was a 'dirty girl'. Shortly after this incident Sarah remembered that her mother had been ill and had been briefly hospitalised. Whilst Sarah's recollection of these early events was somewhat blurred, she established a link between them which was meaningful to her. She began to connect her present symptoms to her first sexual encounter with a man and her enjoyment of it. Having sex before marriage was anathema to her mother, just as masturbation clearly had been. As a child Sarah appeared to have linked masturbation with something that was dirty but also with something that deeply upset her mother. In her child's mind she had linked her masturbation with her mother's illness; she felt unconsciously that she had made her mother ill because she had upset her due to her masturbation.

As an adult, Sarah's first sexual experience triggered her feelings of guilt and through her symptom she was expressing her dilemma: 'if I have sex I'm dirty so I must wash myself or my mother will get very ill and die'. The desire to have sex conflicted with Sarah's internalised prohibitions against sex and her neurotic symptom was her compromise solution. By washing her hands Sarah temporarily managed to appease her feelings of guilt as well as her internalised mother whose voice was telling Sarah she was a 'dirty girl', just as she had told her when she was a little girl.

Sarah's story highlights the function of neurotic symptoms: they serve to protect us from an unconscious emotional ambivalence. Although they may relieve us of some anxiety they nonetheless generate their own problems. In Sarah's case the handwashing was both the solution as well as a problem. In an attempt to maintain our psychic equilibrium, McDougall (1990) argues that we employ a number of different strategies including the creation of a neurosis, a psychosis, a work of art, a dream or a psychosomatic symptom.

In thinking about the development of any kind of neurotic symptom, we need to bear in mind that in attempting to avoid the experience of conflict we develop 'defences' – to which we shall turn in the next chapter – which enable us, to an extent, to keep our conflicting feelings out of conscious awareness. However, what has been repressed or, if you like, defended against, reappears in the form of symptoms. While this suggests a clear, causal link between a repressed event and the emergence of a symptom, in practice things are seldom so simple. Rather, the end product – that is, the symptom or the particular behaviour – cannot be explained by reference to just one cause as often we find that there is more than one. This phenomenon, as we have seen in previous chapters, is referred to as overdetermination.

The inevitability of conflict

The location of psychic pain within a psychological context with conflict as an inevitable concomitant of human existence arose from Freud's belief that neurotic conflict was itself unavoidable given the contradiction between internal desire and external constraints. This view of neurosis stands in sharp contrast to other psychological theories (such as, for example, the behavioural hypothesis that neurosis is unnecessary and merely the result of learning experiences which can be 'unlearned' through negative reinforcement). Even though it would be fair to say, given the inevitability of conflict, that it is normal to at least be mildly neurotic, it is even *more* normal, as it were, to not recognise such traits within ourselves. Yet, to do this is to both appreciate the conflicts we all share as human beings as well as to understand our own highly individualised ways of managing such conflicts. Neurosis, as Anthony Storr said, 'is not so much a matter of possessing a particular type of psychopathology as of being overwhelmed by that psychopathology, or of being unable to make effective use of it' (1979: 151).

Chapter 16
How do I cope with the pain?

Some natural sorrow, loss or pain
That has been and may be again

Wordsworth

The language of pain

As we saw in the last chapter, the experience of conflict and of psychic pain are considered to be, within psychoanalytic theory, inevitable concomitants of human existence since there is a constant struggle between the forces represented by the id, ego and superego. This is known as *intrapsychic conflict*. As we have also seen, Freud considered that one consequence of intrapsychic conflict is the experience of anxiety. So as to reduce anxiety the ego seeks to ameliorate conflict. In order for us then to fully appreciate the nature of neurosis we will examine in this chapter the theory of defence mechanisms, that is the ways in which we attempt to ward off the experience of anxiety.

Before we can begin to consider the strategies we employ to deal with our conflicts and the psychic pain they give rise to, it is helpful to clarify briefly the nature of this pain. To speak of psychic pain may give the misleading impression that psychic or mental pain is quite clearly distinct from physical pain. Such a view was popular in the nineteenth century but now reflects a reductionistic anachronism of mind/body dualism which is considered by many to be an unhelpful way of making sense of our experience of pain. While a migraine, for example, is experienced as bodily pain, its cause lies neither exclusively nor necessarily in human physiology. Moreover, there is a growing literature which implicates organic determinants in what we might regard as mental or psychic pain, as in the case of schizophrenia, as well as that which highlights the role of psychological factors in physical problems, as in the lowering of the immunological shield when under stress so that we are more susceptible to viruses and infections. Such work underscores the importance of an appreciation of the 'dynamic interpenetration between mind and body' (Erskine and Judd, 1994).

The link between mind and body is nowhere more evident than in psychosomatic problems where the physical symptoms are undisputed but where they also frequently reveal a neurotic story. In considering psychosomatic problems we need to guard against the tendency to slip into a position of either biological or psychological reductionism. There are people whose physical problems, asthma for instance, are indisputably real but who may nonetheless at times unconsciously manipulate the physical symptoms to meet psychological ends.

> Samuel is an 11-year-old boy who has suffered from asthma for a number of years. He is described by his parents and teachers as a shy child who has difficulty making friends. He is very close to his parents and prefers spending time with them.
>
> Samuel was the victim of bullying in his primary school. This was managed very effectively by the school and in his final year there he did not experience any further problems. Following his transfer to secondary school, Samuel's asthma worsened. He had increasingly frequent asthma attacks early in the morning which led the parents to keep him at home. Over time a very clear pattern emerged which led the parents to seek professional help.
>
> It soon became apparent that the increase in Samuel's asthma attacks was related to his increased anxiety about transferring to secondary school. Samuel was very frightened of the bigger boys in the school and feared a repetition of the bullying yet he was unable to share his worries with his parents. In place of talking Samuel gave expression to his anxiety through bodily symptoms which, in turn, served the function of also keeping him at home with his parents, thereby avoiding the anxiety provoking situation at school.

By giving expression to our anxieties through bodily symptoms it is as if we short-circuit verbal communication. Rather than telling his parents that he is anxious about being apart from them, the child, as in Samuel's case, may unconsciously bring on an asthma attack which, in turn, provokes the desired response in the parents. This process is by no means uncommon. If we think hard enough most of us could probably identify at least one instance when a headache or gastric problems occurred in lieu of a conscious acknowledgement that we were feeling troubled, angry or anxious. Psychosomatic potentiality exists in all of us. We all tend to somatise, that is to convert our conflicts and anxieties into bodily symptoms, when the internal or external circumstances in our life overwhelm our usual psychological ways of coping (McDougall, 1989). Repression is the precondition for the construction of symptoms which are themselves none other than substitutes for what is being repressed.

The meaning of symptoms

If we can accept the premise that psychic pain may be translated into psychological as well as physical symptoms, the next question we need to consider is the meaning of symptoms. Just as Freud held that dreams had both a manifest and latent meaning, the same applies to symptoms. Symptoms undoubtedly have a painful manifest reality. Sarah's symptoms of compulsive handwashing (see Chapter 15) were experienced by her as distressing just as Samuel who brought on an asthma attack just before he knew he would have to go to school was undeniably in pain. However, such symptoms often also contain a latent reality which, if grasped, lends psychological significance to the person's distress.

In a general sense we might say that symptoms reveal as much as they conceal about what is troubling us. They often carry many meanings which defy the wish to find a direct and clear correspondence between a symptom and an underlying, often unconscious, conflict. As with dreams, however, we need to take the time to unravel their meaning. Just as dreams can be understood as communications to others and to ourselves, the same may be said of symptoms. Symptoms carry messages with varied destinations. The recurring headaches we might get may be both communicating to us that something is troubling us, while also giving a partner the message that we need to be left alone or that important changes in a relationship are required.

Hamburg (1989), a psychoanalytic clinician, has pointed out that the construction of a symptom is a 'creative act of mental architecture'. In dismantling the particular symptomatic structure we may have erected, attention needs to be paid both to its benefits and costs. Symptoms allow us to express our conflicts in a way that does not directly challenge consciousness. They thus serve a protective, or defensive, function and are adaptive in the sense that they allow us to carry on with our lives, even if often only temporarily, without having to face up directly to what is deeply distressing us. The main problem with symptoms, however, is that, as Freud (1917) stressed, they use great amounts of psychic energy both in their creation and in the subsequent struggles that we engage in to fight the symptom itself. What was originally a solution often becomes itself a problem.

Defence mechanisms

The translation of psychological concerns into symptoms is but one of the means we have available to avoid consciously having to think about that which ostensibly troubles us at an unconscious level. Indeed, psychoanalysis alerts us to the existence of many other strategies which we employ to cope with psychic pain. Throughout Freud's writings and those of his followers, there are numerous references to defensive processes whose aim is precisely to ward off conflict and the ensuing anxiety.

In dreams, unconscious conflict or feelings may be expressed in distorted, disguised, form so as to avoid the experience of anxiety. The defences assumed by the ego to resolve intrapsychic conflict are said to be similar. The concept of *defence mechanism* refers to a process designed to avoid danger and hence anxiety which is the product of perceived danger. Defences falsify reality in order to avoid situations which are perceived as dangerous. The kinds of situations that we are likely to experience as dangerous include, for example, the loss of a loved person; the loss of love from an important figure or behaviour which conflicts with the demands of our superego.

In 1926, Freud revised and broadened the concept of defence which he had previously conceived of as synonymous with repression and recognised repression as just one of many defence mechanisms. Let us remind ourselves that repression refers to the confinement to the unconscious of thoughts, images and memories which if allowed into consciousness would give rise to anxiety. Sometimes certain facts may be remembered but their connection or their emotional significance or value to us may be repressed. This relates to what we might identify as a sense of 'emotional cut-offness' – someone who recounts a traumatic experience with none of the expected accompanying emotions. Conflict may then arise when the person encounters a new experience which is somehow connected with what was previously repressed. Here we often find a tendency on the part of the repressed in the unconscious to use this new experience as an opportunity for its outlet – it finds what is called a *derivative*.

Let us take as an example someone who has just been through a divorce and appeared at the time to be very matter-of-fact about it. This same person may later experience a bereavement which may act as a derivative. The experience of the later loss serves to reactivate the feelings of loss associated with the divorce which they had, at the time, repressed. However, the attempt by the repressed material to find a derivative and hence an outlet may fail. This may then give rise to a tendency to repress any event associatively connected with the originally repressed event. In the case of the divorced individual, this might lead to a repression of other events which, if acknowledged, would remind them of their repressed feelings of loss (for example, events or places which might be associated with the partner). Because repressed material continues to exist in the unconscious and may develop such derivatives, repression is not a once and for all process but requires a constant input of psychic energy so as to maintain it (Fenichel, 1946).

We all need at times to defend ourselves from certain ideas, thoughts, fantasies and feelings that arouse anxiety. Defences are at times successful in helping us to avoid the experience of anxiety; at other times, however, they are insufficient and anxiety may overwhelm us. The most useful way to make sense of the various mechanisms of defence which we shall now review is therefore to think about how you usually manage difficult and uncomfortable feelings or thoughts and then see if your strategies fit into any of the categories outlined below.

Let us now look at some of the more common mechanisms of defence:

Projection involves attributing states of mind to someone else. Although we may project both good and bad qualities into others we more readily project those aspects of ourselves (qualities, feelings and wishes) which give rise to conflict within us and hence that we seek to disown. Essentially, it involves two separate processes. Firstly, something, say a feeling, is projected into someone else. Secondly, projection involves relating to that person as if they actually embodied the projection. For example, if we project anger into someone, we would then relate to that person as if they were in fact angry and thereby set in motion a dynamic with them. In this way, even though the particular feeling may be disowned, split off, we nonetheless remain connected with the recipient of our projections. In addition the other person may actually identify with our projection and behave in a manner consonant with its content. One of the undesirable consequences of projection is that the person who projects no longer relates to the recipient of the projection as a separate person with their own feelings and thoughts but, on the contrary, may actually control and force the other to enact the role required of them.

Projection may be used when there is a need to 'evacuate', in fantasy, a painful state of mind which is too difficult to manage. This defence allows the person to get rid of unwanted parts of the self and the recipient of the projections acts as a kind of container for the disowned parts.

Projection also refers to a primitive mode of communication: by projecting a particular state of mind into another person we can communicate with them, unconsciously, about this state of mind. It represents a roundabout way of communicating our feelings to others when it is difficult to do so verbally. Projection is therefore not exclusively used in the service of defence as it is the very process which underlies our capacity for empathy, for putting ourselves in someone else's shoes. In the normal course of events projection is a fluid process so that we may project and then take back projections in a flexible manner. Problems arise when the projected parts remain lodged in the recipient as this prevents the integration of our experiences and feelings.

Mary, a 36-year-old woman who was experiencing some difficulties with her partner, was unable consciously to acknowledge that there were problems.

Yet she was behaving very aggressively towards her partner. She, however, spent considerable time talking about a friend whom she experienced as very aggressive towards her. Mary felt very angry about this as she did not feel she deserved to be treated in this manner and she added that she thought her friend's recent aggression might be due to stress.

Mary eventually realised that she was in fact talking about herself but that she had initially found it difficult to assume responsibility for her own anger and aggression towards her partner because she feared the relationship might end. However, such was the strength of her feelings that she had to dispose of them somehow and her friend who was at the time under considerable stress herself became the recipient of Mary's projections. Once she was able to reclaim her projections Mary could begin to address the difficulties in her relationship.

Introjection is the process of attributing an aspect of another person to ourselves. While this is at first adaptive in childhood as it involves taking into ourselves the 'goodness' that we experience as coming from others and on which we may then model ourselves, it may be used defensively if our identification with the other person is so all-encompassing that we no longer treat the other as a separate person with their own thoughts and feelings. Such a defence may be used, for example, in instances where the individual may fear abandonment and needs to feel in control of the other person to the extent that, through introjection, they create the illusion of merger, of being at one with the other person.

Linda had known her friend Anna since childhood. They had gone to school together and now studied at the same university and shared a flat. Linda, who was the person I knew, came from a rather chaotic family background. Her parents had both had various affairs as she was growing up and advocated an 'open relationship'. While on one level Linda espoused similar values to her parents and at times proudly described her parents as 'liberated', on a deeper level Linda had found the openness of her parents' marriage quite unsettling. She described having been an anxious child who in fact had found it difficult to form enduring friendships. Anna was an exception and Linda felt very close to her. When she spoke about her it was at times difficult to know whether she was talking about herself or Anna as they seemed indistinguishable. If Anna was upset Linda also felt upset and would recount Anna's own upsetting experiences as if she had actually lived through the experience herself.

Problems emerged in Linda's relationship with Anna soon after they began university. Anna met a boyfriend and started to enjoy her new social life on the campus. Linda, who was far more introverted than Anna, found it difficult to join her and felt very threatened by Anna's new independence She could not tolerate the differences between her and Anna which were now becoming clearer and consequently she found it hard to accept that Anna was in fact enjoying her life. On the contrary, Linda felt Anna was unhappy and needed her help. This was a projection of Linda's own feelings as she was threatened with the loss of her friend.

Linda had introjected Anna to such an extent that she could no longer distinguish what she felt from what Anna felt. Her introjection was a defensive measure against the fear of abandonment – a fear Linda had struggled with from early on as she witnessed her parents coming and going with different partners. There had been very little stability in her early years and seemingly little acknowledgement by Linda's parents of her own needs.

Isolation refers to instances when disturbing experiences are broken up into different components, are isolated, so that their links with other thoughts and with the rest of an individual's experiences are severed. An example of this was given earlier in this chapter in the hypothetical case of the divorced man where there was a detachment between affect (emotions) and thought.

Reaction formation is the transforming of a disturbing idea into its opposite. For example, a person's homophobia may be understood as a reaction formation in light of the person's disowned homosexual feelings which are experienced as unacceptable and are therefore turned into their opposite.

Undoing refers to the use of actions or thoughts to neutralise, to undo, something that was said, done or thought. This defence contains a magical aspect. An example of undoing is Sarah's compulsive handwashing (see Chapter 15) where the symptom served to 'undo' her guilt at having had sexual intercourse.

Displacement is the process of substituting or detaching intensity from an idea, event or person, which is then passed on, or attributed to, a substitute related to the original through a series of associations. For example, people who are worried about their health may displace their preoccupation and anxiety about this on to their work which may represent an aspect of their life about which they are worried but over which they may feel more in control

Conversion refers to the process of transforming psychic conflict into somatic symptoms. The psychosomatic examples given earlier in this chapter illustrate this process.

Denial is the distortion of our perception of some aspect of external reality. For example, the terminally ill person, struggling to come to terms with eventual death, may deny that he is going to die and continue to make plans for the future.

Identification with the aggressor is a defence highlighted by Anna Freud (1936) to describe a process which enables the individual to cope with overwhelming threat. It involves taking on the identity of that which is feared. For instance, the child who is beaten by his parents may in turn be aggressive towards other children. In so doing he is turning round the distressing experience of being a victim into one where he becomes the powerful aggressor.

Splitting refers to a process which aims to keep apart two thoughts or feelings which the individual is unable to hold on to at one and the same time. This defence mechanism is, according to Klein, centrally involved in the earliest defensive strategies available to the child. Children split their objects so that parental images are separately invested, in fantasy, with wholly good or bad qualities and intentions. Splitting therefore refers essentially to the way in which objects come to be divided into their good and their bad aspects.

The above list is by no means exhaustive and in thinking about your own use of defences you will most probably have found that you use a variety. In addition to the mechanisms of defence described here we might add any strategy that we employ that results in a reduction of anxiety and ideally its disappearance altogether. Indeed, modes of defence are as varied as psychic life itself. Nevertheless, common to them all is that in employing defence mechanisms, the ego is saying 'no' to whatever is being defended against. To this extent, we could say that denial, in its colloquial sense, is intrinsic to all defence (Brenner, 1981).

In ideal circumstances the conflicts we experience are resolved through our active attempts to find constructive solutions which will ameliorate the conflict or remove it altogether. Although we may use such conscious coping strategies quite successfully, changing ourselves and our lives is no easy task, as we shall see in the next chapter, and we sometimes prefer to avoid our conflicts rather than face them head on. Indeed, to the extent that Freud and his followers would converge on the assumption that we are all neurotic to some degree it follows that we all also employ defences to deal with psychic pain and conflict. They are a part of the healthy repertoire of all of us, since we all need to ward off conflict and anxiety. That which distinguishes the everyday use of defences from what might be regarded as its more pathological use is the rigidity or intensity with which defences are used and therefore the extent to which they preclude us from consciously facing up to our pain and resolving our conflicts.

Chapter 17
Why is it so hard to change?

Things do not change, we change.

Henry Thoreau

Short cuts to change

We live in a society seduced by the possibility of personal change. There are certain changes we can now actually buy, such as plastic surgery which offers the opportunity of permanently altering physical aspects of our being. We can also transform our appearance through dieting, exercising or changing the colour of our hair, for example. From all sides we are bombarded with images which associate a particular style with success and happiness. Probably all of us aspire to some kind of personal happiness and when we are presented with the ready-made packaged happiness that such media images offer us, we may easily fall into the trap of believing that if we change how we look, where we eat or who we socialise with we will also find our happiness. Image consultants, plastic surgeons and cosmetic tycoons are some of the twentieth century fairy godmothers who, with their magic wand, promise to transform us.

Physical changes in our appearance may of course lead to psychological change – that is, in the way we feel about ourselves. Looking good makes us feel good but are such changes only skin deep? This is a difficult question to answer as there are those who, following plastic surgery, for instance, profess to feel much happier within themselves. As there are no sufficiently long-term follow-up studies of the psychological well-being of such individuals, it is difficult to know how enduring the reported changes actually are. On a more mundane level, common enough, however, is the story of the person who feels down, decides to lose some weight, temporarily feels better then feels down again or very quickly puts on the weight again. How many amongst us have also gone out on a shopping spree to deflect a vague

175

feeling of depression? While shopping, we may temporarily be distract-
ed and even enjoy the experience. However, we are often facing a
quite different reality when the excitement wears off and we return
home surrounded by our recent acquisitions but ultimately none the
happier for it.

> Sandra, a 31-year-old woman, came into therapy because she was feeling
> depressed. She had been on various diets in order to lose weight as she
> believed that if she was slimmer she would not feel depressed. Indeed, sev-
> eral of the initial sessions were taken up with Sandra's descriptions of her
> many attempts and devices to lose weight. If she lost a few pounds she
> always felt better and this she used as evidence that the solution to her
> depression was to be on a permanent diet. However, Sandra found it very
> difficult to adhere to the regimes she set herself and would typically regain
> the weight she had struggled so hard to shed and would subsequently feel
> even more depressed as she felt herself to be a failure.
>
> Although Sandra had ostensibly sought therapy to help her address her
> feelings of depression it soon became clear that she found it very hard to
> reflect on her feelings and the stressful life events she had been confronted
> with over the two years prior to starting therapy, such as the loss of her
> mother, who had died of cancer, and the loss of her job, from which she
> had been made redundant. In some respects the solution she had found to
> her problem, that is to lose weight, promised a quick result, even if a tem-
> porary one, which served to reinforce an unhelpful pattern of behaviour.
> Sandra's body was the only tangible thing that she felt she could change,
> that she had some control over, unlike the other areas of her life where she
> felt so much out of control.

At some time or another we all make recourse to some diversionary
technique to distance ourselves from our feelings, hoping that they will
go away in time. For some the answer will be found in some form of
medication or other drugs, for others in attempts to change that which
is most tangible in their life – for instance their appearance, their job,
where they live or even the decor at home. For others still the answer
may lie in some of the shorter-term forms of psychotherapy or group
experiences, some of which offer no more than a 'quick fix' approach
to psychological problems. As we saw in the last chapter, we also have
numerous defences at our disposal which help us to deal with psychic
pain and therefore to bring about some change in how we feel. Even
though their exclusive use invariably gives rise to other problems they
represent means of adjusting to intolerable internal and external situations.

In the main the strategies that have been mentioned represent just
short cuts to the solution of problems we experience at a much deeper
level within ourselves and they tend to lead us to dead-ends. Some of
the most prevalent values found in Western culture reinforce the
human tendency to opt for the solution which will bring about change
with the least amount of personal effort and distress.

In the West we have evolved increasingly ingenious ways of speeding up everything we do and so reducing our expenditure of energy, both physical and psychic. From the microwave oven to the ever more sophisticated computer, we seek the quickest answer to our needs. The same tendency can be traced when we consider personal problems. When we feel unhappy, depressed or anxious the tension which we experience leads us to want to discharge it as quickly as possible and we therefore seek the quickest solution to our dilemma. Such solutions tend, typically, to involve the avoidance of a direct confrontation with the source of our distress. On the whole, all these options involve the investment of our energy in running away from ourselves and what deeply troubles us so that the meaning of our depression or our anxiety remains untapped. In some individual instances any one of the above options may bring about a measure of relief and satisfaction or even happiness but in the majority of cases they are options which attack the symptom, as it were, without paying attention to its causes. Just as bad workmanship may leave cracks through which water will eventually leak, our quick solutions also require repeated attention to the emotional leaks and merely reinforce the problem.

However, even when we repeatedly face the same dead-end and profess never to find ourselves in the same predicament in future we, time after time, return yet again to these old ways of coping and repeat the same patterns. Such behaviour seemingly flies in the face of common sense. If a child burns his hand on a fire he will learn in most cases, through the painful experience, never to place his hand in a fire again. So what is it that leads us to repeat our mistakes, to maintain the status quo even when we are crying out for change in our lives?

The gain in pain

In addition to the socio-cultural factors which, it has been suggested, encourage quick solutions rather than reflection and understanding, there are other psychological factors that may help us to appreciate the painstaking path to personal change. Freud was well aware of self-defeating patterns of behaviour in his patients which he believed resulted from a fixation to particular periods in their past as though they really were unable to free themselves from it and therefore to engage with the present in a more constructive and pleasurable way. As an example of this tendency, Freud cited one of his female patients who had remained fixated to an erotic attachment to her father which had started during the years prior to puberty. As an adult she became ill and failed to marry. She did not feel that she could marry as long as she was ill.

Freud understood his patient's predicament in terms of her *need* to be ill so as to not have to marry and hence she could remain with her father. Freud's understanding of the situation in these terms led to an important hypothesis which is quite widely accepted even outside the psychoanalytic field, namely that however distressing a symptom or a given life situation may be, there may yet be some gain, a kind of pay-off, for the individual which helps to explain the deadlock with regard to personal change. It is also often the case that the forces underlying self-defeating and self-destructive behaviour are frequently so potent that their cost in terms of personal distress does not appear to act as a powerful enough deterrent. For instance, the suffering that symptoms impose may assuage a person's unconscious guilt or their 'need to suffer' as Freud put it, or the disabling nature of symptoms may help the person to sidestep other situations which are likely to generate conflict. In satisfying such unconscious needs the symptoms act as a strong reinforcer. Let us turn to an example to look at the notion of gain in more detail.

> Veronica is a middle-aged woman who had been in a very unsatisfying relationship for 17 years. She had married comparatively late and had only one child who was 16 years old. Her husband worked very hard in his own business and was experienced by Veronica as quite self-absorbed, taking little interest in her. Veronica had herself managed to sustain her career even though she had taken several years off when her daughter was very young. She had very much enjoyed being a mother and had wanted another child but her husband had not been keen on the idea. Veronica had been quite depressed about this but had nonetheless managed to carry on with her life, deriving a lot of enjoyment from her relationship with her daughter and her sister, to whom she felt very close and who lived nearby.
>
> Around the time that her daughter turned 16 and was beginning to talk about leaving home, Veronica's sister left London as her husband was posted abroad. Veronica, who had up until that time enjoyed a very active life, started to experience quite disabling panic attacks which, over a period of time, worsened to the point that she simply felt unable to leave her house. She withdrew from all her activities and stopped working. She became quite depressed but in spite of the help and encouragement of her friends, her symptoms showed no improvement. Her daughter felt obliged to postpone her plans of moving out as she felt she should look after her mother as she was well aware that her father would not spend any time with her. The doctor eventually referred Veronica for psychological help. A year after the onset of the panic attacks, Veronica still complained of them even if she now managed to go out if accompanied by her daughter.
>
> When I met Veronica for the first time she struck me as a most unhappy woman who had lived with her distressing symptoms for some time. However, even when she accepted professional help it really seemed as though there was something holding Veronica back even though she consciously said that she wanted to get better.
>
> Through family therapy sessions it became clear that Veronica was terrified by the prospect of losing her daughter as it would mean having to face

her unhappy marital relationship which she had managed to avoid by investing so much of herself in her daughter's life and her relationship with her sister. When she was faced with the possibility of losing both of them, Veronica literally panicked. However, what served to trigger the symptoms – the impending loss of her two closest companions – was no longer what maintained the problem. Veronica's symptoms also served, at least in part, the function of ensuring that her daughter would not leave home. Veronica had achieved her unconscious goal as her daughter had indeed remained with her and to this extent the symptoms were reinforced by this positive outcome. To get better had become equated at an unconscious level with losing her daughter and being left alone to face her marital problems. Veronica's story thus highlights the benefits that may be derived from neurotic symptoms. In the midst of her undeniable distress, Veronica obtained a measure of gratification while remaining unaware that this was in fact happening.

The compulsion to repeat

Professionals working with individuals seeking help for psychological problems are repeatedly confronted with how difficult it is to change no matter how distressing their predicament might be. However, not only do people remain in intolerable situations but some actually appear to be compelled to repeat the same maladaptive patterns in their lives, as if they recreated or searched for situations which could bring only unhappiness and which often represent a re-enactment of earlier relationships and dynamics (see Chapter 13). Freud called this phenomenon the *compulsion to repeat*. While all analysts would agree that this is a commonly observed pattern there is nonetheless considerable disagreement as to how one can explain it. Freud's own view was that the compulsion to repeat reflected an individual's attempt to master anxiety, relating to an earlier period, that would otherwise be too overwhelming. This was in keeping with his views on the nature of traumatic dreams where, for instance, following an accident, the person may repeatedly dream about the accident. Freud understood such repetitive dreams as attempts to master the anxiety retrospectively.

Clinical work with individuals whose life histories provide ample evidence of the repetition of destructive patterns of behaviour and relationships highlights the way in which the repetition of these dynamics also contains the hope that, *this time around*, they will overcome their difficulties and break the pattern. The compulsion to repeat is a most fascinating phenomenon as it challenges us with the existence of behaviour whose aim appears to be ostensibly self-destructive even if it may well represent an unconscious attempt at mastery. Indeed this led Freud to concede that there does exist in us a compulsion to repeat which overrides the pleasure principle which was believed to rule our instinctual life (see Chapter 1). The evidence of self-destructive tendencies in people reveals that vast quantities of the aggressive instinct are sometimes directed inwards and Freud therefore saw the compulsion to repeat as a manifestation of the Death instinct.

Anchored in our past, in dynamics of which we are not always conscious or that we do not fully understand, we may find ourselves repeating mistakes or specific patterns. Once they occur they usually make us wonder how we ever managed to find ourselves, once again, in a similar position, yet it is clear that this happens. Whether one accepts Freud's own understanding of the compulsion to repeat or not, it is nonetheless a phenomenon which we frequently observe and one that accounts for the great difficulty that some people seem to experience in their attempts to change.

> Frances had been an only child. Her father had died when she was 18 months old and her mother had been left alone to care for her. Frances recalled her mother as having always been very depressed. She had been admitted to hospital for the first time when Frances was 3 years old and had received ECT (electroconvulsive therapy) for her depression. As a child, Frances had thus not only lost her father but she had also been physically separated from her mother, as well as feeling that her mother had not been emotionally available for her. Indeed, Frances remembered having to sit with her mother who at times cried inconsolably, hoping that she would eventually get better. For her part, Frances had tried desperately to please her mother as she so much wanted to make her happy.
>
> As an adult, Frances had found herself repeatedly attracted to rather withdrawn, depressed men and in these relationships Frances' role closely mirrored the one she had adopted with her mother; she would work hard at pleasing them, for instance surprising them with tickets for holidays abroad, hoping that she could make them happy. While at times Frances' tactics produced the desired effect, the consequences of her efforts were short-lived and her partners would revert to what she experienced as their self-absorption which excluded her. She would then feel abandoned and lonely, feelings she was more than familiar with.
>
> As Frances explored her predicament, it appeared that each time she developed a new relationship with a man, with whom she then recreated aspects of her early relationship with her mother, Frances hoped that, this time round, she could make a difference and manage to 'cure' her partner of his depression. This represented her attempt to reverse the situation which she had experienced as so painful as a child.
>
> Underlying Frances' attempts to bring back to life her partners, as it were, were feelings of omnipotence, that is her fantasy that she had the power to 'cure' her partners just as she had striven to do with her mother. As a child she had believed that if she were different her mother would be happier. To this end Frances had tried very hard to be what she imagined her mother needed while ignoring her own needs. Letting go of this omnipotent fantasy involved acknowledging the loss of her father and her mother and relinquishing the hope that one day her mother would be different – a hope which invariably led to disappointment and distress.

The psychological cost of change

Although an increasing number of people seek psychotherapy nowadays with the conscious intention and motivation to change there are often unconscious forces within us which oppose change, which keep up the neurotic conflict and thus maintain the status quo. Even if inhibiting or self-defeating, many of the strategies we employ to deal with psychic pain seemingly hold more appeal than the long and arduous path of self-exploration. The temptation is all too often to seek to change or manipulate factors external to ourselves.

Personal change is difficult to achieve because it involves facing up to aspects of ourselves, our relationships and our lives generally that are painful. It confronts us with feelings, thoughts and fantasies which, most of the time, we would rather not think about – who, after all, likes to think about their envious or destructive feelings? The difficulty inherent in personal change is reflected in the often quoted phrase amongst those who are in psychotherapy of some kind that 'it has to get worse before it gets better'.

Change is always painful, not only because of the challenges it poses, but also because it always involves loss. This is true even when the change is towards something positive or desirable. To move on is at once to let go of something past in order to get to something new and different. It may involve relinquishing ties with others which, even if they were themselves a source of pain, are nonetheless difficult to break, perhaps because we had invested so much of ourselves in these relationships. Changing also involves acknowledging the loss of the time we will never regain. If we spent years in an unsatisfying relationship, we will have to face up to the time we may feel we wasted and the opportunities missed. Change thus comes at a price and only you can ultimately decide which price you are able or willing to pay: that of neurotic symptoms and other self-defeating patterns of behaviour or that of change. If it is the latter we can begin to think about what might help along the way. In the next chapter we will therefore consider the role that psychoanalysis as a form of therapeutic treatment can play in helping us to change.

Chapter 18
How can psychoanalysis help me change?

No doubt fate will find it easier than I to relieve you from your illness. But you will be able to convince yourself that much will be gained if we succeed in transforming your hysterical misery into common unhappiness.

Freud

The birth of psychoanalysis as a treatment method

In 1895 an important text in the history of psychoanalysis was published, *Studies in Hysteria*, which included case histories of patients treated by both Freud and his colleague, Joseph Breuer (Breuer and Freud, 1895). These case histories are of great historical import as they document the evolution of a treatment method for psychological problems which emphasised the therapeutic effects of simply allowing the patient to express their feelings freely and of listening. Indeed, it was one of Breuer's patients, Anna O., who referred to this method as the 'talking cure'.

An underlying assumption in their work, as we saw in Chapter 1, was the contention that hysterical symptoms were psychological rather than physiological in origin. In their collaboration, Freud and Breuer suggested that in order to relieve their patients of their 'hysterical misery', the patients had to release bottled-up feelings. They observed that by allowing them to talk freely about their feelings and fantasies, symptoms disappeared and the patients improved. This led them to believe that the symptoms were actually fed by blocked energy. The process of recalling and then expressing such feelings was termed *abreaction*.

Their early discoveries were made while Freud and Breuer were using hypnosis as their main approach to treatment. Freud's dynamic approach to repression led him to postulate that the causes of his patients' symptoms could be recovered from the unconscious just as apparently forgotten memories of the hypnotic trance could be recalled. However, Freud gradually moved away from the use of hypnosis as he soon realised that he simply could not induce a hypnotic trance in all his patients. His own approach evolved through the influence of the work of two French hypnotists, Leibelault and Bernheim. Their method consisted of applying gentle pressure on the patient's forehead using the hand. This was known as the *pressure method*. Adopting their technique Freud applied the pressure of his hand on his patients' foreheads as he invited them to concentrate by reclining in a comfortable couch, shutting their eyes and often quite literally *insisting* that memories would appear. Freud worked on the assumption that his patients knew at some level everything that was causing their distress and that it was really only a matter of encouraging them to communicate this.

Over time Freud developed his fundamental rule, and the cornerstone of his technique, *free association*, whereby his patients were asked to share all their thoughts as they came to mind without any regard for logic or order. Freud was well aware of the demand he placed on his patients and he wrote, 'In confession, the sinner tells us what he knows; in analysis the neurotic has to tell more' (1926: 289). Freud insisted on the rule of free association because he realised that whatever the seemingly plausible reasons for the appearance in his patients' conscious minds of certain thoughts or images, these were used, as it were, by deeper forces pressing for expression. In encouraging patients simply to share everything that came to mind Freud hoped to be led to their inner conflicts through their associations. In free associating patients certainly reveal a lot about themselves, their aspirations, fears, fantasies – often far more than would be the case if the therapist asked many questions or structured the therapeutic session more. Free association is, however, really an ideal towards which the patient strives but in practice it is very difficult indeed to share all the contents of our thoughts. Nonetheless the principle of free association underpins all current psychoanalytic practice.

While Freud certainly encouraged his patients to freely associate, he was soon confronted by their reluctance to do so. Over time he became aware of a force within the patient which opposed the treatment. He understood this as a *resistance* to treatment – the same force which prevented unconscious ideas from becoming conscious. The purpose of this resistance was, according to Freud, one of defence. His patients' claims that they did not know something were understood by Freud as their 'not wanting to know'. The primary task of the therapy was therefore to overcome the resistance thereby allowing the patient's gaps in memory to be filled in.

Since Freud, psychoanalysis has continued to be applied to the treatment of psychological problems. The question of whether this method of treatment is one that brings about change has generated considerable interest over the years and we shall return to this later in this chapter. In the first instance, however, we will examine the aims of psychoanalytic treatment as well as the means through which analysts strive to achieve their therapeutic aims. After all, before we can ask the question 'does psychoanalysis work? it is important to have some understanding at least in theory of how it claims to work.

On the question of psychoanalytic cure

It is a well-known fact that analysts shirk from using the concept of cure in their written work. This dread of 'pathological therapeutic zeal' – to use Greenson's (1967) telling phrase – has been inherited from Freud who was no therapeutic optimist. Moreover, Freud was far less interested in psychoanalysis as a therapeutic system than as a tool for understanding both the individual and society. As far as Freud was concerned, psychoanalysis should be valued for its contributions to a science of human being rather than for any quick results as regards personality change or the alleviation of neurotic symptoms. Freud was in fact somewhat pessimistic about the possibility for cure and the quote at the beginning of this chapter encapsulates what he believed any analysis could achieve: no more than to transform 'hysterical misery into common unhappiness'.

Freud's pessimism is in keeping with his belief in the inevitability of human conflict and suffering (see Chapter 15). Repression, as we have seen, is considered integral to our survival in a social world which confronts us daily with the impracticability of living our life under the sway of the pleasure principle. The aim of psychoanalysis as a therapy was therefore not, according to Freud, the reduction of suffering but centred on the necessity of living with one's limitations and conflicts. Psychoanalysis thus sets itself as its principal task to reveal conflict but offers no particular suggestion regarding its resolution. The analytic attitude which ideally is not partisan to any particular direction that the patient's life should take, stands in sharp contrast to other forms of psychotherapy, such as cognitive-behavioural therapy, where the aim of bringing the patient's thinking in line with so-called rational, logical argument is made quite explicit.

In practice, most analysts consider it their professional duty not to make any promise of cure to their patients. This is partly because they are anxious not to give reassurance, something which, while giving temporary encouragement, seldom solves problems but may, on the contrary, obscure the patient's problems. It is also because the results of the psychoanalytic process are genuinely unpredictable. Indeed, Freud noted that we should 'not be surprised if the difference between a person who has not and a person who has been analysed is, after all, not so radical as we endeavour to make it and expect and assert that it will be' (Freud, 1937: 329). This may seem a somewhat surprising statement coming from the founder of psychoanalysis itself as it reflects his own cautiousness regarding the scope of psychoanalytic treatment. Given the length and cost of an analysis it may also sound rather worrying and certainly encourages us to take a close look at the outcome of psychoanalytic treatment – a point to which we shall return later in this chapter.

The aims of psychoanalysis

The aims of psychoanalytic treatment have shifted over the years along with the changing conceptualisations of the nature of psychological problems (Steiner, 1989). In Freud's early period he subscribed to a model of dammed-up libido where problems arose largely as a result of sexual inhibitions. The aim of psychoanalysis was then to free the patients from their inhibitions so as to allow for a discharge of the libido. While then for Freud the primary aim of psychoanalytic treatment had originally been to make the unconscious conscious, his later structural formulation of the mind in terms of id, ego and superego emphasised the need to modify defences; to reduce the pressures from the superego so that the patient could become less frightened of the superego; and in general to strengthen the ego: 'where id was there shall ego be', as Freud put it. He believed that the analyst and the patient's weakened ego needed to become allies against the instinctual demands of the id and the conscientious demands of the superego (Freud, 1938). Within this model psychological problems were understood to result from conflict. Those analysts subscribing to this model aim primarily to extend, through the psychoanalytic process, the patients' knowledge of themselves in the hope that with such knowledge – their 'insight' – they may be able to make choices which are not exclusively ruled by neurotic needs, so that new compromises and solutions can be explored. It is argued that if patients have some understanding of their unconscious processes they can construct a more realistic internal world, less distorted by projections and misperceptions.

More recent developments in psychoanalysis, influenced by Kleinian ideas, stress the aim of psychoanalysis as that of helping the patient achieve psychic reintegration by reclaiming parts of the self which have been split off and projected into others because they could not be managed. Psychoanalytic treatment therefore strives to help the patient to understand the process underlying such projections so as to minimise them.

The analytic relationship: transference and counter-transference

Although the various psychoanalytic schools stress different aspects and may be said to have different aims, they nonetheless all converge on the importance of the relationship between analyst and patient which is considered to be an essential, if not the most important, feature of the psychoanalytic process. The analytic relationship, as it is usually referred to, can become as complex as any intimate relationship. The patient may experience intense feelings of anger, hate, envy, love, sexual attraction and many others, towards the analyst.

The analyst, in turn, may also experience a similar array of emotions towards the patient. At times the analyst's feelings are understood as arising in response to unconscious communications by the patient. The patient may, for example, unconsciously use the analyst through projection in such a way that the analyst ends up feeling angry during the session while the patient may disown any such feeling in himself. At other times the feelings experienced by analysts in relation to their patients merely reflect what Freud called their 'blind spots'. He used this term to refer to those occasions when analysts were unable to deal well with those aspects of the patient's communication and behaviour which impinged on unresolved problems or vulnerabilities of their own. For example, an analyst who has just suffered a bereavement may find it difficult to attend to a patient's material relating to feelings of loss. The analyst's feelings towards her patients are termed *counter-transference*. The term is used to refer both to the feelings that the patient engenders in the analyst as well as to those feelings experienced by the analyst towards the patient which pertain to him very personally.

The patient's feelings towards the analyst are, in turn, termed *transference*. This is usually further divided into the positive and the negative transference which refer respectively to the positive and negative feelings which the patient transfers on to the analyst. As we saw in Chapter 4, the term transference has both general and specific meanings. We shall concern ourselves here only with its specific meaning in the context of the analytic relationship where it refers to a special phenomenon[9] which arises between patient and analyst. Freud first used the term when he was reporting on his own attempts to elicit verbal associations from his patients. He noted changes occurring in the

[9]Strictly speaking Freud saw transference as a hypothetical intraspychic process. He used the term to refer to the transference of *intensity* connected to an unconscious idea on to a pre-conscious mental representation. When the pre-conscious content is the image of the analyst we have transference in the clinical sense but Freud understood this to be a special case of a more general psychological process.

course of treatment in the patient's attachment to him, changes which involved strong emotional components. These feelings were regarded as transference coming about as a consequence of a 'false connection'. Transferences came to be considered as new 'editions' of the impulses and fantasies which were aroused during the process of analysis, replacing some earlier person in the patient's life with the person of the analyst.

At first this new discovery disturbed Freud as he saw his method of psychoanalysis becoming increasingly more complicated. It was only in 1909 that he remarked that transference was not an obstacle to analysis but might play a positive role as a therapeutic agent. In time he came round to the opinion that transference was in fact necessary to the psychoanalytic process, so much so that he believed that those patients who were unable to develop a transference relationship with their analyst, for instance psychotic patients, were actually untreatable through psychoanalysis.[10] Notwithstanding its importance, Freud also warned practitioners of the powerful erotic charge of the transference which creates the need for a professional ethic that prevents analysts from taking advantage of the seductive potential of the analyst–patient relationship.

Since Freud there has been a strong tendency within psychoanalysis towards a widening of the concept, whereby transference is used to denote *any* feeling that the patient may harbour towards their analyst (Sandler et al., 1973). Even though there are differences in the use of the concept and consequently in the sense that is made of the patient's communications to the analyst, the analysis of transference is the centrepiece of mainstream psychoanalytic treatment. Its importance lies in the fact that in transferring feelings on to the analyst – which are understood to be repetitions of feelings originally directed at some other significant figure from the patient's past – the patient recreates with his analyst such experiences rather than remembering them consciously. This time round, however, the patient and the analyst can try to understand the meaning of such experiences and the feelings associated with them so that light may be shed on their significance to the whole of the patient's personality and his way of handling interpersonal situations. The following example illustrates this and provides a sketch of a negative transference.

> John is a young man who sought therapy as he was feeling depressed and was experiencing difficulty with his work. At the time of his birth his parents had both been very busy with their own lives, entrusting him to the care of various nannies and eventually sending him to boarding school at a young age. Through the recollections John had of the period spent at boarding school it became clear that he had not enjoyed the experience and had felt rejected by his parents, particularly his mother. In fact, John held rather conflicting views about women generally, feeling on the one hand that they

[10] Nowadays, psychoanalytic treatment is offered to patients whom Freud had not believed could be analysed (e.g. psychotic patients).

should have as many opportunities as men, but on the other hand frequently expressing the belief that a woman's place was with her children. However, whenever this topic emerged in the session he was very defensive, denying that he felt any resentment towards his mother for having invested so much of her time in her career.

John had been in therapy for some time when he arrived one day feeling very distressed. He became very angry with me and accused me of not doing my job properly. He had previously hinted at his dissatisfaction with me but when encouraged to explore these feelings he had been somewhat resistant, denying that he harboured any such negative feelings. On this occasion, however, he was very clearly angry with me. On that day he had apparently telephoned to tell me he would be late for his session but as soon as the receiver had been picked up and he said hello, he claimed that I had replaced the receiver. He had waited several minutes before ringing again and this time round no one answered the telephone. He believed that I had purposely not answered as I had better things to do and that I was not really interested in him and, given this, he felt that I was not fit to practise. The truth of the matter was that there was a fault on the line and I had no way of knowing that John had tried to contact me. This 'fact' was, however, not as relevant as the intensity of John's feelings and his fantasies about me and my feelings and commitment towards him.

John's feelings of rejection when he failed to get a response over the telephone and his fantasy that I was not really interested in him and not fit to be a therapist were very meaningful. These were analysed by reference to his own feelings of rejection by his mother, his anger at her for sending him away to boarding school and his own sense that she had not been a 'good enough' or fit mother. When John was eventually able to reflect on what had happened he was then able to explore further his relationship with his mother and his feelings about her which he had previously transferred on to me. The absence of any retaliation on my part in response to John's quite virulent attacks on me, and my willingness to register his projections and to give them meaning in the context of his relationship with his mother, assisted John in the painful task of integrating his hatred for his mother with his own loving feelings towards her.

Transference, as the above example illustrates, is a 'reliving of the past, a misunderstanding of the present in terms of the past' (Greenson, 1967: 28). The analysis of transference is the pivot upon which the entire structure of psychoanalytic practice rests. It is an inspired and useful concept as the analysis of transference can be a very powerful tool for bringing to the fore in a very immediate way the patient's conflicts, as in John's case. However, it is unfortunately also a concept in the name of which many psychoanalytic sins have been committed as it tends to place the person of the analyst beyond the reality testing of the patient. It is not difficult to see how an analyst could attribute any feelings the patient may have towards him to transference thereby exculpating himself from his part in at times perhaps provoking particular feelings in the patient because of his own difficulties or 'blind spots'. While it is important to acknowledge the potential for such misuse it is not the case that the interpretation of the patient's material in the light of transference is invariably abusive but merely that it is open to abuse.

All approaches to psychotherapy involve some kind of relationship between the patient and the therapist but psychoanalysis is unique in its primary emphasis on the relationship as an agent of change. It therefore provides the most comprehensive literature on this subject and a framework within which to make sense of the complex dynamics that may transpire in the analytic relationship.

The 'real' relationship between analyst and patient

It would be wrong to assume that the only aspect of the relationship which brings about change is the transference relationship. There is also what we might call the 'real' relationship between patient and analyst known as the *working or treatment alliance*. This essentially refers to the contract and rapport which is established between patient and analyst, which enables the patient to use the analysis contructively. The ability to establish and maintain a good rapport with a patient not only depends on the analyst's skills but also rests on less readily quantifiable factors such as their own idiosyncrasies of character as well as those of the patient, of course.

The question of the analyst's own personality and its relevance to the process and outcome of analysis has been comparatively neglected. Yet, it would be surprising if this were not at least a factor in the melting pot of the analytic encounter. Freud, however, argued that the analyst should act like a 'blank screen' to the patient so that the patient could freely project on to the analyst any feelings or attitudes which could then, in turn, be used to elucidate the nature of the patient's relationships outside of the consulting room. To this extent Freud held that the analyst therefore should not reveal anything about their person. This introduces a paradox into the analytic relationship for while, as Budd (1994) points out, it is clearly believed to be of therapeutic importance, it is forged by the deliberate abstinence of the analyst who does not divulge his personal thoughts, sits out of sight and usually does not answer direct questioning – a process which can not only feel most unusual as it breaches so many of the expectations we have of how people communicate with one another, but which can also be experienced as quite persecutory and anxiety provoking.

The therapist as a blank screen is an ideal, however, that is never attainable. Indeed, Klauber (1981) argued that it is the analyst's personality which partly determines the unique manner in which each analyst approaches his or her work, for example, whether they tend to be silent or to intervene much more actively. A wealth of information about analysts is in fact conveyed to patients by the way they dress, choose to decorate their room, their general manner and what they choose to focus on or not in their patients' material. This is true even of those analysts who do their best to remain as neutral as possible and to provide a similarly neutral physical environment. The caricature of the silent, neutral analyst seldom bears a direct relation to how many analysts behave with their patients. While many strive to impinge as little as possible on their patients' space, some have great difficulty in actually remaining silent *enough* and Freud's ideal of neutrality is interpreted by analysts in many different ways. The emphasis on the analyst's neutrality has not always been helpful as it has obscured the reality of the fact of the analyst as a co-participant in the process and how her participation invariably affects the patient.

Interpretation: lending meaning to inner chaos

Important though it is, the relationship with the analyst is not the only process on which psychoanalytic treatment rests. In addition to the establishment of a relationship psychoanalysis, through its use of *interpretation*, offers patients a scheme or system of thought which enables them to make some sense out of their distress. Strictly speaking, to interpret in the analytic sense means to make an unconscious phenomenon conscious (Greenson, 1967). Interpretations help the patient to become aware of the unconscious meaning, source or cause of his feelings, thoughts and behaviours.

While interpretations seldom immediately get rid of symptoms, they do provide important relief from our fear of chaos and meaninglessness. As we saw in Chapter 4, one of the most important characteristics of the psychoanalytic process is that it offers a method of semantic interpretation rather than a direct treatment for neurotic symptoms. It offers the patient new concepts and information which allow for meaningful connections between symptoms and experiences that may have been, up until that point, mysterious. The creation of a powerful explanatory model acts as a means of reducing tension, replacing confusion with a greater degree of clarity.

The term 'interpretation' may give the misleading impression that when in analysis the patient tells the analyst his thoughts and dreams and the latter simply interprets these in light of the patient's past history. This makes it sound as though the patient is a passive recipient waiting for the analyst to dispense the 'truth' or the answer which will explain psychic pain away. Although this may well be the patient's wish or his fantasy or indeed may reflect the analyst's belief about her role, most analysts do not interpret their role in this manner. Rather it is the patient ideally who arrives at his own interpretations through the process of exploring how he feels and making links between the past and the present. The analyst will of course at times point out certain patterns, or emphasise something the patient has said which he appears to be glossing over but may in fact be quite important, while at other times he may highlight inconsistencies in thoughts or feelings which reflect underlying conflicts.

The holding environment

By not encouraging the patient to take any one particular direction in their life but leaving him to find his own way, the analyst offers the patient a very privileged space without any pressure to conform to anyone's wishes or needs. Equally integral to the process of psychoanalytic treatment is the protection of this space which is ensured through the provision by the analyst of a *secure frame*. This refers to the physical boundaries of the relationship which are established through the provision of a space where analyst and patient can meet, where confidentiality can be assured, where the analyst can be relied upon to turn up on time, at the same time week after week, as well as to finish the sessions on time, and to remain neutral in the sense that what the patient says, feels or fantasises about is responded to impartially by the analyst.

The frame of the analytic relationship is also referred to as the *holding environment*, an expression which highlights its containing function – just as mothers provide the baby with such an environment which maximises the opportunities of physical and psychic survival and growth. The importance of this frame cannot be overstated. It is a concrete expression of the boundaries of the analytic relationship, of the containment the analyst can offer the patient – an indication of what the patient can expect from his analyst and can therefore come to rely on.

The safety or otherwise of the so-called container is communicated in practical terms through the respect of the boundaries of the analytic relationship. An analyst who starts his sessions late or cancels sessions repeatedly is conveying a very different message to the one who strives to adhere to the ideal boundaries. This is not a matter of being pedantic or inflexible – accusations often levelled at analysts who are very strict about their boundaries – but on the contrary such an attitude of respect for the boundaries reveals an appreciation of the importance of stability and reliability for the patient's personal development. For those individuals who have experienced losses, unsettled childhoods or grew up in an unpredictable family environment, the safeguarding of the boundaries of the analytic relationship by the analyst may represent the very first experience of a person and an environment which can be trusted and depended upon. It offers a safe psychological space where patients may explore their deepest longings and fears.

The analyst's function to an extent mirrors the early parental function with its emphasis on responding to the patient's needs without impinging on them. Indeed, Bion, a Kleinian analyst, drew a parallel between the mother's containing function – which allows her to receive the raw intensity of her baby's projections, to empathise and bear with them thereby rendering them eventually containable by the baby – and the analyst's function of receiving, containing and transforming the patient's communications which helps the patient eventually to internalise the capacity to bear feelings and to think about them.

The analogies frequently drawn in the literature between the analyst's function and the maternal function lend to the analytic relationship a regressive, infantile quality and this may raise concerns about the potential for exploitation of the patient. To an extent the analytic 'set-up' does invite a degree of regression – most concretely evident in the use of the couch on which the patients lie and the rule of free association, itself a regressive phenomenon, urging the patient to suspend ordinary censorship, to abandon strict logic and coherence in their communications. However, it should most certainly not exploit it. When used therapeutically the regression enables the patient to explore infantile longings and anxieties which shape, to an extent, present relationships and attitudes to life.

It is a sad reflection of human nature that the analytic relationship, as with any relationship, is open to abuse but this is not specific to psychoanalytic treatment. However, it has been argued that the analytic process, through its use of interpretations and the fostering of a transference relationship, places the analyst in a more powerful position than in other forms of therapy. That there is a power imbalance is true, but this is an intrinsic feature of any therapeutic relationship. The actual abuse of this power merely reflects an aspect of human behaviour which is all the more shocking when it occurs in the context of a relationship which sets itself up as offering a measure of healing.

Does psychoanalysis work?

Having reviewed some of the central features of the psychoanalytic process, we can now turn our attention to the question of whether psychoanalysis, as a method of treatment, actually works. In attempting to assess the effectiveness of psychoanalysis as a method of treatment the focus has been on whether or not this approach actually relieves neurotic symptoms. Yet in practice, Storr (1979) points out, both patient and analyst know that once analysis has started the question of relief of symptoms tends to become less and less relevant. One reason for this is that many of the patients who have traditionally presented themselves for intensive psychoanalysis seldom have clear-cut symptoms but are more likely to be suffering from a general sense of malaise, their problems being most accurately described as 'problems in living' (Szasz, 1965). The aim with such patients is not the relief of a particular symptom but changes in attitude towards life generally and towards themselves more specifically. The focus of concern in psychoanalytic treatment is nowadays, for many analysts, not the removal of symptoms, but the person as a whole. The emphasis is on an understanding of both their internal and external world – the discovery of their own individual 'truth'.

The expectation that neurotic phenomena might actually be curable comes from a belief that neuroses are unnecessary, as for example in the hypothesis that they are the result of learning experiences, and that they can be 'cured' by manipulating environmental contingencies or by restructuring one's cognitions. However, as we have seen, psychoanalysis argues that neurotic conflict is inevitable in the contradiction between internal desire and external constraints. This is rooted in a quite different philosophy of life – one where 'life is lived in pain: there is necessarily conflict between what may be desired and what may be achieved. Hunting for happiness is not a project it [psychoanalysis] can accede to because it is itself the most radical critic of the formulation of such a project' (Frosh, 1987: 68). Indeed, Storr (1966) has argued that the psychoanalytic procedure is inherently impossible if it sets itself up to provide some new way of being that is genuinely mentally healthy or 'cured'. Moreover, he suggests that the states of perfection labelled 'emotional maturity', 'integration' or 'self-realisation' are mythical and simply reflect 'goals towards which we may legitimately strive, but at which we never arrive' (Storr, 1971: 152).

While these are important considerations they should not detract attention away from the equally important question of what one can reasonably expect from psychoanalytic treatment. This has been the focus of concern of comparative outcome studies, which have attempted to compare different psychotherapeutic approaches with one another to see which, if any, is more effective. Such studies only include the evaluation of psychoanalytic psychotherapy as opposed to psychoanalysis proper. The latter usually consists of four to five sessions per week over several years. The former, while taking its theoretical core and its practical techniques from psychoanalysis, differs from it in several respects. The major changes are in the greater activity of the therapist, the frequency with which the patient is seen (anything from one to three sessions per week) and the length of treatment (it may be less than one year but usually it extends over a longer period of time).

The stereotypical response given by a significant number of analysts and psychoanalytic psychotherapists to outcome research is that it is not meaningful. Indeed, the evaluation of psychotherapy is inextricably linked to individual views on science and scientific method, on the nature of 'meaningful' questions, on how far the complex phenomena of psychotherapy can be scientifically investigated and, not least, on how one defines a successful outcome, that is whether one is 'cured'. It is, however, not only the psychoanalytically oriented therapists who view outcome research with scepticism. Such research has been equally criticised by the humanistic schools who claim that in so far as psychotherapy is a deeply personal experience, the empirical study of psychotherapy will be of limited value (Graham, 1987). However, while such arguments need to be considered, there are obvious scientific, moral, political and financial reasons for at least attempting to carry out outcome research. The primary advantage of comparative outcome studies is that they place into the empirical arena the many conflicting and hyperbolic claims made about the superiority of one approach over another. Furthermore, the value of knowing the relative efficacy of alternative techniques, the differences in the range or type of outcomes produced, and the process through which such outcomes are achieved, encompass critical theoretical and practical questions. In accepting the potential value of such research investigators must, however, defend against the temptation to demonstrate what is easily demonstrable rather than what is important and always bear in mind the limitations of such an enterprise.

Among the many questions that psychotherapy research addresses, none has attracted as much interest and controversy as comparative outcome studies. At the outset these studies were largely descriptive, anecdotal and uncontrolled. Gradually, beginning in the 1950s, a number of attempts were made to introduce control or comparison groups. Over the ensuing years such studies became more methodologically sophisticated. Despite the methodological advances, the findings from such studies have been mixed. The same studies are often simultaneously praised and criticised on methodological grounds and are frequently cited in support of different conclusions. The cumulative knowledge from such studies is at best difficult to assess. To complicate matters further, by comparison with other forms of therapy, psychoanalytical psychotherapies have not been adequately evaluated. This is partly because of the general psychoanalytical scepticism towards such research alluded to earlier but also because psychoanalysis has traditionally been the prerogative of a privileged few in the private sector where scientific evaluation has not been on the agenda. The shorter term psychoanalytic therapies which are available in the public sector are still relatively new and have not yet been extensively researched and evaluated.

Despite the plethora of purportedly different psychotherapeutic treatments, influential reviews of comparative outcome research which include psychoanalytically oriented approaches appear to support the conclusion that outcomes of diverse therapies are similar (Stiles et al., 1986; Watts, 1989). While there is now a general consensus over the greater effectiveness of psychotherapy compared with no treatment, no such consensus exists over the effectiveness of the diverse therapies. Most reviews have, however, returned the verdict that no substantial differences in effectiveness have been found amongst the different therapies (Smith et al., 1980). Although some behavioural therapists have argued that behavioural therapies are more effective when compared with psychoanalytic therapies, on balance, studies of better than average quality show little advantage of behavioural over verbal methods in the treatment, for example, of depression or anxiety (Lambert et al., 1986; Barkham, 1990). Moreover, an interesting review of treatments for depression showed that once the influence of the investigator's allegiance to a particular type of therapy was controlled for (by using independent raters who judged investigator allegiance by examining comments provided in the introductory sections of each study) there remained no evidence for the relative superiority of any one approach (Robinson et al., 1990). Such a bias was also noted earlier by Smith and colleagues who found that the results of comparisons between therapies varied according to the theoretical preferences of the investigator.

On the basis of the evidence currently available it would certainly appear that the outcomes of psychoanalytically based therapies and other therapies, with clinical populations, are roughly equivalent (see Lemma, 1991, for a more extensive review of such research; Culverwell et al., 1994). The apparent equivalence of outcomes that has been noted by many researchers may reflect a failure of comparative outcome studies to measure the particular changes that differentiate treatments. It is also important to consider a neglected perspective on the question of effectiveness, namely the one distinguishing the effects of treatment from their value. Different psychotherapies may have powerful effects that are valued differently by different people (Stiles, 1983). In this respect an important research question is *what* are the effects of different types of therapy rather than *which* effect is best.

The idea that psychotherapy should produce consensually recognised improvements may rest, as Stiles suggests, on an inappropriate analogy with medicine. The medical model blurs the distinction between the effects of treatment and the values of these effects because medical treatment is generally tailored to the correction of some deviation which is more or less the same for everybody and is generally desired. However, psychological 'normality' is heterogeneous and behaviour varies widely across roles and cultures. What works for one person with regard to psychotherapy may well not work for another.

Psychoanalysis and psychoanalytic psychotherapy as forms of treatment undoubtedly have a place amongst a range of psychological therapies. Not everyone, however, benefits from them. It would be desirable, but presently not possible, to specify exact criteria regarding who is most likely to benefit. This is a question that needs to be researched further. Although we are clearly lacking such criteria psychoanalysis is certainly not the type of therapy suited to someone who is merely seeking symptomatic relief but has no desire to understand himself or to someone who does not believe in the existence of unconscious mental life. In a general sense such approaches appear to be more suited to relatively non-focal psychological problems, that is, for example, people who complain of more general anxiety as opposed to a very specific anxiety resulting from a phobia. And, as was mentioned earlier, such approaches are particularly relevant to those individuals who find an exploratory approach to their dilemmas and concerns more attractive.

Where to next?

A commonly held view by the sceptics of psychoanalysis is that psychoanalytic treatment 'seems to produce a good many more converts that cures' (Crews, 1993: 55). The question of 'cure', as we have seen in this chapter, raises a number of important issues, not least what is meant by it. Whatever we mean by cure, it is certainly not possible to guarantee that psychoanalysis, or any other form of psychological therapy for that matter, will help you change or 'cure' you of disabling symptoms. Psychoanalysis is by no means a panacea for all ills.

The aim of this book has not been to 'convert' you to a psychoanalytic way of thinking about your emotional life but rather to present to you an outline of core psychoanalytic concepts and their wider applications. However, if the ideas presented in this book make sense to you, if by the time you have reached this chapter you have made some meaningful links between your own experiences and some of the ideas we have examined, then psychoanalysis or psychoanalytic psychotherapy may well be worth exploring if you are considering personal therapy. How you then evaluate the changes that engagement in such a therapy may bring about will depend ultimately on your own values, on what matters to you. As Kovel writes: 'It cannot be too strongly emphasised that the changes [resulting from psychotherapy] can never be measured by some absolute standard, but only through the way a person evaluates his life. In other words, the "better way" is the way one values' (1976: 70).

Further reading

This book is but a drop in the ocean of the vast and rich psychoanalytic literature which awaits you, if you feel that psychoanalysis has something to offer you. My suggestions for further reading reflect my own personal tastes but in compiling this list I also have in mind the need to acquaint oneself gradually with the literature. The aim of the list is to give you some guidance towards those books which will broaden and deepen your understanding of psychoanalysis and some of the notions that have been presented in this book. The list is very selective but aims to cover both theoretical and more applied texts. Some of the books have already been referred to in the main text.

In beginning this list I can only wholeheartedly encourage you to read Freud himself. Not only is he a good writer who expresses his ideas clearly (with the exception of a few papers which are rather dense and not for the faint-hearted!), but as he has been frequently misrepresented by others, it is advisable to go back to the original source and judge for yourself. A good starting point is the collection of some of Freud's most important papers that can be found in *The Essentials of Psychoanalysis* (1986) London: Penguin Books. You might find it helpful in order to grasp Freud's own thoughts to read a basic introductory text on Freud. I can but highly recommend Christopher Badcock's *Essential Freud* (1988), London: Blackwell, which offers an engaging and lively introduction to Freudian concepts.

Alongside Freud's own works, it is very enlightening and interesting to read one of his biographies, such as Peter Gay's *Freud: A Life for Our Time* (1988), London: J.M. Devil & Sons. I would also highly recommend a book which examines the impact of Freud's Jewish roots on his theorising especially in relation to his views on female psychology, *The Riddle of Freud* (1987) by Estelle Roith, London: Tavistock Publications. Complementing the last book with a more thorough critique of psychoanalytic views on women is Juliet Mitchell's *Psychoanalysis and Feminism* (1974) London: Penguin and Nancy Chodorow's *Femininities, Masculinities, Sexualities: Beyond Freud*

(1994), London: FAB. On the subject of male sexuality, you will find some interesting papers in the edited collection by Andy Metcalf and Martin Humphries (1985) *The Sexuality of Men*, London: Pluto Press. The article by Tom Ryan is especially relevant to a psychoanalytic perspective. A more advanced text but nonetheless very illuminating on the question of the construction of masculinity is Stephen Frosh's (1994) *Sexual Difference: Masculinity and Psychoanalysis*, London: Routledge. For books on psychoanalysis and homosexuality refer to the books mentioned in the chapter in this book, especially the one by Noreen O'Connor and Joanna Ryan (1993) *Wild Desires and Mistaken Identities*, London: Virago.

It is important in considering psychoanalytic concepts to have some idea about the research which has attempted to study them. An excellent book which focuses on experimental research in psychoanalysis is Matthew Erdelyi's *Psychoanalysis: Freud's Cognitive Psychology* (1985), New York: Freeman & Co.

Although the present text has focused mainly on Freud's ideas there have clearly been many developments since his time. A most promising field has been that of 'object-relations' theory. Unfortunately there are no easy introductory texts on this. However, if you have reached this stage of exploration you will no doubt not be intimidated by the academic textbook by J.R. Greenberg and S.S. Mitchell (1983) *Object Relations in Psychoanalytic Theory*, Cambridge, Mass: Harvard University Press, which offers a scholarly introduction to object relations theory. For an engaging and thorough review of the developments in the Independent tradition in British psychoanalysis dip into Eric Rayner's (1991) *The Independent Mind in British Psychoanalysis*, London: FAB.

Melanie Klein is a most important theorist in the history of psychoanalysis and deserves to be read. However, her own writing is rather dense and laden with terminology which can be rather offputting. I therefore do not suggest you start with it. It is better to read an introduction to her work first – such as Hanna Segal's *Introduction to the work of Melanie Klein* (1973) London: Karnac. A good accompaniment to this last book is the one by Robert Hinshelwood *Clinical Klein* (1994) London: FAB, which covers basic Kleinian concepts and illustrates them with clinical material.

If, after reading this book, you are left in any doubt about the significance of early relationships to adult development, or if this is an area of particular interest, you will find it most stimulating to read an excellent collection of papers on attachment edited by Colin Murray-Parkes, Joan Stevenson-Hinde and Peter Harris (1991) *Attachment Across the Life Cycle*, London: Routledge.

A broader psychoanalytic perspective on developmental milestones and conflicts can be gained by dipping into a series of short books on children at different ages entitled *Understanding your [1, 2, 3, etc.]*

year old, London: Rosendale Press. Each book, written by a child psychotherapist, devotes itself to a specific age group and offers a simple and clear overview of children's development from a broadly psychoanalytic perspective.

Psychoanalytic ideas are best grasped when explored in the context of their applications to everyday concerns and to clinical problems. This book has attempted to give you a flavour of psychoanalytic ideas at work but if you would like to get some sense of how such ideas might be applied to clinical work, I will direct you to two eminently readable and deeply touching books. The first, by Ann Alvarez (1992), *Live Company*, London: Routledge focuses on psychoanalytic work with severely deprived and autistic children. The second, by Valerie Sinason (1991) *Mental Handicap and the Human Condition*, London: FAB, concerns itself with the application of psychoanalytic ideas to working with people with learning difficulties. My reasons for selecting these two books out of the sheer wealth of clinically oriented books are by no means arbitrary. These books highlight the scope of psychoanalytic approaches to psychotherapy with client groups which have been traditionally neglected in favour of more medicalised, behavioural or purely social interventions. They are also both clearly written and invite us to consider aspects of ourselves which we would generally prefer not to think about. In addition to these two books I encourage you to read Robert Langs' (1991) *Take Charge of your Emotional Life*, New York: Harry Holt & Co., which offers an eminently readable introduction to how you might best deploy your 'unconscious wisdom'.

Last but not least a book for those amongst you who are considering psychotherapy for yourselves. Joel Kovel's 'A Complete Guide to Therapy' (1976), London: Pelican, covers psychoanalytic approaches alongside humanistic and behavioural ones and provides a balanced overview of the field.

Enjoy your reading ... much, much more awaits you!

References

Alvarez, A. (1982). *Live Company*. London: Routledge.

Balint, E. (1993). Unconscious communication between husband and wife. In Ruszczynski, S. (Ed.) *Psychotherapy with Couples*. London: Karnac.

Barkham, M. (1990). Research in individual therapy. In Dryden, W. (Ed.) *Individual Therapy: A Handbook*. Milton Keynes: OUP.

Bettelheim, B. (1984). *Freud and Man's Soul*. New York: Vintage Books.

Bollos, C. (1987) *The Shadow of the Object*. London: Free Association Books.

Boscolo, L. and Bertrando, P. (1993). *The Times of Time*. New York: Norton.

Bowlby, J. (1989). *A Secure Base*. London: Routledge.

Brazelton, T.B. and Cramer, B.G. (1991). *The Earliest Relationship*. London: Karnac.

Brenner, C. (1969). Dreams in clinical psychoanalytic practice. In Flanders, S. (Ed.) (1990). *The Dream Discourse*. London: Routledge.

Brenner, C. (1981). Defence and defence mechanisms. *Psychoanalytic Quarterly* 1, 557–569.

Breuer, J. and Freud, S. (1895). *Studies in Hysteria*. London: Penguin.

Britton, R. (1989). The missing link: parental sexuality in the Oedipus Complex. In Britton, R., Feldman, M. and O'Shaughnessy, E. (Eds) *The Oedipus Complex Today*. London: Karnac.

Brown, D.E. (1991). *Human Universals*. New York: McGraw-Hill.

Brown, G. and Harris, T.O. (1978). *Social Origins of Depression: A Study of Psychiatric Disorder in Women*. London: Tavistock Publications.

Budd, S. (1994). Transference revisited. In Budd, S. and Sharma, U. (Eds) *The Healing Bond*. London: Routledge.

Cantlie, A. (1994). Psychoanalysis and anthropology: applied or misapplied? *The Psychoanalysis Newsletter* 14, 2–7.

Cassidy, J. and Kobak, R. (1988). Avoidance and its relationship to other defensive processes. In Belski, J. and Nezworski, T. (Eds) *Clinical Implications of Attachment*. Hillsdale, NJ: Erlbaum.

Chodorow, N. (1978). *The Reproduction of Mothering*. Univ. California Press.

Chodorow, N. (1989). *Feminism and Psychoanalytic Theory*. Cambridge: Polity.

Chodorow, N. (1994). *Femininities, Masculinities, Sexualities: Beyond Freud*. London: Free Association Books.

Crews, F. (1993) The unknown Freud. *New York Review of Books* 18 November, 55–66.

Culverwell, A., Agnew, R., Barkham, M., Hardley, G., Rees, A., Shapiro, D.,

Reynolds, S., Halstead, J., Stiles, W. and Harrington, V. (1994). The second Sheffield psychotherapy project: some initial findings and their clinical implications. *Clinical Psychology Forum* 72, 5–8.

Cunningham, R. (1993). When is a pervert not a pervert? *British Journal of Psychotherapy* Vol. 1.

Dixon, N. (1981). *Preconscious Processing*. London: Wiley.

Egeland, B., Carlson, E. and Sroufe, A. (1993). Resilience as process. *Development and Psychopathology* 5, 517–528.

Eichenbaum, L. and Orbach, S. (1982). *Outside In – Inside Out*. London: Penguin.

Ellenberger, H.F. (1970). *The Discovery of the Unconscious*. New York: Basic Books.

Ellis, M. (1994) Lesbians, gay men and psychoanalytic training. *Free Associations* 4(4), 501–517.

Erdelyi, M. (1985). *Psychoanalysis: Freud's Cognitive Psychology*. New York: Freeman & Co.

Erskine, A. and Judd, D. (Eds) (1994). *The Imaginative Body*. London: Whurr.

Evans, D. (1995). Current criticisms of psychoanalysis. *The Psychoanalysis Newsletter* 15, 7–16.

Farrell, B.A. (1981). *The Standing of Psychoanalysis*. Oxford: OUP.

Feldman, M. (1989). The Oedipus Complex: manifestations in the inner world and the therapeutic situation. In Britton, R., Feldman, M. and O'Shaughnessy, E. (Eds) *The Oedipus Complex Today*. London: Karnac.

Fenichel, O. (1946). *The Psychoanalytic Theory of Neurosis*. London: Routledge.

Fonagy, P. (1992). The theory and practice of resilience. Paper presented at the 1992 conference of the Association of Child Psychology and Psychiatry, York, England.

Fonagy, P. (1994). A psychoanalytic understanding of memory and reconstruction. *Psychotherapy Section Newsletter* 16, 3–20.

Foucault, M. (1981). *The History of Sexuality*. Harmondsworth: Penguin.

Fraiberg, S. (1974). *Selected Writings of Selma Fraiberg*. Ohio State University Press.

French, T.M. and Fromm, E. (1964). *Dream Interpretation*. New York: Basic Books. In Flanders, S. (Ed.) (1990). *The Dream Discourse*. London: Routledge.

Freud, A. (1936). *The Ego and The Mechanisms of Defence*. London: Karnac.

Freud, S. (1900). *The Interpretation of Dreams*, Vol. 9. London: Penguin.

Freud, S. (1905). *Three Essays on Sexuality*, Vol. 7. London: Penguin.

Freud, S. (1909). *Analysis of a Phobia in a Five Year Old Boy*, Vol. 8. London: Penguin.

Freud, S. (1914). *On Narcissism*, Vol. 11. London: Penguin.

Freud, S. (1915). *The Unconscious*, Vol. 11. London: Penguin.

Freud, S. (1917a). *The Paths to the Formation of Symptoms*,Vol. 1. London: Penguin.

Freud, S. (1917b). *Fixation to Traumas in The Unconscious*, Vol. 1. London: Penguin.

Freud, S. (1919). *Lines of Advance In Psychoanalytic Therapy* , Standard Edition, Vol. 24. London: Hogarth Press.

Freud, S. (1920). *Beyond the Pleasure Principle*, Vol. 10. London: Penguin.

Freud, S. (1921). *Group Psychology and the Analysis of the Ego*, Vol. 12. London: Penguin.

Freud, S. (1923). *The Ego and the Id*, Vol. 10. London: Penguin.

Freud, S. (1924). *The Loss of Reality in Neurosis and Psychosis*, Vol. 10. London: Penguin.

Freud, S. (1926). *The Question of Lay Analysis*,Vol. 15. London: Penguin.

Freud, S. (1932). *Revision of the Theory of Dreams*, Vol. 2. London: Penguin.

Freud, S. (1937). *Analysis Terminable and Interminable*, Standard Edition, Vol. 23. London: Hogarth Press.

Freud, S. (1938). *An Outline of Psychoanalysis*, Vol. 15. London: Penguin.

Friedman, R. (1988). *Male Homosexuality: A Contemporary Psychoanalytic Perspective*. New Haven: Yale University Press.

Friedman, R. and Downey, J. (1993). Neurobiology and sexual orientation: current relationships. *Journal of Neuropsychiatry and Clinical Neurosciences* 5, 131–153.

Frosh, S. (1987). *The Politics of Psychoanalysis*. London: Macmillan.

Frosh, S. (1994). *Sexual Difference: Masculinity and Psychoanalysis*. London: Routledge.

Furman, E. (1994). Early aspects of mothering: what makes it so hard to be there to be left? *Journal of Child Psychotherapy* 20(2), 149–164.

Gardner, H. (1985). *The Mind's New Science: A History of Cognitive Revolution*. New York: Basic Books.

Gay, P. (1988). *Freud: A Life for Our Time*. London: J.M. Devil & Sons.

Goffman, J. and Krokoff, L. (1989). Marital interaction and satisfaction – a longitudinal view. *Journal of Consulting and Clinical Psychology* 57(1), 47–52.

Goodyear, I. (1990). *Life Experiences, Development and Childhood Psychopathology*. London: John Wiley & Son.

Graham, A. (1987). *The Human Face of Psychology*. Milton Keynes: OUP.

Greenberg, R. and Perlman, C. (1975). A psychoanalytic dream continuum: the source and function of dreams. In Flanders, S. (Ed.) (1993) *The Dream Discourse Today*. London: Routledge.

Greenson, R. (1967). *The Technique and Practice of Psychoanalysis*. London: Hogarth Press.

Grunberger, B. (1991). Narcissism and the analytic situation. In Sandler, J., Person, E.S. and Fonagy, P. (Eds) *Freud's 'On Narcissism' – An Introduction*. New Haven: Yale University Press.

Hamburg, P. (1989). Bulimia: the construction of a symptom. In Bemporad, J. and Herzog, D. (Eds) *Psychoanalysis and Eating Disorders*. New York: Guilford Press.

Hinshelwood, R. (1994). *Clinical Klein*. London: Free Association Books.

Horney, K. (1937). *The Neurotic Personality of our Time*. London RKP.

Hurry, A. (1994). Homosexuality, biology and the work of Richard Isay. *Journal of the British Association of Psychotherapists* 37, 123–129.

Jaynes, J. (1976). *The Origins of Consciousness in the Breakdown of the Bicameral Mind*. Boston: Houghton Mifflin.

Jones, E. (1925). Mother-right and the sexual ignorance of savages. *International Journal of Psychoanalysis* 6, 109–130.

Jones, E. (1955, 1958, 1974). *Sigmund Freud: Life and Work*. London: Hogarth.

Jukes, A. (1993). *Why Men Hate Women*. London: Free Association Books.

Kaplan, L. (1991). *Female Perversion*. London: Penguin.

Kernberg, O. (1983). *Internal World and External Reality*. New York: Aronson.

Khan, M. (1963). The concept of cumulative trauma. *Psychoanalytic Study of the Child* 18, 283–306.

Kirsner, D. (1990). Mystics and professionals in the culture of American Psychoanalysis. *Free Associations* 20, 85–104.

Klauber, J. (1981). *Difficulties in the Analytic Encounter*. London: Free Association Press.

Klein, M. (1930). The importance of symbol-formation in the development of the ego. *International Journal of Psychoanalysis* 11, 24–39.

Kline, P. (1981). *Fact and Fantasy in Freudian Theory*. London: Methuen.

Kline, P. (1988). *Psychology Exposed*. London: Routledge.

Kline, P. (1989). Objective tests of Freud's theories. In Coleman and Beaumont (Eds) *Psychology Survey*, 7. London: Wiley.

Kovel, J. (1976). *A Complete Guide to Therapy*. London: Penguin.

Kraemer, S. (1994). The post natal development of fathers: how do they cope with their new roles? *Clinical Psychology Forum* 64, 21–25.

Lambert, M.J., Shapiro, D.A. and Bergin, A.E. (1986). The effectiveness of psychotherapy. In Garfield, S.L. and Bergin, A.E. (Eds) *Handbook of Psychotherapy and Behaviour Change*. New York, Wiley.

Langs, R. (1988). *Decoding your Dreams*. London, Unwin Hyman.

Langs, R. (1991). *Take Charge of your Emotional Life*. New York: Henry Holt & Co.

Langs, R. (1993). *Science, Systems and Psychoanalysis*. London: Karnac.

Lemma, A. (1991). *Clinical Psychology and Psychoanalysis – Irreconcilable Differences?* Unpublished M.Phil. Thesis. Cambridge University.

Lerner, H. (1988). *Women in Therapy*. New York: Jason Aronson.

Limentani, A. (1977). The differential diagnosis of homosexuality. *British Journal of Medical Psychology* 50, 209–216.

Lyons, E. (1993). Husbands and wives: the mysterious choice. In Ruszczynski, S. (Ed.) *Psychotherapy with Couples*. London: Karnac.

Lyons-Ruth, K., Connell, D., Zoll, D. and Stahl, J. (1987). Infants at social risk: relations among infant maltreatment, maternal behaviour and infant attachment behaviour. *Developmental Psychology* 23(2), 223–232.

Main, M. and Weston, D. (1981). The quality of the toddler's relationship to mother and father; related to conflict behaviour and the readiness to establish new relationships. *Child Development* 52, 932–940.

Malinowski, B. (1961). *Sex and Repression in Savage Society*. Cleveland: World.

Marmor, J. (1982). Homosexuality and disturbances of sexual orientation. In Friedman, A., Kaplan, H. and Sadwick, B. (Eds) *Comprehensive Textbook of Psychiatry*. Baltimore: Williams & Wilkins.

Masson, J. (1984). *Freud: The Assault on Truth*. London: Faber & Faber.

McDougall, J. (1980). *Plea for a Measure of Abnormality*. London: Free Association Books.

McDougall, J. (1989). *The Theatre of the Body*. London: Free Association Books.

Murray, L. and Stein, A. (1989) The effects of postnatal depression on the infant. *Ballières Clinical Obstetrics and Gynaecology* 3(4), 921–933.

Murray-Parkes, C., Stevenson-Hinde, J. and Harris, P. (1991). *Attachment Across the Life Cycle*. London: Routledge.

Neville, S. (1993). *Narcissism: A New Theory*. London: Karnac.

O'Connor, J. and Ryan, J. (1993). *Wild Desires and Mistaken Identities*. London: Virago.

Olivier, C. (1989). *Jocasta's Children*. London: Routledge.

Ostow, M. (Ed.) (1982). *Judaism and Psychoanalysis*. New York: Ktav.

Person, E.S. (1980) Sexuality as the mainstay of identity: psychoanalytic perspectives. In Stimpson, C. and Person, E. (Eds) *Women: Sex and Sexuality*. Chicago: University of Chicago Press.

Person, E.S. (1989). *Love and Fateful Encounters*. London: Bloomsbury.

Pincus, L. (1962). *The Marital Relationship as a Focus for Casework*. London: Institute for Marital Studies.

Piontelli, A. (1992). *From Foetus to Child*. London: Routledge.

Quinton, D. and Rutter, M. (1985a). Parenting behaviour of mothers raised in care. In Nicol, A. (Ed.) *Longitudinal Studies in Child Psychology and Psychiatry*. Chichester: Wiley.

Quinton, D. and Rutter, M. (1985b) Family pathology and child psychiatric disorder: a four year prospective study. In Nicol, A. (Ed.) *Longitudinal Studies in Child Psychology and Psychiatry*. Chichester: Wiley.

Quinton, D., Pickles, A., Maugham, B. and Rutter, M. (1993). Partners, peers and pathways: assortative pairing and continuities in conduct disorder. *Development and Psychopathology* 5, 763–783.

Raphael-Leff, J. (1991). *Psychological Processes of Childbearing*. London: Chapman and Hall.

Rayner, E. (1991) *The Independent Mind in British Psychoanalysis*. London: Free Association Books.

Reik, T. (1941). *Of Love and Lust*. New York: Aronson.

Robert, M. (1977). *From Oedipus to Moses: Freud's Jewish Identity*. London: RKP.

Roberts, G. (1991). Delusional beliefs and meaning in life: a preferred reality? *British Journal of Psychiatry* 1559 (Suppl. 14), 19–28.

Robinson, L.A., Berman, J.S. and Neimeyer, R.A. (1990). Psychotherapy for the treatment of depression: a comprehensive review of controlled outcome research. *Psychological Bulletin* 108(1).

Roith, E. (1987). *The Riddle of Freud*. London: Routledge.

Rose, S. (1992). *The Making of Memory*. London: Bantam Books.

Rosen, I. (1979). The personal psychoanalytic theory of perversion. In Rosen, I. (Ed.) *Sexual Deviation*. London: OUP.

Ryan, J. (1983). Psychoanalysis and women loving women. In Cartledge, S. and Ryan, J. (Eds) *Sex and Love*. London: The Women's Press.

Rycroft, C. (1979). *The Innocence of Dreams*. London: Hogarth Press.

Sandler, J., Dare, C., and Holder, A. (1973). *The Patient and the Analyst*. London: Karnac.

Sartre, J.P. (1956). *Being and Nothingness*. New York: Washington Square Post.

Smith, D. (1985). Freud's developmental approach to narcissism: a concise review. *International Journal Psychoanalysis* 66, 489–497.

Smith, D. (1991). *Hidden Communications*. London: Routledge.

Smith, M.L., Glass, G.V. and Miller, T.L. (1980). *The Benefits of Psychotherapy*. London: John Hopkins Press.

Socarides, C. (1979).The psychoanalytic theory of homosexuality. In Rosen, I. (Ed.) *Sexual Deviation*. London: OUP.

Spanjaard, J. (1969). The manifest dream content and its significance for the interpretation of dreams. In Flanders, S. (Ed.) (1990). *The Dream Discourse*. London: Routledge.

Spinelli, E. (1989). *The Interpreted World*. London: Sage.

Spinelli, E. (1993). The unconscious: an idea whose time has come? *Journal of the Society for Existential Analysis* 4, 19–47.

Spiro, M. (1982). *Oedipus in the Trobriands*. Chicago: University of Chicago Press.

Sroufe, A. and Fleeson, J. (1988). The coherence of family relationships. In Hinde, R. and Stevenson-Hinde, J. (Eds) *Relationship within Families: Mutual Influences*. Oxford: OUP.

Steiner, J. (1989). The aim of psychoanalysis. *Psychoanalytic Psychotherapy* 4(2), 109–120.

Stern, D. (1977). *The First Relationship. Infant and Mother*. Cambridge, Mass: Harvard University Press.

Stern, D. (1993). Acting versus remembering in transference love and infantile love. In Person, E.S., Haselin, A. and Fonagy, P. (Eds) *On Freud's 'Observations On Transference Love'*. New Haven: Yale Univ. Press.

Stevens, R. (1983). *Freud and Psychoanalysis*. London: OUP.

Stiles, W.B. (1983). Normality, diversity and psychotherapy. *Theory, Research and Practice* 20(2), 183–188.

Stiles, W.B., Shapiro, D.A. and Elliott, R.K. (1986). Are all psychotherapies equivalent? *American Psychologist* 42, 165–188.

Stoller, R.J. (1975). *Perversion: The Erotic Form of Hatred*. London: Karnac.

Storr, A. (1966). The concept of cure. In Rycroft, C. (Ed.) *Psychoanalysis Observed*. London: Penguin.

Storr, A. (1979). *The Art of Psychotherapy*. London: William Heinemann Medical Books.

Stubrin, J. (1994). *Sexualities and Homosexuality*. London: Karnac.

Symington, N. (1993) *Narcissism: A New Theory*. London: Karnac.

Szasz, T. (1965). The concept of transference. *International Journal of Psychoanalysis* 44, 432–443.

Szasz, T. (1978). *The Myth of Psychotherapy*. Syracuse University Press.

Trevarthen, C. (1980). The foundations of intersubjectivity: development of interpersonal and co-operative understanding in infants. In Olson, D.R. (Ed.) *The Social Foundations of Language and Thought*. New York: Norton.

Wachtel, P. (1972). *Psychoanalysis and Behaviour Therapy*. New York: Basic Books.

Ward, E. (1984). *Father–Daughter Rape*. London: The Women's Press.

Watts, F. (1989). *The Efficacy of Clinical Application of Psychology: An Overview of Research*. Wales: Shadowfax.

Weiner, A. (1985). Oedipus and the ancestors. *American Ethnologist* 12, 758–762.

Winnicott, D. (1941).The observation of infants in a set situation. In Winnicott, D. (1958) *Through Paediatrics to Psychoanalysis, Collected Works*. London: Karnac.

Wollheim, R. (1991). *Freud*. London: Fontana Press.

Index